Principles of Risk Management and Insurance

Principles of Risk Management and Insurance

Dheeraj Razdan

CYBER TECH PUBLICATIONS
4264/3, Ansari Road, Daryaganj, New Delhi-110002 (India)
Ph.: 011-23244078, 011-43559448 Fax: 011-23280028
E-Mail: cyberpublicationsdelhi@yahoo.com
Website: www.cybertechpublications.com

PRINCIPLES OF RISK MANAGEMENT AND INSURANCE

Dheeraj Razdan

First Edition 2010

Published by : Asian Offset Printers

G.S. Rawat for **Cyber Tech Publications**
4264/3, Ansari Road, Daryaganj, New Delhi-110002 (India)
Ph.: 011-23244078, 011-43559448 Fax: 011-23280028
E-Mail: cyberpublicationsdelhi@yahoo.com
Website: www.cybertechpublications.com

Preface

There is a basic shift in the paradigm of risk management practices and has placed greater emphasis on the successful identification, quantification, mitigation, control and financing of risk. Evolving concepts of risk are leading to complex management perspectives requiring an integrated view of the finances and operations of a corporation. Today's risk manager must generate a comprehensive context of risks faced by the enterprises. The process of risk management involves the following: Recognition and understanding, measurement and, monitoring and control. In order to effective risk management, a comprehensive risk management policy has to be formulated incorporating a detailed structure of limits and guidelines to be followed and a Strong Management Information System (MIS) build up for continuous monitoring and reporting of risk exposures.

Every agency, college, university, board and commission of the Connecticut State Government is subject to risk. Risk management plays a vital role in helping to avoid, minimize and control the adverse effects of accidental loss. The objective of this manual is to familiarize you with the importance of the risk management function in Connecticut State Government. This manual will acquaint you with the State Insurance and Risk management Board, the services offered and provide you with the appropriate tools to effectively manage the risk to which your operations are exposed. This manual has been developed to provide you with an easy to use format so you can use risk management principles throughout your everyday operations.

—Author

CONTENTS

1

INTRODUCTION TO RISK MANAGEMENT

Risk Management is a broad field encompassing numerous specializations: Enterprise Risk Management, Financial Risk Management and Operational Risk management to name a few. While the tools and methods for measuring and treating exposure to risk differ somewhat by specialization, the principles of risk management are the same in all.

The principles of risk management are a set of practices utilized by business to manage its exposure to risk, reach its objectives and goals, and to guide its conduct to meet expectations and concerns of the public interest, labor relations, human safety, the environment, and the laws governing business practices.

The Principles of Risk Management are risk assessment and risk control. Where risk assessment identifies, quantifies and prioritizes exposure to risk, risk control manages exposure to risk on a continuous basis.

Part of risk control, naturally, is an ongoing assessment of risk exposure that assures business its plans are correct for the most current risk climate.

The principles of risk management have been firmly established as an essential set of management functions. Clearly, assessing and controlling exposure to risk minimizes the adverse impact of risk on the organization's resources, earnings, and cash flows.

The Risk Management Assessment

Three key processes, cornerstones among the principles of risk management, comprise the risk management assessment. Identify exposure to risk; Analyze the risk, meaning measure the likelihood and severity of impact; Prioritize risk.

When exposure to risk has been identified, quantified and prioritized, treatments for the organization's exposure to risk can be devised.

Risk Control

Another key principle in risk management is Risk Control. Managing and controlling an organization's exposure to risk usually involves the following: risk mitigation, contingency planning and close managerial supervision of the combined risk management effort so that adjustments can be made to continually improve the efficiency of the endeavor over time and guard against untreated exposure.

One of the essential processes in risk management is assessing an organization's exposure to risk. That process is aptly named the Risk Management Assessment Identifying an organization's exposure to risk is only the beginning. A true assessment of risk means that each risk must be evaluated for its probability of occurrence and its potential impact. Owners of risk must be identified, and their responsibilities must be determined.

The Risk Management Assessement is a fact finding mission in support of the planning and development of a risk management strategy. No meaningful approach to risk management can be achieved without a thorough and painstaking assessment of an organization's exposure to risk.

Risk Management Assessment Challenges

Risk can be defined as uncertainty. Measuring the likelihood and the impact of an adverse event can be difficult - a serious challenge in risk management assessment. Events can represent high probability risk, low probability risk, high potential for loss and low potential for loss. Exact measurements for both probability and potential loss are usually impossible, introducing uncertainty best battled by experience. Treatments for these exposures must be managed based on the information generated by the risk assessment and considered against an organization's objectives and goals.

Risk Management Assessment Benefits

When faced with limited resources, especially time, the risk management process breaks down without a thorough assessment. Business moves quickly - more quickly now than ever before. At decision time, the risk management strategy developed from planning the treatment of risk evaluated during the risk management assessment should be in place to guide and instruct decision makers. The great benefit of effective risk management assessment can be seen in rapid responses that accurately account for an organization's objectives - made possible through effective risk management assessment.

RISK MANAGEMENT INSURANCE

Recognizing and assessing areas at risk in your business is the beginning. Once a risk issue is discovered, a strategy must be devised to manage that risk. Among the treatments are avoiding the risk, acccpting (retaining) the risk, reducing (mitigating) the negative effect of the risk and risk transfer. Risk transfer is accomplished through risk management insurance. A well rounded risk management strategy will utilize each of these treatments where applicable.

Risk transfer through risk management insurance is a common method of obtaining financial protection against potential loss. Our risk management consultants can help you identify insurable risk areas. Moreover, we will show you how to minimize your risk management insurance cost through correct use of all available treatment options and through educational initiatives proven to reduce events that result in loss.

Maximizing Your Risk Management Insurance Dollar

Risk Management Insurance can alleviate loss from everything from fire and labor disputes, to product liability, lawsuits and publicity disasters. For many types of risk, insuring against financial loss is the best option. In addition, we will show you ways that you can reduce the cost of your risk management insurance. To reduce your total insurance cost while still protecting against disasters, reduce the likelihood of negative events through proactive programs that manage information and feature accurate training for all employees at point of risk positions. Again, reducing the probability of loss can reduce your risk managment insurance costs.

RISK MANAGEMENT PLANNING

At the heart of Risk Management Planning is information. Planning in risk management is not possible without understanding where and how your entity is exposed to risk, how those exposures relate to your organization's goals and objectives and the expected effect of all possible methods of treatment - acceptance, avoidance, mitigation and transfer - on both the specific risk and on organizational objectives.

Effective risk management planning requires an accurate description of the risk and its causes, the impact should an adverse event occur and the identities of the risk owners and their assigned responsibilities. Documentation can be critical. Owners of risk must understand the treatment of each risk and the actions necessary to implement those treatments.

Risk Management Planning Follows the Risk Assessment

Most of the information so vital to effective risk management planning is generated during the risk assessment. A risk assessment identifies risk, measures its potential impact - including any impact on an organization's objectives. Risk assessment is a cornerstone among the principles of risk management.

RISK MANAGEMENT SERVICES

From simple lost sales to a major disaster, exposure to risk is a business reality. Your risk management measures should be as real as the issues they are meant to address. Our experts are here to help. What level of support do you need? Our risk management consultants are seasoned professionals who provide excellent service and the most up to date risk management training. We can even embed our experts directly into your business.

Risk Management: Risk Assessment

Our experienced risk management consultants will work with you to identify and quantify your exposure to risk.

We provide detailed summaries that define your risk and effective risk management strategies to help you control events that could result in loss. Our special focus partners are niche experts that can furnish reviews and recommendations in areas such as credit, finance and information technology at risk.

Risk Management: Risk Mitigation

Loss happens. But, it can be managed, mitigated, reduced, and in some cases avoided altogether. Our team of risk management experts can help you reduce potential losses.

We can help you establish proactive mitigation in the form of risk management programs that can reduce the frequency and severity of events such as workplace accidents, loss of property and more. We can also help you to establish a business continuity plan that will help you get back in business in the event of a major disaster.

Loss Analysis & Loss Financing Evaluation

Our risk management services include evaluating your business objectives and current conditions to prioritize your efforts and minimize your risk management insurance cost.

The effective use of deductibles, retentions and appropriate policy limits can ensure that your earnings are protected at the lowest cost. We will review financial alternatives with you to be certain that your risk management strategy firmly safeguards your earnings.

RISK MANAGEMENT SOLUTIONS

The right Risk Management Solution for your business is the one tailored to your services, practices, objectives, risk profile and risk appetite. Our approach to risk management is an in depth procedural method to assist you in selecting from a broad range of services to be sure that you get exactly what you need based on your specific circumstances.

Risk Management Solutions Require a Risk Management Strategy

Through discussions with executive management and stakeholders, we can help you define your risk management strategy. That strategy becomes the guiding force in the decisions made by managers at all organizational levels, from parents to subsidiaries to partners.

Risk Management Solutions Help to Ensure Stability

Effective risk management solutions identify your at risk areas, quantify potential loss and establish plans for control and migation. Our solutions include establishing controls and safeguards for all of your areas at risk. We'll help you to ensure the stability of your business.

Our risk management consultants methodically identify potential losses, evaluate risk control and risk financing alternatives and assist you in the implementation of corrective actions. We will develop a customized program that ensures you are getting the most value from your account team and from your risk management dollars.

RISK MANAGEMENT STRATEGY

Developing a complete Risk Management Strategy means generating an organized approach for treatment of all exposures to risk from the organizational perspective. Following a risk management assessment, following the planning of specific treatments for specific risks, an organization must develop a comprehensive risk management strategy for treating risk that best serves the objectives and goals of the organization as a whole.

Risk Management Strategy: Challenges

Through the assessment, analysis and planning stages, such treatments as avoidance, retention, reduction and transfer will have been evaluated for specific risks. Evaluating the effect of these treatments on organizational objectives, in light of organizational priorities, can be a difficult and time consuming endeavor. Getting it right is one of the most difficult challenges when developing a risk management strategy.

Tailored Risk Management Solutions

Our experienced risk management professionals have served as consultants for a number of Fortune 1000 clients, many multi-national, and can be invaluable in helping you shape your risk management strategy to best serve organizational goals and objectives. Your risk management strategy should be and - with our risk management expertise - can be tailored to your exact needs.

RISK MANAGEMENT TRAINING

Risk Management Training can provide decision makers and managers the skills needed to perform their risk related duties effectively. When your managers and decision makers lack specific risk management expertise, invest in them. Provide them with risk management training.

In most organizations, those pressed into the role of risk managers have backgrounds in everything other than risk management. Many owners of risk are decision makers in their own departments who have little if any experience with risk management concepts, methods and goals. Risk management training can help you keep your key people in key positions while expanding their capabilities.

Who Needs Risk Management Training?

Simple: Anyone charged with identifying, reporting, evaluating or managing an exposure to risk needs risk management training. Your executives, managers, project managers, decision makers and systems specialists are typically responsible for some aspect of your organization's overall risk management effort. You can best protect your organization from risk by providing them the skills necessary to perform their risk management related tasks.

PROJECT RISK MANAGEMENT PRINCIPLES

The principles of project risk management can be stated very simply. Any project organisation is subject to risks. One which finds itself in a state of perpetual crisis, is failing to manage risks properly.

Failure to manage risks is characterised by inability to decide what to do, when to do it, and whether enough has been done. Risk Management is a facet of Quality, using basic techniques of analysis and measurement to ensure that risks are properly identified, classified, and managed.

Risk management is the systematic process of managing an organization's risk exposures to achieve its objectives in a manner consistent with public interest, human safety, environmental factors, and the law. It consists of the planning, organizing, leading, coordinating, and controlling activities undertaken with the intent of providing an efficient pre-loss plan that minimizes the adverse impact of risk on the organization's resources, earnings, and cash flows.

In my view the mosthelpful definition is that given by Larry Krantz, Chief Executive of Euro Log Ltd here in the UK. Larry says that 'A risk is a combination of constraint and uncertainty'. We all face constraints in our projects, and also uncertainty. So we can minimise the risk in the project either by eliminating constraints (a nice conceit) or by finding and reducing uncertainty.

The illustration plots uncertainty against constraint. The curved line indicates the 'acceptable level of risk', whatever that may be in the individual case.

The risk may be reduced to an acceptable level by reducing either or both of uncertainty and constraint. In practice, few people have the opportunity to reduce constraint, so most focus on the reduction of uncertainty.

It is also worth noting from the diagram that total elimination of risk is rarely achieved. So we have to consider how to manage that remaining risk most effectively. There are two stages in the process of Project Risk Management, Risk

Assessment and Risk Control. Risk Assessment can take place at any time during the project, though the sooner the better. However, Risk Control cannot be effective without a previous Risk Assessment.

Similarly, most people tend to think that having performed a Risk Assessment, they have done all that is needed. Far too many projects spend a great deal of effort on Risk Assessment and then ignore Risk control completely.

Risk Assessment has three elements:

Identify Uncertainties

Explore the entire project plans and look for areas of uncertainty.

Analyse Risks

Specify how those areas of uncertainty can impact the performance of the project, either in duration, cost or meeting the users' requirements.

Prioritise Risks

Establish which of those Risks should be eliminated completely, because of potential extreme impact, which should have regular management attention, and which are sufficiently minor to avoid detailed management attention.

In the same way, Risk Control has three elements, as follows:

Mitigate Risks

Take whatever actions are possible in advance to reduce the effect of Risk. It is better to spend money on mitigation than to include contingency in the plan.

Plan for Emergencies

For all those Risks which are deemed to be significant, have an emergency plan in place before it happens.

Measure and Control

Track the effects of the risks identified and manage them to a successful conclusion.

THE ELEMENTS OF PROJECT RISK MANAGEMENT

In Project Risk Management Principles we have seen an overview of the principles involved.

This article takes a deeper view of the elements of both Risk Assessment and Risk Control, and proposes some whimsical considerations which we believe are worthy of serious thought.

The Elements of Risk Assessment

We have shown these elements as three separate branches of the same tree. This is correct, but it is important to remember that the process is in fact an iterative one, and the Risk Assessment is only completed when the Assessors and Project Manager are satisfied that any undetected risks are now insignificant.

Identify Uncertainties (and Constraints)

Explore the entire project plans and look for areas of uncertainty or constraints. It is not possible to stress too often that "The project will be late." is not a risk, it is an impact. We need to crawl over the plans to search for things which could make the project late. The risk could be expressed as "We have underestimated the likely duration of task xxx." Some examples of areas of uncertainty are:

- Failure to understand who the project is for
- Failure to appoint an executive user responsible for sponsoring the project
- Failure to appoint a fully qualified and supported project manager
- Failure to define the objectives of the project
- Failure to secure commitments from people who are needed to assist with the project
- Failure to estimate costs accurately
- Failure to specify very precisely the end users' requirements

- Failure to provide a good working environment for the project
- Failure to tie in all the people involved in the project with contracts or Documents of Understanding

Analyse Risks

The probability of occurrence of a risk, which is another way of saying how uncertain the success of the task would be, against the Impact. By Impact we mean the severity of the effect on either the budget, the timeliness of project completion, or the ability of the project to meet the users' requirements. Whether the severity of Impact or the Probability is high or low is a matter for the judgement of the Risk Assessor and the Project Manager - even with rational method involved we are still talking of an art! We have classified the four sectors of the graph, perhaps whimsically, as:

Tigers

High Probability, High Impact. These are dangerous animals and must be neutralised as soon as possible.

Alligators

Low Probability, High Impact. These are dangerous animals which can be avoided with care. However, we all remember the old joke that it is difficult to remember when one is up to the arise in alligators that the original objective was to drain the swamp.

Puppies

High Probability, Low Impact. We all know that delightful pup will grow into an animal which can do damage, but a little training will ensure that not too much trouble ensures.

Kittens

Low Probability, Low Impact. The largest cat is rarely the source of trouble, but on the other hand a lot of effort can be wasted on training it! List each of your identified Risks, decide on the probability occurrence of each, and define the expected impact on schedule, budget, and ability to meet the users' requirements.

Prioritise Risks

By now you have really done this. Tigers have to be neutralised i.e. the risks must be mitigated early on. Alligators have to be watched, and there must be an action plan in place to stop them from interfering with the project. Puppies similarly have to be watched, but less stringently and with less urgent containment plans. Kittens can be ignored at the peril of the project manager.

THE ELEMENTS OF RISK CONTROL

Mitigate Risks

You would do this for all those risks categorised above as Tigers. We can mitigate risks by reducing either the probability or the impact. Remember that we identified the risk by seeking uncertainty in the project.

The probability can be reduced by action up front to ensure that a particular risk is reduced. An example is to employ a team to run some testing on a particular data base or data structure to ensure that it will work when the remainder of the project is put together around it. The technique of building a pilot phase of the project is an example of risk mitigation. Unfortunately it often fails, because the team works closely with the pilot user group, and then thinks that all the problems are solved for the roll out. This is rarely the case.

Plan for Emergencies

By performing the risk assessment, we know the most likely areas of the project which will go wrong. So the project risk plan should include, against each identified risk, an emergency plan to recover from the risk.

As a minimum, this plan will name the person accountable for recovery from the risk, the nature of the risk and the action to be taken to resolve it, and the method by which the risk can be spotted. A risk which has been mitigated may still be a significant and dangerous risk - it is rare for a tiger to be converted to a kitten by action before the event. These will require emergency plans as well as alligators and puppies.

Kittens can probably be allowed to play at will, provided we are satisfied they really are kittens!

Measure and Control

The owner of each risk should be responsible to the project manager to monitor his risk, and to take appropriate action to prevent it from going on, or to take recovery action if the problem does occur. Nothing can be controlled which cannot be measured. In a project there are three things which can always be measured - the schedule, the cost, and the users satisfaction.

Risk management is a structured approach to managing uncertainty related to a threat, a sequence of human activities including: risk assessment, strategies development to manage it, and mitigation of risk using managerial resources.

The strategies include transferring the risk to another party, avoiding the risk, reducing the negative effect of the risk, and accepting some or all of the consequences of a particular risk.

Some traditional risk managements are focused on risks stemming from physical or legal causes (e.g. natural disasters or fires, accidents, death and lawsuits). Financial risk management, on the other hand, focuses on risks that can be managed using traded financial instruments.

The objective of risk management is to reduce different risks related to a preselected domain to the level accepted by society. It may refer to numerous types of threats caused by environment, technology, humans, organizations and politics. On the other hand it involves all means available for humans, or in particular, for a risk management entity (person, staff, organization).

Some Explanations

In ideal risk management, a prioritization process is followed whereby the risks with the greatest loss and the greatest probability of occurring are handled first, and risks with lower probability of occurrence and lower loss are handled in descending order. In practice the process can be very difficult, and balancing between risks with a high probability of occurrence but lower loss versus a risk with high loss but lower probability of occurrence can often be mishandled.

Intangible risk management identifies a new type of risk - a risk that has a 100% probability of occurring but is ignored by the organization due to a lack of identification ability. For example, when deficient knowledge is applied to a situation, a knowledge risk materialises. Relationship risk appears when ineffective collaboration occurs. Process-engagement risk may be an issue when ineffective operational procedures are applied. These risks directly reduce the productivity of knowledge workers, decrease cost effectiveness, profitability, service, quality, reputation, brand value, and earnings quality. Intangible risk management allows risk management to create immediate value from the identification and reduction of risks that reduce productivity.

Risk management also faces difficulties allocating resources. This is the idea of opportunity cost. Resources spent on risk management could have been spent on more profitable activities. Again, ideal risk management minimizes spending while maximizing the reduction of the negative effects of risks.

Steps in the Risk Management Process

Establish the Context

Establishing the context involves

- Identification of risk in a selected domain of interest
- Planning the remainder of the process.

Mapping out the following:

- the social scope of risk management
- the identity and objectives of stakeholders
- the basis upon which risks will be evaluated, constraints.
- Defining a framework for the activity and an agenda for identification.
- Developing an analysis of risks involved in the process.
- Mitigation of risks using available technological, human and organizational resources.

Identification

After establishing the context, the next step in the process of managing risk is to identify potential risks. Risks are about events that, when triggered, cause problems. Hence, risk identification can start with the source of problems, or with the problem itself. Source analysis Risk sources may be internal or external to the system that is the target of risk management. Examples of risk sources are: stakeholders of a project, employees of a company or the weather over an airport. Problem analysis Risks are related to identified threats. For example: the threat of losing money, the threat of abuse of privacy information or the threat of accidents and casualties. The threats may exist with various entities, most important with shareholders, customers and legislative bodies such as the government. When either source or problem is known, the events that a source may trigger or the events that can lead to a problem can be investigated. For example: stakeholders withdrawing during a project may endanger funding of the project; privacy information may be stolen by employees even within a closed network; lightning striking a Boeing 747 during takeoff may make all people on board immediate casualties.

The chosen method of identifying risks may depend on culture, industry practice and compliance. The identification methods are formed by templates or the development of templates for identifying source, problem or event. Common risk identification methods are:

Objectives-based risk identification Organizations and project teams have objectives. Any event that may endanger achieving an objective partly or completely is identified as risk.

Scenario-based risk identification In scenario analysis different scenarios are created. The scenarios may be the alternative ways to achieve an objective, or an analysis of the interaction of forces in, for example, a market or battle. Any event that triggers an undesired scenario alternative is identified as risk. Taxonomy-based risk identification The taxonomy in taxonomy-based risk identification is a breakdown of possible risk sources. Based on the taxonomy and knowledge of best practices, a questionnaire is compiled. The answers to the questions reveal risks. Taxonomy-based risk identification in software industry can be found in CMU/SEI-93-TR-6.

Risk Charting This method combines the above approaches by listing Resources at risk, Threats to those resources Modifying Factors which may increase or reduce the risk and Consequences it is wished to avoid. Creating a matrix under these headings enables a variety of approaches. One can begin with resources and consider the threats they are exposed to and the consequences of each. Alternatively one can start with the threats and examine which resources they would affect, or one can begin with the consequences and determine which combination of threats and resources would be involved to bring them about.

Assessment

Once risks have been identified, they must then be assessed as to their potential severity of loss and to the probability of occurrence. These quantities can be either simple to measure, in the case of the value of a lost building, or impossible to know for sure in the case of the probability of an unlikely event occurring. Therefore, in the assessment process it is critical to make the best educated guesses possible in order to properly prioritize the implementation of the risk management plan.

The fundamental difficulty in risk assessment is determining the rate of occurrence since statistical information is not available on all kinds of past incidents. Furthermore, evaluating the severity of the consequences (impact) is often quite difficult for immaterial assets. Asset valuation is another question that needs to be addressed. Thus, best educated opinions and available statistics are the primary sources of information. Nevertheless, risk assessment should produce such information for the management of the organization that the primary risks are easy to understand and that the risk management decisions may be prioritized. Thus, there have been several theories and attempts to quantify risks. Numerous different risk formulae exist, but perhaps the most widely accepted formula for risk quantification is:

Rate of Occurrence Multiplied by the Impact of the Event Equals Risk

Later research has shown that the financial benefits of risk management are less dependent on the formula used but are more dependent on the frequency and how risk assessment is performed. In business it is imperative to be able to present the findings of risk assessments in financial terms. Robert Courtney Jr. (IBM, 1970) proposed a formula for presenting risks in financial terms. The Courtney formula was accepted as the official risk analysis method for the US governmental agencies. The formula proposes calculation of ALE (annualised loss expectancy) and compares the expected loss value to the security control implementation costs (cost-benefit analysis).

Potential Risk Treatments

Once risks have been identified and assessed, all techniques to manage the risk fall into one or more of these four major categories:

- Avoidance (eliminate)
- Reduction (mitigate)
- Transference (outsource or insure)
- Retention (accept and budget)

Ideal use of these strategies may not be possible. Some of them may involve trade-offs that are not acceptable to the organization or person making the risk management decisions. Another source, from the US Department of Defense, Defense Acquisition University, calls these categories ACAT, for Avoid, Control, Accept, or Transfer. This use of the ACAT acronym is reminiscent of another ACAT (for Acquisition Category) used in US Defense industry procurements, in which Risk Management figures prominently in decision making and planning.

Risk Avoidance

Includes not performing an activity that could carry risk. An example would be not buying a property or business in order to not take on the liability that comes with it. Another would be not flying in order to not take the risk that the airplane were to be hijacked. Avoidance may seem the answer to all risks, but avoiding risks also means losing out on the potential gain that accepting (retaining) the risk may have allowed. Not entering a business to avoid the risk of loss also avoids the possibility of earning profits.

Risk Reduction

Involves methods that reduce the severity of the loss or the likelihood of the loss from occurring. Examples include sprinklers designed to put out a fire to reduce the risk of loss by fire. This method may cause a greater loss by water damage and therefore may not be suitable. Halon fire suppression systems may mitigate that risk, but the cost may be prohibitive as a strategy. Modern software development methodologies reduce risk by developing and delivering software incrementally. Early methodologies suffered from the fact that they only delivered software in the final phase of development; any problems encountered in earlier phases meant costly rework and often jeopardized the whole project. By developing in iterations, software projects can limit effort wasted to a single iteration. Outsourcing could be an example of risk reduction if the outsourcer can demonstrate higher capability at managing or reducing risks. In this case companies outsource only some of their departmental needs. For example, a company may outsource only its software development, the manufacturing of hard goods, or customer support needs to another company, while handling the business management itself. This way, the company can concentrate more on business development without having to worry as much about the manufacturing process, managing the development team, or finding a physical location for a call center.

Risk Retention

Involves accepting the loss when it occurs. True self insurance falls in this category. Risk retention is a viable strategy for small risks where the cost of insuring against the risk would be greater over time than the total losses sustained. All risks that are not avoided or transferred are retained by default.

This includes risks that are so large or catastrophic that they either cannot be insured against or the premiums would be infeasible. War is an example since most property and risks are not insured against war, so the loss attributed by war is retained by the insured. Also any amounts of potential loss (risk) over the amount insured is retained risk. This may also be acceptable if the chance of a very large loss is small or if the cost to insure for greater coverage amounts is so great it would hinder the goals of the organization too much.

Risk Transference

Many sectors have for a long time regarded insurance as a transfer of risk. This is not correct. Insurance is a post event compensatory mechanism. That is, even if an insurance policy has been effected this does not mean that the risk has been transferred. For example, a personal injuries insurance policy does not transfer the risk of a car accident to the insurance company. The risk still lies with the policy holder namely the person who has been in the accident. The insurance policy simply provides that if an accident (the event) occurs involving the policy holder then some compensation may be payable to the policy holder that is commensurate to the suffering/damage.

Means causing another party to accept the risk, typically by contract or by hedging. Insurance is one type of risk transfer that uses contracts. Other times it may involve contract language that transfers a risk to another party without the payment of an insurance premium. Liability among construction or other contractors is very often transferred this way. On the other hand, taking offsetting positions in derivatives is typically how firms use hedging to financially manage risk.

Some ways of managing risk fall into multiple categories. Risk retention pools are technically retaining the risk for the group, but spreading it over the whole group involves transfer among individual members of the group. This is different from traditional insurance, in that no premium is exchanged between members of the group up front, but instead losses are assessed to all members of the group.

Create a Risk Management Plan

Select appropriate controls or countermeasures to measure each risk. Risk mitigation needs to be approved by the appropriate level of management. For example, a risk concerning the image of the organization should have top management decision behind it whereas IT management would have the authority to decide on computer virus risks.

The risk management plan should propose applicable and effective security controls for managing the risks. For example, an observed high risk of computer viruses could be mitigated by acquiring and implementing antivirus software. A good risk management plan should contain a schedule for control implementation and responsible persons for those actions.

According to ISO/IEC 27001, the stage immediately after completion of the Risk Assessment phase consists of preparing a Risk Treatment Plan, which should document the decisions about how each of the identified risks should be handled. Mitigation of risks often means selection of Security Controls, which should be documented in a Statement of Applicability, which identifies which particular control objectives and controls from the standard have been selected, and why.

Implementation

Follow all of the planned methods for mitigating the effect of the risks. Purchase insurance policies for the risks that have been decided to be transferred to an insurer, avoid all risks that can be avoided without sacrificing the entity's goals, reduce others, and retain the rest.

Review and Evaluation of the Plan

Initial risk management plans will never be perfect. Practice, experience, and actual loss results will necessitate changes in the plan and contribute information to allow possible different decisions to be made in dealing with the risks being faced. Risk analysis results and management plans should be updated periodically. There are two primary reasons for this:

- to evaluate whether the previously selected security controls are still applicable and effective, and

- to evaluate the possible risk level changes in the business environment. For example, information risks are a good example of rapidly changing business environment.

Limitations

If risks are improperly assessed and prioritized, time can be wasted in dealing with risk of losses that are not likely to occur. Spending too much time assessing and managing unlikely risks can divert resources that could be used more profitably. Unlikely events do occur but if the risk is unlikely enough to occur it may be better to simply retain the risk and deal with the result if the loss does in fact occur. Prioritizing too highly the risk management processes could keep an organization from ever completing a project or even getting started. This is especially true if other work is suspended until the risk management process is considered complete. It is also important to keep in mind the distinction between risk and uncertainty. Risk can be measured by impacts x probability.

Areas of Risk Management

As applied to corporate finance, risk management is the technique for measuring, monitoring and controlling the financial or operational risk on a firm's balance sheet. See value at risk. The Basel II framework breaks risks into market risk (price risk), credit risk and operational risk and also specifies methods for calculating capital requirements for each of these components.

Enterprise Risk Management

In enterprise risk management, a risk is defined as a possible event or circumstance that can have negative influences on the enterprise in question. Its impact can be on the very existence, the resources (human and capital), the products and services, or the customers of the enterprise, as well as external impacts on society, markets, or the environment.

In a financial institution, enterprise risk management is normally thought of as the combination of credit risk, interest rate risk or asset liability management, market risk, and operational risk. In the more general case, every probable risk can have a pre-formulated plan to deal with its possible consequences (to ensure contingency if the risk becomes a liability). From the information above and the average cost per employee over time, or cost accrual ratio, a project manager can estimate:

- the cost associated with the risk if it arises, estimated by multiplying employee costs per unit time by the estimated 8ime lost (cost impact, C where C = cost accrual ratio * S).
- the probable increase in time associated with a risk (schedule variance due to risk, Rs where Rs = P * S):

Sorting on this value puts the highest risks to the schedule first. This is intended to cause the greatest risks to the project to be attempted first so that risk is minimized as quickly as possible. This is slightly misleading as schedule variances with a large P and small S and vice versa are not equivalent. (The risk of the RMS Titanic sinking vs. the passengers' meals being served at slightly the wrong time).

- the probable increase in cost associated with a risk (cost variance due to risk, Rc where Rc = P*C = P*CAR*S= P*S*CAR)
- sorting on this value puts the highest risks to the budget first.
- see concerns about schedule variance as this is a function of it, as illustrated in the equation above.

Risk in a project or process can be due either to Special Cause Variation or Common Cause Variation and requires appropriate treatment. That is to re-iterate the concern about extremal cases not being equivalent in the list immediately above.

Risk Management Activities as Applied to Project Management

In project management, risk management includes the following activities: Planning how risk management will be held in the particular project. Plan should include risk management tasks, responsibilities, activities and budget.

Assigning a risk officer - a team member other than a project manager who is responsible for foreseeing potential project problems. Typical characteristic of risk officer is a healthy skepticism. Maintaining live project risk database. Each risk should have the following attributes: opening date, title, short description, probability and importance. Optionally a risk may have an assigned person responsible for its resolution and a date by which the risk must be resolved. Creating anonymous risk reporting channel. Each team member should have possibility to report risk thathe foresees in the project. Preparing mitigation plans for risks that are chosen to be mitigated. The purpose of the mitigation plan is to describe how this particular risk will be handled – what, when, by who and how will it be done to avoid it or minimize consequences if it becomes a liability. Summarizing planned and faced risks, effectiveness of mitigation activities, and effort spent for the risk management.

Risk Management and Business Continuity

Risk management is simply a practice of systematically selecting cost effective approaches for minimising the effect of threat realization to the organization. All risks can never be fully avoided or mitigated simply because of financial and practical limitations. Therefore all organizations have to accept some level of residual risks. Whereas risk management tends to be preemptive, business continuity planning (BCP) was invented to deal with the consequences of realised residual risks. The necessity to have BCP in place arises because even very unlikely events will occur if given enough time. Risk management and BCP are often mistakenly seen as rivals or overlapping practices. In fact these processes are so tightly tied together that such separation seems artificial. For example, the risk management process creates important inputs for the BCP (assets, impact assessments, cost estimates etc). Risk management also proposes applicable controls for the observed risks. Therefore, risk management covers several areas that are vital for the BCP process. However, the BCP process goes beyond risk management's preemptive approach and moves on from the assumption that the disaster will realize at some point.

2

INSURANCE IN BUSINESS AND TRADE

Although almost all businesses need to buy insurance, for most it is ancillary to their main trade. As the 1980 report said: There are certain mischiefs in the law of nondisclosure which apply equally whether the insured is a consumer or a businessman who is not constantly concerned in his business activities with the insurance market. Neither consumers nor ordinary businessmen who are not in the insurance market have the knowledge or experience to identify all facts which may be material to insurers. Both are therefore to this extent in need of protection and both may properly be regarded as consumers visàvis insurers.

The British Insurance Law Association also stressed this point: "a tradesman insuring his business is in as much need of protection as when he is insuring his home". Lord Justice Longmore argued that the fact the insurance industry accepts that the strict law needs to be modified for consumers suggests strongly that it should also be modified for businesses: How can it be right that a lawyer insuring his home and household possession can rely on the more relaxed test of nondisclosure under the Statements of Practice, but the small trader, eg the garage owner or the fishmonger insuring his premises, cannot?

In 1980, the English Law Commission pointed to harsh cases involving small businesses, especially where the nondisclosed issue related to moral hazard. For example, in

Locker & Woolf Ltd v Western Australian Insurance Co, a fire claim was rejected on the grounds that the applicant had not revealed that the partnership had previously been refused motor cover. We do not think that many people running noninsurance businesses would understand the full extent of the duty of disclosure that the law requires. They are unlikely to understand, for example, that they must volunteer information about criminal offences their employees have committed, or any previous rejection for insurance. Brokers or inhouse expertise

That said, many applicants will be advised by brokers, and some may have specialist staff. This is sometimes also true for consumers, but with business insurance it is much more common.

In our Scoping Paper we drew attention to the type of problem that can arise where an applicant for insurance discloses material facts to an intermediary and the intermediary fails to pass on that information to the insurer. We intend to address this issue in a later paper – it does not form part of current discussions.

More generally we do not think that the involvement of an intermediary should affect the test of materiality, though it may affect the standard of disclosure that can be expected from an insured.

Supporting Trust and Confidence in the Market

Even for large commercial risks, the insurance market is built on trust and generally accepted standards of market practice. We are concerned that the law undercuts rather than supports accepted market practice. Let us take the example of avoidance. Avoidance is an appropriate remedy for conduct involving some form of dishonesty, but the law allows it to be used where an insured has acted innocently or inadvertently in making an untrue statement or failing to disclose a fact that is known to be material.

Insurance solicitors dealing with high value claims justify the current law on the ground that it is necessary to prevent sharp dealing. As one solicitor put it: Time and again [nondisclosure] isn't inadvertent. A commercial decision has been made: this will not be insured if we tell the whole truth. And in those circumstances the sanction [of avoidance] should remain.

It is often said that the full remedy of avoidance will only be applied if there is some element of fraud or dishonesty. We were told that good market practice is that an insurer will honour an insurance contract unless there is some element of dishonesty on the part of the insured.

I always advise my clients that if they get a whiff of nondisclosure or misrepresentation, basically the panel or court has to think there is a bit of a stitchup here. You don't really avoid for technical nondisclosure.

However, if the law permits insurers to avoid for purely technical nondisclosure, it is inevitable that some insurers will take the point. When we asked one firm whether insurers would ever attempt to avoid a policy for an innocent nondisclosure, this is the answer we received: Some would, especially in a climate where money is tight. I suspect that they still would. Yes. And what also there is the potential for with the big commercial [risks]... they're subscribed to by three, five, twenty different insurers. And you could have three or four who are perhaps looking at insolvency problems or whatever and will in truth seize on any opportunity they can.

So... to take comfort in the thought that the market as a whole will not take the point on innocent disclosure– you might be surprised really. There would be a risk that some parts of it would. When we asked whether that particular firm would attempt to avoid for an innocent nondisclosure, we were told that they would if instructed to: That is the current law, so we would, yes... We wouldn't really have a choice.

If the insured had indeed acted fraudulently, we need have little sympathy. However, if the law provides insurers with a strong financial incentive to attempt to avoid even where there was no fraud, it is inevitable that some insurers in some circumstances will use the weapon they have been given. This has the potential to undercut more ethical insurers and to undermine confidence in the UK market. It can contribute to the perception that the law in this country is unduly insurerfriendly.

The Insurer is Judge and Jury

A particular complaint is that while reputable insurers will not avoid for innocent misrepresentation or nondisclosure, they may do so if they suspect fraud, even if they cannot prove it. This effectively allows them to be "judge and jury in their own cause". In other contexts the courts have roundly condemned provisions that, in effect, oust their jurisdiction.

All or Nothing Remedies

Under the current law, an insurer may avoid whenever it can show that, had it known the information, it would only have altered a single term of the contract, a term which need not have any connection with the disputed claim. Moreover, the current law, does not permit half measures. An insurer cannot pay a claim and avoid for the future, or accept liability for a proportion of the claim.

It must either seek to avoid completely, or waive all rights to a remedy. As one solicitor put it: There are avoidance cases where... you have to say to the [insurer] client, I'm sorry, you've got one remedy, and the client may say – 'that's very heavy – we don't particularly want to go that far'... If they don't, they lose the remedy completely. So it's pay or avoid... It means [the insurers] have to avoid or abandon their right. And they have shareholders and people.

Even in cases where it seems right to allow an insurer some remedy, avoidance can appear to be excessively harsh. Lord Justice Longmore makes this point, quoting *Kausar v Eagle Star*: Avoidance for nondisclosure is a drastic remedy. It enables the insurer to disclaim liability after, and not before, he has discovered that the risk turns out to be a bad one~ it leaves the insurer without the protection which he thoughthe had contracted and paid for... I do consider that there should be some restraint in the operation of the doctrine.

In practice, of course, most cases are resolved through some sort of settlement. The insurer alleges nondisclosure and misrepresentation~ the insured denies that the fact is material, or pleads that it was a mere expectation or belief, held in good faith. After some horsetrading, a settlement is reached. Lawyers acting for insurers worried that if the law was changed to provide proportional remedies the insurer would have to start by offering more, and would end up paying more: Instead of going into negotiations saying we are paying nothing and end up paying half, we would say we would pay a third and end up paying two thirds. Inevitably, most cases will be resolved through bargaining conducted in the shadow of the legal rules. Our concern is that the current legal rules have little connection to fairness or market expectations, but instead provide insurers with a weapon that can be wielded simply to reduce the size of a settlement.

Pooling of Risks

It is frequently said that the law is too much in favour of the insurer, and that it needs to be rebalanced in favour of the insured. We think that the question of balance between insurer and insured is one that must be approached with great care.

In our view the question is not really whether the law favours one or other party too much. It is whether the rules that will be applied when the parties have not made a different agreement (for example, have not agreed that the insurer may not avoid for innocent misrepresentation) represent a fair or efficient balance. To put it another way, had both parties known of the potential issue in advance, what would they have agreed?

To the best of our knowledge, the insurance market is fully competitive in terms of price. Putting it simply, the insured gets what it pays for. If the law is to be changed so as to give the insured more rights for example, by preventing the insurer from avoiding the contract on the ground of an innocent misrepresentation or nondisclosure, there will be a marginal increase in the cost of policies, since insurers will now be obliged to pay out on some policies that under the old law they might have avoided. However, whether the market is less competitive depends on the preferences of insureds. If it is true that insurers will normally pay in such a case unless there is a suggestion of fraud, and that fraud is rare, the increase is likely to be low. While some insureds may prefer to pay slightly less and take the risk that their policy is avoided because of a purely innocent, nonnegligent misrepresentation on their part, others may prefer to pay a slightly higher premium to have this risk transferred to the pool of risks covered by the insurer.

The Parties are Free to Agree what they Want

An argument often made against reform is that it is unnecessary because the current law is not compulsory~ if insureds don't like it, they can ask for better terms in their policy. In other words, the market will take care of any problem without the need for reform.

No doubt there are insureds who are sufficiently sophisticated to study very carefully the terms offered by potential insurers and who bargain for changes in their favour. It is quite clear from the cases and from the many sad histories supplied to us that there are large numbers of business insureds who do not. They may have no expertise in insurance law and may simply not be able to understand the effect of the policy offered.

They may not be able to afford expert advice or may rationally take the view that the chances of a problem occurring are low enough that it is not worthwhile to spend time or money doing so. If they are not important customers, then even if they are aware of the difficulties they may be unable to persuade the insurer to write a special policy just for them. That is a quite understandable reaction on the part of the insurer, since for many types of relatively lowvalue insurance, writing and administering policies on different terms may be uneconomic. But whatever the reason, if the insured would in fact have been willing to pay a sufficient additional premium to cover the cost of the improvement in cover plus the regular profit element, there is a form of market failure – the terms of the contract are inefficient.

Thus the question is whether the rules for business insurance can be made to correspond more closely to what insureds want– and, given the generally high standards of the vast majority of insurers, insureds probably think that they are getting when they buy insurance in the UK market.

Mandatory or Default Rules

The rules we have proposed for consumer insurance would be mandatory rules to the extent that the parties would not be free to vary them in favour of the insurer. We need to consider whether whatever rules are thought appropriate for business insurance should be similarly mandatory, should be merely default rules that the parties are free to vary or should be semimandatory in the sense that they can be varied provided that the change from the default rules is "fair". (That is the test applied to consumer contracts in general, though not to the 'core terms', under Unfair Terms in Consumer Contracts Regulations 1999.)

In general terms we do not favour mandatory rules for business insurance contracts. We think it is important to preserve freedom of contract unless there is a very good reason to depart from it. Nor do we favour applying a fairness test, except perhaps for insurance contracts with small businesses. 8 The reason is quite simply the uncertainty that such controls can create. Thus we think that for business insurance contracts in general, any proposed rules should be default rules that can be disapplied by contrary agreement.

It may be argued that this will defeat the object of reform insurers will simply write their contracts to reflect the old law. Most insurance contracts are on standard terms~ all we would be achieving would be an alteration in the standard terms.

We do not think that this is true, nor that, if it were, it would necessarily follow that reform is pointless. First, we think most insurers would be reluctant to reduce the rights of the insured from the legal norm without discussing the matter expressly with the insured. Most insurers are rightly proud of their reputation and it would do their reputation no good at all to be found to have taken away the insured's "new rights" by means of a standard term that was not expressly agreed by the parties. And of course if the parties do freely agree to revert to the position under the old law, there can be no objection. That is what freedom of contract means.

Secondly, having to insert special terms to revert to the previous position at least gives the insured a chance to discover what is happening by reading the terms. If they object, they can then try to bargain for something better. Indeed, we hope that the publicity that would inevitably surround any change in the law of insurance would positively encourage insureds to ask insurers: are my rights under the new Insurance Act fully protected?

Lastly, insurers may be reluctant to try to reduce the insured's rights by means of standard clauses for fear that they may not work. It has to be remembered that the courts will interpret the terms of the insurance contract, when there is doubt, in favour of the insured (under the contra proferentem rule) but they will do so against the background of the existing law.

In other words, if a provision merely leaves in place the insurer's current rights, it is unlikely to be given a narrow interpretation. But were the law to be changed to give the insured more rights, a clause excluding those rights would probably be read narrowly. The insurer would have to use very clear words. We do not think this would be inappropriate. The parties should be free to agree what they want but insureds should be left in no doubt where they stand.

Keeping UK Law Competitive

The insurance industry makes a significant contribution to the invisible earnings of the UK. However, we have been told that in recent years the London market in particular has lost a large amount of international business, and that this has been partly as a result of the state of insurance contract law.

It has been suggested that from the perspective of brokers or policyholders, other jurisdictions provide a more attractive legal regime. Bermuda, France and Norway are amongst the countries mentioned. To date, definitive figures on the loss of business have proved elusive. Furthermore, one observer suggested that the loss was a positive development: Yes, we've lost 40% of the business but it was the 40% we wanted to lose!

Nevertheless, we would like to explore how reforms in the law might support the UK insurance industry and therefore invite views on this issue.

It is our tentative proposal that the law affecting business insurance should be changed to give the insured certain additional rights, but that the rules should in general not be mandatory.

NONDISCLOSURE

In Part 6 we tentatively proposed that consumers should no longer have a residual duty of disclosure. 9 Rather, insurers should have to ask for the information they need. They should be entitled to ask questions in general terms ("Are there any other facts that we ought to know?") but the answers given should be judged by what the reasonable consumer would think was being asked about. Thus if the consumer reasonably thought that a fact they did not reveal was not material, the insurer would have no remedy.

Should the same apply to business insurance? Although there is no such duty in several of the jurisdictions that compete with the UK (such as New York), our tentative view is that it would not be right to abolish the residual duty of disclosure for businesses. There are two reasons for this.

First, the duty of disclosure has become part of the way the UK business insurance market works. For many business policies, there is no proposal form. Instead the broker presents the risk, and the underwriter relies on the broker and client to present that risk honestly. It would be possible to distinguish insurance that was preceded by a proposal form (whether a paper form or on a website) and insurance where there was no such form, and require disclosure only in the latter. However we would prefer, if possible, not to set arbitrary boundaries between types of insurance. These always cause problems in marginal cases.

Secondly, we think that business insurance in general is probably subject to a much greater variety of risks than is consumer insurance. That would make it much harder for the insurer to ask questions about all the relevant risks.

Thirdly, while not all business insurance is done through intermediaries who can advise as to what is required, a far greater proportion of it is. This means that the risk of an insured not realising that it has a general duty to disclose is reduced.

We still think that it would be appropriate to expect insurers, as a matter of good practice, to warn insureds about the duty to disclose when it is reasonable to think that the insured may not be aware of the need, particularly on renewal. This might well be the case with many kinds of business insurance written on an annual basis. But we doubt it is necessary to provide a legal remedy, such as preventing the insurer from avoiding, for failure to do so.

We tentatively propose that the duty of disclosure should continue to apply to business insurance contracts in general.

REDEFINING MATERIALITY

Different Degrees of Sophistication

In 1980, the Law Commission recommended reform not just for consumers but for all insureds outside the marine, aviation and transport markets. Although the gap between what an underwriter understands to be material and what a policyholder understands to be material is greatest for consumers, the injustice is not confined to consumer policies. Small and medium businesses may also have little understanding of insurance, and in some cases will be less protected than are consumers. As we have seen, small businesses make relatively little use of the Financial Ombudsman Scheme. Even if a small business does use the scheme, the Statements of Practice will not necessarily be applied~ so only some will be granted consumerstyle protection. Medium businesses with a turnover of £1 million or more do not have the right to use an ombudsman at all.

Overdisclosure

There is even an argument that the current law operates against the interests of insurers in that they get too much information when the insured is sophisticated.

The duty of disclosure is so wide and, to many insureds, so imprecise that an insured may conclude that the safest option is to give the insurer all the information it is able to gather. We have been told that applicants often provide insurers with more information than they are able to process. As one experienced insurance lawyer put it: We are now at the stage where commercial brokers are tending to walk into underwriters with three CDs and tell them, 'it's all in there'.

We were told, for example, about a South American highways authority that provided the insurer with a survey report on each road, in Spanish: "It took us 2 weeks to get it translated". With the development of information technology, the problem is likely to increase. To some extent, if the parties have the ability to transmit large quantities of information, they will. However, we think that a narrower test of what is material just might do less to encourage the present tendency to inundate the insurer with information.

Modify the Duty

Our tentative view is that the ambit of the duty of disclosure should be modified in business cases, to include only what a reasonable insured in the circumstances would understand to be material to the underwriter in question. We think this test is sufficiently flexible to adapt to the many different circumstances in which insurance is used and sold. The same test should apply in cases of misrepresentation.

In many insurance markets, in particular where both parties are knowledgeable about insurance and what is likely to be relevant, the effect of this change would be minimal. One advantage of a "reasonable insured test" is that it is flexible enough to cope with a variety of policyholders. In the more sophisticated markets, where both insurers and insured are professionally represented, we would expect almost no difference between what a reasonable insurer and a reasonable insured would regard as material. Here the two tests are effectively synonymous. As the gap between the two sides grows, so does the effect of the reform. A reasonable insured test has the advantage that it does not require legislators to define arbitrary lines by, for example, distinguishing businesses by their size or level of sophistication. As the British Insurance Law Association put it in their 2002 report, the test would enable the court to differentiate between the duty of a large industrial company with a professional insurance department, as compared with a small company on an industrial estate where the insured's knowledge of insurance law may well be very limited.

In assessing what a reasonable insured in the circumstances would understand to be material to the underwriter in question, a court could also take into account whether the policyholder had received professional advice from an intermediary.

The Nature of the Evidence

We have been told that there are advantages in the present "prudent underwriter" test, because the issue of what underwriters think is material may be determined by expert evidence from the industry. Solicitors acting for insurers can locate expert underwriters and ask them to give evidence in court. They expressed concern that a reasonable insured test was inherently uncertain. In the absence of any recognised "reasonable insureds" to give evidence, they thought it would merely invite the judge to substitute his or her own opinion for that of the industry.

In 1980, the Law Commission saw the prominence granted to insurers' evidence as a serious criticism of the current law: Such evidence will usually be readily available to the insurers, who will have no difficulty in selecting appropriate witnesses. However the insured will often be at a considerable disadvantage in finding expert witnesses prepared to challenge those of the insurer and the position of such witnesses is often invidious. Some judicial doubt has also been cast on the cogency of such evidence. Under our proposed reform, the actual insurer in question will need to start by showing that the issue was material to them, in that if they had known the truth they would not have entered into the same contract on the same terms.

The judge or arbitrator would then need to determine what the reasonable insured would have understood to be material in the circumstances. We expect that in many cases involving small businesses, judges would indeed draw on their own understanding to ask how a reasonable small business would regard the matter.

However, in more specialist markets, there will still be a need for expert evidence. Where the parties are relying on established practice in the market, we anticipate that this evidence may be given by a range of experienced professionals, including insureds, brokers or underwriters.

Thus for generalist markets, judges could be expected to draw on their own understanding of what a reasonable small business would understand to be material. For specialist markets, evidence about what is reasonable may be given by a range of experienced professionals.

An alternative would be to take up a suggestion we made in relation to consumer insurance. This is that a revised test of materiality might ask whether a reasonable insurer with the same knowledge of the client would expect the insured to understand that a particular matter was relevant. That would once more be a question on which the court mighthear evidence from underwriters and brokers.

Conclusion on Materiality

We tentatively propose that a reasonable insured test of materiality should apply to all business insurance.

This would be a default rather than a mandatory rule of law. In other words, the parties will be free to agree a different test by means of an explicit term in the contract. 12 However, the need to obtain agreement to a different test will, we hope, serve the useful purpose of alerting a prospective policyholder to the importance of the issue. It will then, of course, then be open to that prospective policyholder to ask the insurer to explain exactly what information is required.

DISTINGUISHING BETWEEN FRAUDULENT, INNOCENT AND NEGLIGENT CONDUCT

In Part 6 we distinguish between behaviour that is fraudulent, innocent but negligent, and innocent without negligence. We tentatively conclude that for consumer insurance, avoidance is appropriate where the insured has behaved fraudulently. Where the insured has behaved innocently and reasonably, insurers should take policyholders as they find them. Where the insured has behaved negligently, the law should as far as possible put the parties into the position they would have been in had the facts been stated correctly.

Here we consider whether the same rules should be applied to businesses, or whether there are reasons to treat business insurance differently. We think that there is no case for restricting the insurer's right to avoid the policy (and therefore to refuse to pay any claim) where a business insured has behaved fraudulently. Below we discuss three more difficult issues:

(1) Should the insurer be entitled to a remedy where the insured has behaved innocently and not negligently?

(2) Where the insured has behaved negligently but not fraudulently, should the insurer be granted a proportionate remedy?

(3) Where should the balance of proving fraud lie?

If a proportionate remedy is to be applied, we then consider two ancillary issues: how should the law treat cases where the insurer should have declined the risk~ and what rights should an insurer have to avoid in the future.

Innocent Misrepresentation or Nondisclosure

The first question is whether there should continue to be a legal right to avoid for innocent nonnegligent misrepresentation or nondisclosure.

We have already discussed this in relation to the general issues of trust in the market and the pooling of risks, and it seems unnecessary to repeat what was said there. The basic question is whether in general insureds would prefer to pay the slight increase in premiums that might be involved as the price for knowing that no policy can be avoided for nonnegligent misrepresentation by the insured.

We have considered where the burden of proof should lie. We think that the information available to the insured when it made the misrepresentation or failed to make the disclosure will normally be a matter largely within its own knowledge.

We think it is useful to draw the analogy with Misrepresentation Act 1967, section 2(1), and place the burden of disproving fraud or negligence on the insured.

The Act provides (in effect) that when a misrepresentation has been made, the misrepresentee can recover damages for any resulting loss unless the misrepresentor can prove that, up until the time the contract was made, it had reasonable grounds to believe and did believe that the statement it made was true.

We tentatively propose that when a business insured has acted without negligence in making an incorrect statement or in other ways (such as failing to answer a question), the insurer should have no right to avoid the policy or to refuse to pay a claim under it on that ground.

Negligence: a Proportionate Remedy?

In Part 6 we reach the tentative conclusion that where a consumer proposer has made a negligent misrepresentation, the court should apply a proportionate remedy by asking what the insurer would have done had it known the true facts. In particular:

(1) where an insurer would have excluded a particular type of claim, the insurer should not be obliged to pay claims that would not fall within the exclusion

(2) where an insurer would have declined the risk altogether, the claim may be refused~

(3) where an insurer would have charged more, the claim should be reduced proportionately to the underpayment of premium.

Many insurance lawyers accept the theory behind these proposals. The main concern is how the issues would be determined in practice. Solicitors expressed concern that each side would bring experts to contradict what the other side said: Each side will have an expert each, which will say the opposite of the other. It's not as if they all have rating books and tariffs... In France, for example, there are fixed tariffs. What would actually happen at the box is that we would propose a premium, and the broker would say, 'Oh, that's a bit steep. Charlie down the road does it for half that.' And they would end up with a number without any science at all.

The problems are likely to be greater in relation to business insurance than they would be for consumer insurance. But we do not see them as insuperable. However unscientific the negotiations may be, they would be a more accurate assessment of the loss involved than the current law, which permits unscrupulous insurers to wield a dominant weapon.

A more difficult question is whether in business insurance, where the average insured is far more likely to be aware of what it should be doing, it is desirable to create stronger incentives.

This was the reason given for refusing to apply the discretion to refuse rescission under Misrepresentation Act 1967 section 2(2) to contracts of insurance. If business insureds know that if they make a careless mistake they will not recover anything under the policy, they would have a stronger incentive to be careful. Conversely, insureds may be willing to carry the small increase in premiums necessary to cover the cost of "innocent mistakes" as one of the pooled risks, but may feel very differently about sharing the costs of other people's negligence.

We welcome views on whether the remedy for negligent misrepresentation should be proportionate, in that it should aim to put the insurer into the position it would have been in had it known the true circumstances.

Proving Fraud

We are conscious that this approach would mean that the insurer would only have an incontestable right to avoid the policy and refuse to pay the claim if it could prove fraud, and that fraud is hard to prove.

Where the insured is a company, in particular, it can be extremely difficult to pin down who knew what at which stage, or to impute knowledge to the controlling mind of the organisation. We do not wish to give an advantage to organisations that fail to investigate safety issues properly, or where the directors isolate themselves from matters they should have known about.

We think that these concerns could be eased by two presumptions:

(1) that an insured knew what a person in their position would be expected to know~ and

(2) that if the insurer asked a clear question about the matter, the insured knew that any inaccuracy in their answer was material.

The first presumption is similar to section 18(1) of the Marine Insurance Act 1906, whereby the insured is "deemed to know every circumstance which, in the ordinary course of business, ought to be known by him". Unlike section 18(1), however, it would be rebuttable.

The insured would be able to bring evidence that they did not know the facts, even though they should. However, the burden of proving this would be on the insured. Similarly, if the insured did not think a question was material, it would have to show why not. We ask whether the insured should have to show that it did not know what a person in its position would be expected to know, or alternatively that it did not know why an inaccurate response to a clear question was material.

Further Issues

If it is decided that proportionality should be applied where appropriate, two further questions arise.

Cases where Another Insurer would have Accepted the Risk

For consumers we also asked whether the courts should have an additional discretion. We suggested this may apply where the insurer would have declined the risk, but the policyholder's fault is minor, and other insurers would have accepted the risk at a higher premium.

This may also apply where the misrepresented fact is unrelated to the claim. On balance, we think that such a discretion is more appropriate to consumers than to businesses, but we would welcome advice on the issue.

We ask whether where the insurer would have declined the risk, but the policyholder's fault is minor and other insurers would have accepted the risk at a higher premium, the court should have a discretion to apply a proportionality solution.

Avoidance for the Future

We also asked whether insurers should be entitled to cancel policies for the future in all cases, or only where they would have declined the risk. We noted that the FOS would sometimes require insurers to amend the terms of a policy, and abide by it in the future. Again, we think this may be appropriate only in consumer cases. Our starting point in business cases is that where the insured has made a negligent misrepresentation or nondisclosure, even if the insurer should have to pay a proportion of the claim in question, it should be entitled to cancel the policy for the future. We would expect the insurer to give reasonable notice and return a proportionate part of the premium.

We tentatively propose that negligent misrepresentation or nondisclosure should be a ground on which the insurer may cancel the policy after reasonable notice, without prejudice to claims that have arisen or arise within the notice period.

BASIS OF THE CONTRACT CLAUSES

In Part 6 we propose to abolish basis of the contract clauses in consumer cases. These have been criticised for many years and their use has been outlawed in Australia and New Zealand. We think we would need to enact something along similar lines to prevent evasion of our other proposals.

We think that basis of the contract clauses should be abolished in business contracts, for the same reasons.

There would need at least to be a provision that incorrect answers would not give rise to a remedy for breach of warranty unless there was a term to that effect in the contract itself, rather than merely a "basis of the contract" clause in the proposal form. This is a rule that would have to be mandatory, otherwise the mere insertion of a basis of the contract clause might be taken as a 'contracting out' from all the rules proposed in this section.

We tentatively propose that there should be a mandatory rule that incorrect answers would not give rise to a remedy for breach of warranty unless there was a term to that effect in the contract itself, rather than merely a "basis of the contract" clause in the proposal form.

MARINE, AVIATION AND TRANSPORT INSURANCE

The 1980 report excluded MAT insurance from the scope of its reforms. It argued that the people working in this market were generally professionals "who could reasonably be expected to be aware of the niceties of insurance law". 14 The law was certain and understood, and worked satisfactorily.

However, the Commission accepted that the line between MAT and other insurance was not a clear one, and that some individuals with pleasure craft did need additional protection. The Commission expressed unease with the definitions of MAT used in previous regulations, and suggested some omissions. It also proposed that the Secretary of State should be empowered to vary the definition by regulation.

Here we are not minded to make a distinction between MAT and other forms of insurance, for three reasons.

(1) We are told MAT is no longer regarded as such a separate and distinct form of insurance.

(2) It would be overly complex to require lawyers to apply one law to (for example) major constructions, and quite a different law to ships.

(3) The boundary between MAT and other insurance is extremely difficult to draft. We would not only need to extend protection to consumers who own pleasure craft but also many small leisure businesses and fishermen. The result would be complex regulations, with arbitrary dividing lines.

(4) The difference between full avoidance and a proportional remedy is greatest in the very largest claims, where several million pounds may be at stake. With such large claims, the result of insurance litigation is likely to affect the solvency of the firm, and therefore have knock on consequences not only for shareholders but also for creditors, employees and third party claimants. Even in large sophisticated businesses, information does not always get passed on in the way it should, and the consequences may be borne by people who are not sophisticated at all. There is still a need for the law to reflect accepted notions of fairness and good market practice.

We tentatively propose that our earlier proposals for business insurance should apply to MAT.

THIRD PARTY CLAIMS

It has been suggested to us that proportionality produces an unsatisfactory result where the claim in question relates to the policyholder's liability to a third party. The point in question is whether it is desirable that the rights of a third party are affected by the acts or omissions of the policyholder.

Under the Road Traffic Act 1988 an insurer is obliged to meet thirdparty claims in motor insurance cases, even where a policy has been avoided for misrepresentation or nondisclosure by the policyholder. 15 For most lines of business there is no such protection the third party will have rights only against the policyholder.

If the policyholder is insolvent, the third party can bring a claim direct against the insurer under the Third Parties (Rights against Insurers) Act 1930.

However, defences such as misrepresentation or nondisclosure which are available to the insurer against the policyholder can, however, also be used against a third party. We can see that there may be arguments for giving third parties Road Traffic Act style protection – particularly where insurance is compulsory under statute, contract or professional rules. For example, a professional may be obliged to effect professional indemnity insurance. Such insurance is intended to provide compensation for third parties clients affected by the professional's negligence.

However, we suspect that even in such cases the matter is best left to the relevant professional body. It can decide first whether such insurance should be compulsory and second the terms on which it should be written, which might including modifying the rights of an insurer to rely on misrepresentation or nondisclosure. In doing so, it can take into account the availability or otherwise of such cover in the insurance market.

Our tentative conclusion, therefore, is that we should not extend the existing rights of third parties, but we welcome views on this issue.

REINSURANCE

Our starting point is the principle that the same rules should apply to reinsurance as to insurance unless a good case is made for distinguishing between the two.

We recognise that there are important practical differences between the ways in which insurance and reinsurance are conducted. A member of our Advisory Panel suggested that three matters in particular should be considered:

(1) Much reinsurance is placed under obligatory treaties. If a risk falls within the terms agreed, the insurer is obliged to place it under the treaty and the reinsurer is bound to accept it. Disclosure of the details of individual risks is not typically required.

(2) Facultative business coming in to the London market from abroad is frequently written on a fronting basis, so that the local insurer is simply the conduit for passing the risk to reinsurers. In that situation, the majority of material facts will relate not to the reinsurance itself but to the underlying risk which will have been written under a contract governed by a foreign law with its own disclosure rules.

(3) The parties entering into reinsurance agreements are both conducting insurance as a business and may be assumed to have a level of knowledge significantly greater than that of the typical policyholder.

Nevertheless we ask if there is any reason not to apply our earlier proposals for business insurance to reinsurance.

SMALL BUSINESSES

As we explained earlier, our tentative view is that the residual duty of disclosure should be abolished in consumer cases but retained in business cases. This leaves the question of whether small businesses should be treated as consumers or in the same way as larger businesses? Should a small and unsophisticated business be required to volunteer information to an insurer? Should a proportionate remedy apply in cases of negligent misrepresentation?

The Position of Small Businesses under the FOS Scheme

At present, the FOS makes a distinction between small businesses based on its assessment of the sophistication of the business in question.

The most vulnerable businesses will be treated as consumers, while others will not. For example, in our survey a fish and chip shop was treated in the same way as a consumer, while an insurance broker was not. We found some cases where small businesses had been expected to volunteer information in the absence of questions. For example, the FOS held that a landlord should have revealed that his tenant was unsatisfactory even though the proposal form did not ask about this.

Options for Reform

In the joint Law Commissions' report on Unfair Contract Terms, we recommended that businesses with nine or fewer employees were often particularly vulnerable and required specific protection against unfair contract terms. We have considered whether micro businesses are also vulnerable in applying for insurance. Should they be treated as consumers and only required to answer the questions asked?

The problem with this approach is that some firms may have very few employees but be highly sophisticated. In the context of Unfair Contract Terms, we were told that in the capital markets it was common to use special purpose vehicles to conduct extremely complex deals. We developed several additional tests to exclude such companies, including a provision imposing a value limit on the contracts that could be reviewed and (on the grounds that they are already regulated) excluding all financial services contracts.

The same issues arise in insurance. A ship, for example, may be owned by a oneship company, and be managed using agents rather than employees. Obviously it may not be appropriate to say that an insurance contract affecting the vessel should not be subject to control because it is a financial services contract –that would beg the question of this review.

But otherwise similar exemptions may be needed. So in defining a small business, it would be necessary to look at the turnover and assets of the business, either instead of or as well as the number of employees. Any definition would also need to be based on factors that are transparent to an insurer. An insurer would need to know, for example, how the definition applied to an overseas entity that may be no more than a shell for a particular purpose.

There are two possible approaches. The first is to retain the duty of disclosure for small businesses, but only to the degree that would be reasonable in the circumstances (applying the test of materiality discussed earlier). We think this would enable the FOS to continue to take the approach it currently takes, by deciding that some small businesses are so similar to consumers that they should not be expected to volunteer information. It should also be possible for court to reach the same result, considering all the circumstances of the case.

The alternative would be to consider more sophisticated definitions of small businesses. We were particularly interested in the Norwegian approach, which disapplies the consumer regime when one of five criteria are satisfied:

(a) when the insurance relates to undertakings which at the time of concluding the contract, or at subsequent renewals, meet a minimum of two of the following requirements:

  (1) the number of employees exceeds 250

  (2) the sales earnings are a minimum of NOK 100 million according to the most recent annual accounts

  (3) assets according to the most recent balance sheet are a minimum of NOK 50 million

(b) when the business takes place mostly abroad

(c) when the insurance relates to a ship under duty to register, cf. section 11 of the Maritime Act, or to installations as stated in section 33, subsection one, and sections 39 and 507 of the Maritime Act,

(d) when the insurance relates to aircraft, or

(e) when the insurance relates to goods in international transit, including transportation to and from the Norwegian Continental Shelf.

Using this sort of definition would ensure that foreign businesses and those taking out marine and aviation insurance would still be required to volunteer information. For domestic risks, the definition considers employees, turnover and assets. However, the test is complex, and brings back issues of how to define MAT, for example, that we had hoped to avoid.

We ask to what extent small businesses should be treated in the same way as consumers.

We ask how small businesses should be defined for this purpose.

3

PRESENT SCENARIO

The Law

The law on insurance warranties in general is clearly set out in the Marine Insurance Act 1906. The Act states that warranties must be exactly complied with, whether material to the risk or not. A breach cannot be remedied, but automatically discharges the insurer from liability from that date. By including a "basis of the contract clause" in the proposal form, the insurer may convert every answer given by the proposer into a warranty. This means that any mistake discharges the insurer from all liability under the contract from the outset, even if the mistake is innocent and immaterial to the risk.

The Problems

The provisions of the Marine Insurance Act have the potential to lead to unfair results. They mean that insurers may refuse to pay a claim for actions or omissions that:

(1) *are immaterial to the risk.* For example, an insurer may refuse to pay a claim because the insured innocently said that a lorry was kept at the wrong address, even though this did not increase the risk.

(2) *are only relevant to other risks.* For example, a failure to employ watchmen may discharge an insurer from liability for a storm claim.

(3) *have already been remedied.* For example, once a ship has entered an excluded zone, it remains uninsured even if it leaves that zone as soon as possible.

The problems are exacerbated by the use of basis of the contract clauses. Proposers are unlikely to appreciate the legal effect of a clause giving warranty status to all the answers given on a proposal form.

In 1980 the Law Commission described these results as wrong and unjust. We agree. They are wrong because they do not accord with policyholders' reasonable expectations. If a proposer has given incorrect information but the true position does not alter the risk or reduces it, the policyholder may well not realise that the policy is ineffective. If a policyholder is slow in repairing a fire alarm, they may well think that their fire cover is suspended while the problem persists. However, those unfamiliar with the niceties of insurance law are unlikely to think that this also invalidates their flood cover. Nor are they likely to realise that they will continue without fire insurance after the alarm has been fixed.

Insurers have told us that they would rarely apply the strict letter of the law. They would not, for example, refuse to pay a claim because of a breach that had already been remedied before the loss. It is difficult to know how many claims are turned down each year for breaches of terms that are not causally connected to the loss. Our own small survey of complaints brought to the FOS does not suggest that the practice is widespread, though we note that the FSA reports cases where it has occurred. The case for reform does not depend on evidence of widespread abuse. If insurers no longer think that the Marine Insurance Act 1906 embodies fair principles, this is itself strong evidence that the law should be brought into line with acceptable practice.

In the rest of this part we deal first with basis of the contract clauses, which cause the same problem in all types of insurance. We then consider specific warranties of fact or future conduct.

BASIS OF THE CONTRACT CLAUSES

In our first Issues Paper on Misrepresentation and Non-disclosure we said that basis of the contract clauses should no longer be effective to convert a statement of fact into a warranty in any kind of insurance. Although judges have severely criticised the use of basis of contract clauses for the last 150 years, their use has been consistently upheld. In 1996 the Court of Session justified them on the grounds that the parties are free to agree what they like. We find this unconvincing.

In most cases the insured's signature at the bottom of the proposal form containing a clause stating that "this proposal shall be the basis of the contract between us and the insurers" would not represent a true agreement because the proposer will have no idea of the implications of the statement. An insurer may have good reasons for making cover dependent on particular facts but, if so, it must make this clear to the insured.

The FSA rules (unlike the Statements of Practice they replaced) do not cover basis of the contract clauses, and in any event they are geared primarily to regulation, not to the rights of the individual insured. No doubt the FOS would take a dim view of an insurer who tried to rely on a basis of the contract clause, but as we noted in our first Issues Paper, not all cases can be resolved by the FOS. There is a need for legislation.

At the first working seminar, there seemed to be a widespread consensus that basis of the contract clauses should be rendered ineffective in consumer insurance. There was also considerable support for our argument that they should not be effective in business insurance. However, there was some doubt about our proposal to render them totally ineffective while still permitting the parties to a business policy to vary the rules on when a policy could be avoided for misrepresentation.

SPECIFIC WARRANTIES OF FACT OR FUTURE CONDUCT

How far the injustices inherent in the law on specific warranties of fact or of future conduct have been ameliorated. We saw that because of the Unfair Terms in Consumer Contracts Regulations 1999, and the existence of the FSA regulations and the FOS scheme, the position in consumer insurance is different to that in business insurance. Therefore we consider warranties in consumer insurance before we turn to warranties in business insurance.

Consumer Insurance

The Unfair Terms in Consumer Regulations

The 1993 Directive and the Unfair Terms in Consumer Contracts Regulations 1999 protect consumer insureds against the effect of unfair terms. The regulations are not widely understood, and appear not to have been used to their full potential in insurance cases that fall within the topics covered in this Issues Paper.

We have shown that they can be used to challenge warranties, descriptions of the risk and other forms of exclusion that are either not made obvious to the proposer (for example because the term is just one among many in the small print) or whose meaning or requirements are not clear.

The terms will be open to challenge on the grounds of unfairness unless they are part of the "definition of the main subject matter" and are in plain, intelligible language. We have argued that they cannot be part of the main subject matter unless they are substantially in line with what the consumer reasonably expected.

In other words, the insurer must take reasonable steps to ensure the consumer is aware of warranties, descriptions of the risk and other forms of exclusion. Simply including the warranty or exclusion in the contract documents is not enough.

The effect of the Regulations is not as clear as it should be. The two Law Commissions have already made recommendations to rewrite the Regulations in a clearer and more accessible way, so that the implications behind the Directive are made explicit.

The recommendations have been accepted in principle, subject to a regulatory impact assessment. We believe that if our draft bill were implemented, what is required of insurers would be made significantly clearer.

A consumer may be aware of the existence of a warranty but unaware of its implications. A consumer may realise that the insurer requires certain locks, but not realise that a failure to install these locks discharges the insurer from liability for flooding.

We have argued that the Regulations are very likely to apply to a clause making a term into a warranty if it does not set out the insurer's rights should the warranty be broken, because its effects will almost always be substantially different from what the consumer reasonably expects.

Then it is open to the court to hold the term unfair because it would give the insurer the right to treat itself as discharged for a breach that was immaterial, or where there was no causal link between the breach and the loss for which the claim was made.

However, we do not think that in practice the problem for consumers has been solved by the Regulations. We think that it is important that consumers are protected by a firm rule, that a breach of warranty should not absolve the insurer from liability if the breach was immaterial or there was no causal connection between it and the claim.

The consumer should not be required to make the complex and difficult argument that the term permitting this first is not a core term and secondly is unfair.

The FSA Rules

Is reform of the law along these lines needed? ICOB Rule 7.3.6 currently states that "except where there is evidence of fraud" the insurer may not refuse to meet a claim for a breach of warranty or condition "unless the circumstances of the claim are connected with the breach". However, the FSA rule suffers from two problems.

First, the FSA rule permits an insurer to refuse to pay a claim where there is inconclusive evidence of fraud. This effectively allows insurers to substitute their own opinion for that of the court. While inconclusive evidence of fraud may be a reason for excusing the insurer from a regulatory sanction, it is not a ground on which the insurer should be entitled to reject an individual claim where the breach of warranty and the claim had no causal connection.

It could be argued that insurers should have some discretion not to pay claims where they have robust evidence that nevertheless falls short of proof. We will return to the definition and proof of fraud in a subsequent paper. However, we do not think that the problem insurers have in proving fraud is a good reason for permitting them to retain technical or unmeritorious defences to paying claims. Suppose for example, an insurer suspects (but cannot prove) that a policyholder has inflated the costs of repair following storm damage.

If the insurer refused the claim because the burglar alarm was not working, it could undermine trust on both sides. The insured would be unable to defend themselves on the substance of the charge, while the insurer would not have established the substance of the wrongdoing.

Secondly, the FSA rule does not give the insured a ready remedy. In a private law contract claim, the court would be required to find for the insurer on the basis of strict law. The consumer may then have a claim to damages for breach of statutory duty under section 150(1) on the ground that the insurer should not have taken the point.

However, it is difficult to reconcile this with the strict legal position that an insurer is automatically discharged from liability with no need for further action on its part. It is odd to think that an insurer may be sued for damages for failing to pay a claim for which it is not liable. It must be asked whether any consumer insured would understand the position, let alone actually make a claim.

The Financial Ombudsman Service

Our research did not reveal a case directly on the need for a causal connection between a loss and a breach of warranty. However the case of the stolen bicycle described earlier (which involved an exception rather than a warranty) shows that the Ombudsmen would almost certainly insist that the insurer pay the claim.

We do not think that the existence of the FOS scheme is a sufficient reason for leaving the law as it is, however. The reason is just the same as in other cases we have considered. Not all cases will reach the FOS; and it makes no sense to have different rules for the courts on the one hand and the FOS on the other. This incoherence and complexity alone is a good reason for reform.

Conclusion

It is our conclusion that although the UTCCR, the FSA Rules and the FOS offer valuable protection to consumer insureds in relation to breaches of warranty, there is a clear need for reform of the underlying law in consumer insurance cases.

Business Insurance

The problems with the law on breach of warranty are not confined to consumer insureds. We do not think it accords with the expectation of any class of insureds that the insurer should be discharged by an immaterial breach of warranty, or one that has been cured before any claim arose. Nor would policyholders expect a claim to be rejected on the ground of a breach of warranty that had no connection to the loss. We discuss below whether the parties should be able to agree expressly that a breach of warranty should have such consequences.

However, we do not think that this should be the "default" rule for breach of warranty (that is the rule that will apply if nothing different is provided in the contract).

Neither the FSA rules nor UTCCR cover businesses. For insured businesses, their only protection lies in inviting the court to construe a term to give it a fair meaning. The courts are often prepared to do this, sometimes finding ambiguities in the words used, even when the words appear firm and clear.

However, we do not think that it is an adequate substitute for law reform. The process of reinterpreting the effect of contractual terms can cause considerable complexity and difficulty, as is shown by the case law on whether a notification clause can be an innominate term. And in some cases the courts are prepared to give terms their traditional (harsh) meaning.

The problems caused by the harshness of the law can affect any business, but they appear most severe for small and medium businesses. They may not understand the import of words such as "warranty" and, even if they do, they lack the bargaining position to change the insurer's standard wording. Furthermore, they are particularly vulnerable to legal uncertainty as they lack the legal knowledge and resources to argue cases before the courts. Insurers may therefore be able to use the harshness of the law as set out in the MIA 1906 as a negotiating tool.

Large businesses are more able to protect themselves. They have the resources to understand the issues, and the bargaining position to renegotiate terms. We were told, for example, that one large company refuses to agree to warranties in any circumstances. This does not suggest, however, that reform is unnecessary for large businesses.

Rather it suggests that all businesses might benefit from the change we are proposing. The fact that businesses which are able to do so exclude the rule, and presumably pay any resulting increase in premium, suggests that it is a poor rule in the first place. We conclude that the law on breach of warranty requires reform in all types of insurance. The question is exactly what shape the reform should take.

4

LAWS REGARDING RISK MANAGEMENT

Insurance is a tool used to help manage financial risk. Financial risk can take many forms. There are risks to our investments, liabilities for our actions, and risks to our ability to earn income. There is insurance to manage all these risks. Insurance is a financial agreement entered by two people to protect one against a certain risk. The contract that binds the two parties to certain obligations is known as Policy. The one who buys the insurance is known as policyholder or insured while the party that sells insurance is known as the insurer. From the time the insured signs the policy he/she has an obligation to pay a certain amount of money known as premium.. In this lesson, we will discuss the various laws governing insurance in India.

The Insurance sector in India is governed by Insurance Act, 1938, the Life Insurance Corporation Act, 1956 and General Insurance Business (Nationalization) Act, 1972, Insurance Regulatory and Development Authority (IRDA) Act, 1999 and other related acts.

Objectives

After going through this lesson you should be able to:

- Define the term contract.
- Describe essential features of valid contract.
- Understand meaning of lawful Consideration.

- Define the term 'Consumer'.
- Know the difference between agent and servant.
- Define Complaint Procedure.
- Know redressal of consumer's grievances
- Understand Features of IRDA Act.
- Understand main functions of LIC Act.
- Understand main functions of GIC Act

LESSON 1-GENERAL CONTRACT ACT 1872, LIC ACT 1956 & GIC ACT 1972

Essentials of General Contract (Section 10) of Indian Contract Act 1872

A contract is an agreement made between two or more parties, which the law will enforce.

To be enforceable by law, an agreement must possess the essential elements of a valid contract as contained in Sections 10.

Essential of a valid contract: The contract of insurance, like any other contract must fulfill the following essential requirements of a valid contract as laid down in the Indian contracts act.

A contract is an agreement made between two or more parties, which the law will enforce.

The essential requirements of a valid contract as laid down in the Indian contract act are:

1. *Agreement*: This involves, one party making the offer and the other party accepting it. The acceptance of the offer must be in the writing or given verbally and must be absolute and unconditional and must be communicated to the proposer.
2. *Legal Relationship*: when the two parties enter into an agreement their intention must be create legal relationship between them. With many informal and social agreements, such as, an agreement to give a

friend a lift in one's car, there is never any intention of legal consequences so the agreement for same reason should not be carried out

3. *Lawful Consideration*: The, agreement is legally enforceable, only when the contract is supported by consideration, i.e., 'when both the parties give something in return. In insurance both parties provide consideration. Consideration from the insured to the insurer is the premium while from the insurer to the insured is a promise to compensate the insured or to make certain payment in the event of certain happenings taking place.
4. *Capacity of Parties*: The parties to the agreement must be competent or capable of entering into a valid contract. A person is competent to contract if he is of the age of majority, is sound mind, and is not disqualified from contracting by any law to which he is subject
5. *Free and Genuine Consent*: There must also be a free and genuine consent of the parties to the agreement. If the agreement is induced by 44 coercion, undue influence, fraud misrepresentation etc., there is absence of free consent.
6. *Lawful Object*: The object of the contract must be lawful. Thus, the object of the agreement must not be illegal, immoral, or opposed to public policy. If an agreement suffers from any legal flaw, it would not be enforceable by law. For example a landlord knowingly lets a house to terrorist to carry out his activities, and he cannot recover the rent through the court of law.
7. *Agreement Not Declared Void*: The agreement, though it might possess all the essential elements, must not have been expressly declared void by any law in force in country. Any contract which is contrary to the law of this country is void, such as insurance on goods being traded with an enemy national in times of war.
8. *Certainty and Possibility or Performance*: It is essential the creation of every contract that the terms of agreement

must be certain and not vague, indefinite, or ambiguous. An agreement to do an act impossible in itself cannot be enforced. For example Q agrees with P, to increase his height by magic. This agreement is not enforceable by law.

9. *Legal Formalities*: The agreement maybe either oral or in writing. But if it is in writing, it must comply with the necessary legal formalities as to writing, registration, attestation, and stamp and must be issued under seal.

CONTRACTS WHICH ARE DEFECTIVE

Void agreement: An agreement not enforceable by law is said to be void [sec2 (g)]. A void agreement does not create any legal rights or obligations. It is void ab initio, i.e. from very beginning, for example an agreement with minor. Void contracts: A contracts which legally does not exist is known as void contract. In other words, a contract, which ceases to be enforceable, is void when it ceases to be enforceable. It is valid when it is entered into, but something, which happens subsequently to the formation of the contract makes it void. Example: a contract to import goods from foreign country. It may subsequently become void.

Voidable contract: An agreement which is enforceable by law at the option of one or more of the parties thereto, but not at the option of the other or others, is voidable contract. In other words when either party is in breach of the essential terms of the contract, the other party has a right to consider the contract void. If the aggrieved party may decide to overlook the breach or to waive the breach, the contract on this case is unaffected and remains in full force. Example: Anu promises to sell his watch for Rs. 500. Her consent is obtained by use of force.

The contract is voidable at the option of Anu. She may accept it or reject it. Unenforceable contracts: Unenforceable contracts are those which are neither void nor voidable but which cannot be enforced through the courts. For example, an insurance policy without proper stamp duty cannot be produced as evidence of a contract in court. Unenforceable contracts are fully valid contracts but the parties cannot enforce them through the courts.

Illegal Agreements: Illegal agreements are those agreements, which involve the breaking of some rule of basic public policy and are criminal in nature. An illegal agreement is not only void as between immediate parties but also taints the collateral transactions with illegality.

Essential Feature of Insurance Contracts

The purchasers of Insurance have to enter into a contract, where by one party (insured) agrees to pay to other party (insurer) a certain sum of money, determined on the happening of a certain event in consideration of a certain sum of money caned Premium.

Such a contract is known as "Insurance Contract". Like any other contract, Insurance contract are also governed by the provisions of the law of contract as laid down in The Indian Contract Act, 1872. Therefore they have to fulfill the essential features of a valid contract. The essentials of a valid contract have been discussed earlier.

Life Insurance Corporation Act, 1956

An Act to provide for the nationalization of life insurance business in India by transferring all such business to a Corporation established for the purpose and to provide for the regulation and control of the business of the Corporation and for matters connected there with or incidental thereto.

Some of the important provisions are as follows: —

1. Short title and commencement. —

(1) This Act maybe called the Life Insurance Corporation Act, 1956

(2) It shall come into force on such date as the Central Government may, by Notifications in the Official Gazette, appoint. Definitions: In this Act, unless the context otherwise requires,

  (1) "Appointed day," means the date on which the Corporation is established under Section 3;

(2) "Composite insurer "means an insurer carrying on in addition to controlled business any other kind of insurance business;

(3) "Controlled business" means—

(i) In the case of any insurer specified in sub-clause (a) or sub-clause (b) of clause (9) of section 2 of the Insurance Act and carrying on life insurance business—

(a) all his business, if he carries on no other class of insurance business;

(b) all the business appertaining to his life insurance business, if he carries on any other class of insurance business also;

(c) all his business if his certificate of registration under the Insurance Act in respect of general insurance business stands wholly cancelled for a period of more than six months on the 19th day of January, 1956.

(ii) in the case of any other insurer specified in clause (9) ofsection 2 of the Insurance Act and carrying on life insurance business—

(a) all his business in India, if he carries on no other class of insurance business in India;

(b) all the business appertaining to his life insurance business in India, if he carries on any other class of insurance business also in India;

(c) all his business in India if he certificate of registration under the Insurance Act in respect of general insurance business in India stands wholly cancelled for a period of more than six months on the 19th day of January, 1956.

Explanation.

An insurer is said to carry on no class of insurance business other than life insurance business, if in addition to life insurance business, he carries on only capital redemption business or annuity certain business or both; and the expression" business appertaining to his life insurance business" in sub-clause (i) and (ii) shall be construed accordingly; (iii) in the case of a provident society, as defined in section 65 of the Insurance; Act, all its business; (iv) in the case of the Central Government or a State Government, all life insurance business carried on by it, subject to the exceptions specified in section 44;

(4) "Corporation" means the Life Insurance Corporation of India established under section 3;

(5) "Insurance Act" means the Insurance Act, 1938 (4 of 1938);

(6) "Insurer" means an insurer as defined in the Insurance Act who carries on life insurance business in India and includes the Government and a provident society as defined in section 65 of the Insurance Act;

(7) "Member" means a member of the Corporation;

(8) "Prescribed" means prescribed by rules made under this Act;

(9) "Tribunal" means a Tribunal constituted under section 17 and having jurisdiction in respect of any matter under the rules made under this Act;

(10) All other words and expressions used herein but not defined and defined in the Insurance Act shall have the meanings respectively assigned to them in that Act.

Establishment and incorporation of Life Insurance Corporation of India.—

(1) With effect from such date as the Central Government may, by notification in the Official Gazette, appoint, there shall be established a Corporation called the Life Insurance Corporation of India.

(2) The Corporation shall be a body corporate having perpetual succession and a common seal with power subject to the provisions of this Act, to acquire, hold and dispose of property, and may by its name sue and be sued.

Constitution of the Corporation.—

(1) The Corporation shall consist of such number of persons not exceeding 2 as the Central Government may think fit to appoint thereto and one of them shall be appointed by the Central Government to be the Chairman there of.

(2) Before appointing a person to be a member, the Central Government shall satisfy itself that person will have no such financial or other interest as is likely to affect prejudicially the exercise or performance by him of his functions as a member, and the Central Government shall also satisfy itself from time to time with respect to every member thathe has no such interest; and any person who is, or whom the Central Government proposes to appoint and who has consented to be, a member shall, whenever required by the Central Government so to do, furnish to it such information as the Central Government considers necessary for the performance of its duties under this sub-section.

(3) A member who is in anyway directly or indirectly interested in a contract made or proposed to be made by the Corporation shall as soon as possible after the relevant circumstances have come to his knowledge, disclose the nature of his interest to the Corporation and the member shall not take part in any deliberation or discussion of the Corporation with respect to that contact.

Capital of the Corporation.—

(1) The original capital of the Corporation shall be five crores of rupees provided by the Central Government after due appropriation made by Parliament bylaw for the purpose, and the terms and conditions relating to the provision of such capital shall be such as maybe determined by the Central Government.

(2) The Central Government may, on the recommendation of the Corporation, reduce the capital of the Corporation

to such extent and in such manner as the Central Government may determine.

Functions of the Corporation.—

1) Subject, to the rules, if any, made by the Central Government in this behalf, it shall be the general duty of the Corporation to carry on life insurance business, whether in or outside India, and the Corporation shall so exercise its powers under this Act as to secure that life insurance business is developed to the best advantage of the community.

2) Without prejudice to the generality of the provisions contained in sub-section (1) but subject to the other provisions contained in this Act, the Corporation shall have power —

   (a) To carryon capital redemption business, annuity certain business or reinsurance business in so far as such re insurance business appertains to life insurance business;

   (b) Subject to the rules, if any, made by the Central Government in this behalf, to invest the funds of the Corporation in such manner as the Corporation may think fit and to take all such steps as may be necessary or expedient for the protection or realization of any investment; including the taking over of and administering any property offered as security for the investment until a suitable opportunity arises for its disposal;

   (c) To acquire, hold and dispose of any property for the purpose of its business;

   (d) To transfer the whole or any part of the life insurance business carried on outside India to any other person or persons, if in the interest of the Corporation it is expedient so to do;

   (e) To advance or lend money upon the security of any movable property or otherwise;

(f) To borrow or raise any money in such manner and upon such security as the Corporation may think fit;

(g) To carry on either by itself or through any subsidiary any other business in any case where such other business was being carried on by a subsidiary of an insurer whose controlled business has been transferred to and invested in the Corporation under this Act;

(h) to carry on any other business which may seen to the Corporation to be capable of being conveniently carried on in connection with its business and calculated directly or indirectly to render profitable the business of the corporation;

(i) to do all such things as maybe incidental or conducive to the proper exercise of any of the powers of the Corporation. In the discharge of any of its functions the Corporation shall act so far as maybe on business principles.

Power to impose conditions, etc.—

(1) In entering into any arrangement, under section 6, with any concern, the Corporation may impose such conditions as it may think necessary or expedient for protecting the interest of the Corporation and for securing that the accommodation granted by it is put to the best use by the concern.

(2) Where any arrangement entered into by the Corporation under section 6 with any concern provides for the appointment by the Corporation of one or more directors of such concern, such provision and any appointment of directors made in pursuance there of shall be valid and effective notwithstanding anything to the contrary contained in the Companies Act, 1956 (1 of 1956), or in any other law for the time being in force or in the memorandum, articles of association or any other instrument relating to the concern, and any provision

regarding share, qualification, age limit, number of directorships, removal from office of Directors and such like conditions contained in any such law or instrument aforesaid, shall not apply to any director appointed by the Corporation in pursuance of the arrangement as aforesaid.

(3) Any director appointed as aforesaid shall-

(a) Hold office during the pleasure of the Corporation any maybe removed or substituted by any person by order in writing by the Corporation;

(b) Not incur any obligation or liability by reason only of his being a director or for anything done or omitted to be done in good faith in the discharge of his duties as a director or anything in relation thereto;

(c) Not be liable to retirement by rotation and shall not be taken into account for computing the number of directors liable to such retirement.

Offices, branches and agencies.—

(1) The central office of the Corporation shall be at such place as the Central Government may, by notification in he Official Gazette, specify.

(2) The Corporation shall establish a zonal office at each of the following places, namely, Bombay, Calcutta, Delhi, Kanpur and Madras, and, subject to the previous approval of the Central Government, may establish such other zonal offices as it thinks fit.

(3) The territorial limits of each zone shall be such as may be specified by the Corporation.

(4) There may be established as many divisional offices and branches in each zone as the Zonal Manager thinks fit.

Committees of the Corporation.—

(1) The Corporation may entrust the general superintendence and direction of its affairs and business to an Executive Committee consisting of not more than five of its members and the Executive Committee may

exercise all powers and do all such acts and things as may be delegated to it by the Corporation.

(2) The Corporation may also constitute an Investment Committee for the purpose of advising it in matters relating to the investment of its funds, and the Investment Committee shall consist of not more than eight members of whom not less than four shall be members of the Corporation and the remaining members shall be persons (whether members of the Corporation or not) who have special knowledge and experience in financial matters, particularly, matters relating to investment of funds.

(3) The Corporation may constitute such other Committees as it may thin fit for the purpose of discharging such of its functions as maybe delegated to them.

Funds of the Corporation.—

The Corporation shall have its own fund and all receipts of the Corporation shall be credited thereto and all payments of the Corporation shall be made there from. Audit.—

(1) The accounts of the Corporation shall be audited by auditors duly qualified to act as auditors of companies under the law for the time being in force relating to companies, and the auditors shall be appointed by the Corporation with the previous approval of the Central Government and shall receive such remuneration from the Corporation as the Central Government may fix.

(2) Every auditor in the performance of his duties shall have at all reasonable times access to the books, accounts and other documents of the Corporation.

(3) The auditors shall submit their report to the Corporation and shall also forward a copy of their report to the Central Government.

Annual report of activities of Corporation.—

The Corporation shall, as soon as may be, after the end of each financial year, prepare and submit to the Central Government in such form as maybe prescribed a report giving an account of its activities during the previous financial year, and the report shall also give an account of the activities, if any, which are likely to be undertaken by the Corporation in the next financial year.

General Insurance Contract, 1972

Although Life Insurance was nationalized as early as 1956, general insurance business continued to be in the private sector right up to 1969. In that year the Government imposed strict social control on General Insurance Companies.

This was a prelude to nationalization of General of General Insurance Business. With effect from 13th May, 1971 under the provisions of General Insurance (Emergency Provisions) Act, 1971 the Government of India took over the management of all General Insurance Companies operating in India whether they belonged to Indian or non-Indian shareholders.

Subsequently, the General Insurance (Emergency Provisions) Amendment Act, 1971 was passed withdrawing certain rights of the Directors and Members of the Companies, which they were enjoying under the Companies Act. General Insurance (Nationalization) Act, 1972 shortly followed and with effect from 2nd January, 1973 the provisions of the Act became effective. The functions of the Corporation are enumerated in Section 18 of the Act, some of are as follows:

Functions of Corporation –

(1) The functions of the Corporation shall include:-

(a) The carrying on of any part of the general insurance business, if it thinks it desirable to do so;

(b) Aiding, assisting and advising the acquiring companies in the matter of setting up of standards of conduct and sound practice in general insurance business and in the matter of rendering efficient services to holders of policies of general insurance;

(c) Advising the acquiring companies in the matter of the controlling their expenses including the payment of commission and other expenses.

(d) Advising the acquiring companies in the matter of the investment of their funds;

(e) Issuing directions to acquiring companies in relation to the conduct of general insurance business.

(2) In issuing any directions under sub-section (1), the Cooperation shall keep in mind the desirability of encouraging composition amongst the acquiring companies as far as possible in order to render their services more efficient."

Functions of acquiring companies:-

(1) Subject to the rules, if any, made by the Central Government in this behalf and to its memorandum and articles of association, it shall be the duty of every acquiring company to carry on general insurance business.

(2) Each acquiring company shall so function under this Act as to secure that general insurance business is developed to the best of the community.

(3) In the discharge of any of its functions, each acquiring company shall act so far as may be on business principles and where any directions have been issued by the Corporation shall be guided by such directions.

(4) For the removal of doubts it is hereby declared that the Corporations and any acquiring company may, subject to the rules, if any, made by the Central Government in this behalf, "enter into such contracts of reinsurance treaties as it may think fit for the protection of its interests".

Under Sec. 35, The Central Government may by notification specify the application of the provision of the Insurance Act with such modifications as is deemed necessary to the Corporation and the acquiring companies. The Central Government is also empowered to make rules to carry out the provisions of the Act and such rules may provide for:

(a) Manner in which the profits and other moneys received by the Corporation may be dealt with'

(b) The conditions subject to which the Corporation and the acquiring companies shall carry on general insurance business;

(c) The terms and conditions subject to which any re-insurance contract or treaties may be entered into;

(d) Form and manner in which any notice or application may be made to the Central Government;

(e) The reports which may be called for by the Central Government from the Corporation and acquiring companies; and

(f) Any other matter which is required to be or may be prescribed.

THE INSURANCE ACT, 1938

Earlier to the Insurance Act, 1938, the insurance business was carried by the insurance companies in accordance with the principles of the Company Law, 1913. When the business started growing, the need for an independent law to regulate the insurance business was noticed and a separate Act, the Insurance Act, 1938 was legislated. The Act was used for all purposes relating to both life and general insurance businesses and their regulations. With regards to general insurance, this Act is being used to regulate the marine insurance, fire insurance and other insurances. Further growth of business has made it complex and more legal provisions were required to regulate it.

The Marine Insurance Act, 1963, Public Liability Insurance Act, 1991, Insurance Regulatory and Development Authority Act, 1999 and regulations made by the IRDA are some of the legislations that govern the insurance business.

Short title, extent and commencement.

1. (1)) This Act may be called Insurance Act, 1938.

(2) It extends to the whole of India.

(3) It shall come into force on such date as the Central Government may, by Notification in the Official Gazette, appoint in this behalf.

Definitions.

2. In this Act, unless there is anything repugnant in the subject or context,-

(1) "Authority" means the Insurance Regulatory and Development Authority established under sub-section (1) of section 3 of the Insurance Regulatory and Development Authority Act, 1999;

(2) "Policy-holder" includes a person to whom the whole of the interest of the policy-holder in the policy is assigned once and for all, but does not include an assignee thereof whose interest in the policy is infeasible or is for the time being subject to any condition;

(3) "Approved securities," means-

(i) Government securities and other securities charged on the revenue of the Central Government or of the Government of a State or guaranteed fully as regards principal and interest by the Central Government or the Government of any State;

(ii) debentures or other securities for money issued under the authority of any Central Act or Act of a State Legislature by or on behalf of a port trust or municipal corporation or city improvement trust in any Presidency-town;

(iii) shares of a corporation established by law and guaranteed fully by the Central Government or the Government of a State as to the repayment of the principal and the payment of the divided;

(iv) securities issued or guaranteed fully as regards principal and interest by the Government of any Part B State and specified as approved securities for the purposes of this Act by the Central Government by notification in the Official Gazette; and

(4)"Auditor" means a person qualified under the Chartered Accountants Act, 1949 (38 of 1949), to act as an auditor of companies;

(4A)"Banking company" and "company" shall have the meanings respectively assigned in them in clauses (c) and (d) of sub-section (1) of Section 5 of the Banking Companies Act, 1949 (10 of 1949);

(5) "Certified" in relation to any copy or translation of a document required to be furnished by or on behalf of an insurer or a provident society as defined in Part III means certified by a principal officer of 6E such insurer or provident society to be a true copy or a correct translation, as the case may be;

(5A) "Chief agent" means a person who, not being a salaried employee of an insurer, in consideration of any commission-

(i) Performs any administrative and organizing functions for the insurer, and

(ii) Procures life insurance business for the insurer by employing or causing to be employed insurance agents on behalf of the insurer;

[(5-B) "Controller of Insurance" means the officer appointed by the Central Government under section 2B to exercise all the powers, discharge the functions and performs the duties of the Authority under this Act or the Life Insurance Corporation Act, 1956 (31 of 1956) or the General Insurance Business (Nationalization) Act, 1972 (57 of 1972) or the Insurance Regulatory and Development Authority Act, 1999;]

(6) "Court" means the principal Civil Court of original jurisdiction in a district and includes the High Court in exercise of its ordinary original civil jurisdiction;

(6A)"Fire insurance business" means the business of effecting, otherwise than incidentally to some other class of insurance business, contracts of insurance against loss by or incidental to fire or other occurrence customarily included among the risks insured against in fire insurance Policies;

(6B)"General insurance business" means fire, marine or miscellaneous insurance business, whether carried on singly or in combination with one or more of them;

(7)"Government security" means a Government security as defined in the Public Debt Act, 1944 (18 of 1944);

2[(7A) "Indian insurance company" means any insurer being a company-

(a) which is formed and registered under the Companies Act, 1956 (1 of 1956);

(b)in which the aggregate holdings of equity shares by a foreign company, either by itself or through its subsidiary companies or its nominees, do not exceed twenty-six percent paid-up equity capital of such Indian insurance company;

(c) whose sole purpose is to carry on life insurance business or general insurance business or re-insurance business.

(8) "Insurance company" means any insurer being a company, association or partnership which may be wound up under the Indian Companies Act, 1913 (7 of 1913), or to which the Indian Partnership Act, 1932 (9 of 1932), applies;

(9) "Insurer" means-

(a) any individual or unincorporated body of individuals or body corporate incorporated under the law of any country other than India, carrying on insurance business not being a person specified in sub-clause (c) of this clause which-

(i) carries on that business in India, or

(ii) has his or its principal place of business or is domiciled in India, or

(iii) with the object of obtaining insurance business, employs a representative, or maintains a place of business, in India;

(b) any body corporate [not being a person specified in sub-clause (c) of this clause] carrying on the business of insurance, which is a body corporate incorporated under any law for the time being in force in India; or stands to any such body corporate in the relation of a subsidiary company within the meaning of the Indian Companies Act, 1913 (7 of 1913), as defined by sub-section (2) of section 2 of that Act, and

(c) any person who in India has a standing contract with underwriters who are members of the Society of Lloyd's whereby such person is authorized within the terms of such contract to issue protection notes, cover notes, or other documents granting insurance cover to others on behalf of the underwriters. But does not include a principal agent' chief agent, special agent' or an insurance agent or a provident society as defined in Part III;

(10) "Insurance agent" means an insurance agent licensed under Sec. 42 who receives agrees to receive payment by way of commission or other remuneration in consideration of his soliciting or procuring insurance business including business relating to the continuance, renewal or revival of policies of insurance;

(10A)"investment company" means a company whose principal business is the acquisition of shares, stocks debentures or other securities;

(10B) "Intermediary or insurance intermediary" shall have the meaning assigned to it in clause (f) of sub-section 2 of the Insurance Regulatory and Development Authority Act, 1999 (41 of 1999)

(11) "Life insurance business" means the business of effecting contracts of insurance upon human life, including any contract whereby the payment of money is assured on death (except death by accident only) or the happening of any

(12) "Manager" and "officer" have the meanings assigned to those expressions in clauses (9) and (11), respectively of Section 2 of the Indian Companies Act, 1913 (7 of 1913);

(13) "Managing agent" means a person, firm or company entitled to the management of the whole affairs of a company by virtue of an agreement with the company, and under the control and direction of the directors except to the extent, if any, otherwise provided for in the agreement, and includes any person, firm or company occupying such position by whatever name called.

Explanation. —If a person occupying the position of managing agent calls himself manager or managing director, he shall nevertheless be regarded as managing agent for the purposes of Sec. 32 of this Act;

(13A)"marine insurance business" means the business of effecting contracts of insurance upon vessels of any description, including cargoes, freights and other interests which may be legally insured, in or in relation to such vessels, cargoes and freights, goods, wares, merchandise and property of whatever description insured for any transit, by land or water, or both, and whether or not including warehouse risks or similar risks in addition or as incidental to such transit, and includes any other risks customarily included among the risks insured against in marine insurance policies;

(13B)"miscellaneous insurance business" means the business of effecting contracts of insurance which is not principally or wholly of any kind or kinds included in clause (6A), (11) and (13A);

(14) "Prescribed" means prescribed by rules made under this Act; and

(15) "Principal agent" means a person who, not being a salaried employee of an insurer, in consideration of any commission,—

(i) Performs any administrative and organizing functions for the insurer; and

(ii) Procures general insurance business whether wholly or in part by employing or causing to be employed insurance agents on behalf of the Praviate Comapany

(16) "Private company" and "public company" have the meanings respectively assigned to them in Clauses (13) and (13-A) of Sec. 2 of the Indian Companies Act, 1913 (7 of 1913);

(17) "Special agent" means a person who, not being a salaried employee of an insurer, in consideration of any commission, procures life insurance business for the insurer whether wholly or in part by employing or causing to be employed insurance agents on behalf of the insurer, but does not include a chief agent.

Appointment of Authority of Insurance.

(1) If at any time, the Authority is superseded under sub-section (1) of section 19 of the Insurance Regulatory and Development Authority Act, 1999, the Central Government may, by notification in the Official Gazette, appoint a person to be the Controller of Insurance till such time the Authority is reconstituted under subsection (3) of section 19 of that Act.

(2) In making any appointment under this section, the Central Government shall have due regard to the following considerations, namely, whether the person to be appointed has had experience in industrial, commercial or insurance matter and whether such person has actuarial qualifications. Requirements as to capital.

No insurer carrying on the business of life insurance, general insurance or re-insurance in India on or after the commencement of the Insurance Regulatory and Development authority Act, 199, shall be registered unless he has,-

(i) a paid-up equity capital of rupees one hundred crores, in case of a person carrying on the business of life insurance or general insurance; or

(ii) a paid-up equity capital of rupees two hundred crores, in case of a person carrying on exclusively the business as a reinsurer: Provided that in determining the paid-up equity capital specified under clause (i) or clause (ii), the deposit to be made under section 7 and any preliminary expenses incurred in the formation and registration of the company shall be excluded:

Provided further that an insurer carrying on business of life insurance, general insurance or re-insurance in India before the commencement of the Insurance Regulatory and Development Authority Act, 1999 and who is required to be registered under this Act, shall have a paid-up equity capital in accordance with clause (i) and clause (ii), as the case may be, within sex months of the commencement of that Act.

Deposits

Every insurer shall, in respect of the insurance business carried on by him in India, deposit and keep deposited with the Reserve Bank of India in one of the offices in India of the Bank for and on behalf of the Central Government the amounthereafter specified, either in cash or in approved securities estimated at the market value of the securities on the day of deposit, or partly in cash and partly in approved securities so estimated:-

(a) in the case of life insurance business, a sum equivalent to one per cent of his total gross premium written direct in India in any financial year commencing after the 31st day of March, 2000, not exceeding rupees ten crores;

(b) in the case of general insurance business, a sum equivalent to three per cent of his total gross premium written in India, in any financial year commencing after the 31st day of March, 2000, not exceeding rupees ten crores;

(c) in the case of re-insurance business, a sum of rupees twenty crores Provided that, where the business done or to be done is marine insurance only and relates exclusively to country craft or its cargo or both, the amount to be deposited under this sub-section shall be one hundred thousand rupees only: Provided further that in respect of an insurer not having a share capital and carrying on only such insurance business as in the opinion of the Central Government is not carried on ordinarily by insurers under separate policies, the Central Government may, by notification under Official Gazette, order that the provisions of this sub-section shall apply to such insurer with the modification that instead of sum of rupees twenty lakhs or rupees ten lakhs, as the case may be, the deposit to be made by such insurer shall be such amount, being not less than one hundred and fifty thousand rupees, as may be specified in the said order.

Audit

The balance-sheet, profit and loss account, revenue account and profit and loss appropriation account of every insurer, in the case of an insurer specified in sub-clause (a)(ii) or sub-clause (b) of clause (9) of section 2 in respect of all insurance business transacted by him, and in the case of any other insurer in respect of the insurance business transacted by him in India, shall, unless they are subject to audit under the Indian Companies Act, 1913 (7 of 1913), be audited annually by an auditor, and the auditor shall in the audit of all such accounts have the powers of, exercise the functions vested in, and discharge the duties and be subject to the liabilities and penalties imposed on, auditors of companies by section 145 of the Indian Companies Act, 1913.

This Act not to apply to preparation of account, etc., for periods prior to this Act coming into force.

Nothing in this Act shall apply to the preparation of accounts by an insurer and the audit and submission thereof in respect of any accounting year which has expired prior to the commencement of this Act, and notwithstanding the other provisions of this Act, such accounts shall be prepared, audited and submitted in accordance with the law in force immediately before the commencement of this Act.

Investment of Assets

(1) Every insurer shall invest and at all times keep invested assets equivalent to not less than the sum of-

(a) the amount of his liabilities to holders of life insurance policies in India on account of matured claims, and

(b) the amount required to meet the liability on policies of life insurance maturing for payment in India, less-

(i) the amount of premiums which have fallen due to the insurer on such policies but have not been paid and the days of grace for payment of which have not expired, and

(ii) any amount due to the insurer for loans granted on and within the surrender values of policies of life insurance maturing for payment in India issued by him or by an insurer whose business he has acquired and in respect of which he has assumed liability, in the manner following, namely, twenty-five per cent of the said sum in Government securities, a further sum equal to not less than twenty-five per cent of the said sum in Government securities or other approved securities and the balance in any of the approved investments specified in sub-section (1) of section 27A or, subject to the limitations, conditions and restrictions specified in sub-section (2) of that section, in any over investment.

(2) For the purposes of subsection (1),—

(a) the amount of any deposit made under section 7 or section 98 by the insurer in respect of his life insurance business shall be deemed to be assets invested or kept invested Government securities;

(b) The securities of, or guaranteed as to principal and interest by, the Government of the United Kingdom shall be regarded as approved securities other than Government securities for a period of four years from the commencement of the Insurance (Amendment) Act, 1950 (47 of 1950), in the manner and to the extenthereinafter specified, namely:—

(i) during the first year, to the extent of twenty-five per cent in value of the sum referred to in sub-section (1);

(ii) during the second year, to the extent of eighteen and three fourths per cent in value of the said sum;

(iii) during the third year, to the extent of twelve and a half per cent in value of the said sum; and

(iv) during the fourth year, to the extent of six and a quarter per cent in value of the said sum: Provided that, if the Authority so directs in any case, the securities specified in clause (b) shall be regarded as approved securities other than Government securities for a longer period than four years, but not exceeding six years in all and the manner in which and the extent to which the securities shall be so regarded shall be as specified in the direction;

(c) Any prescribed assets shall, subject to such conditions, if any, as may be prescribed, be deemed to be assets invested or kept invested in approved investments specified in sub-section (1) of section 27A.

(3) In computing the assets referred to in subsection (1),—

(a) any investment made with reference to any currency other than the Indian rupee which is in excess of the amount required to meet the liabilities of the insurer in India with reference to that currency, to the extent of such excess; and

(b) any investment made in the purchase of any immoveable property outside India or on the security of any such property, shall not be taken into account: Provided that nothing contained in this sub-section shall affect the operation of sub-section (2): Provided further that the Authority may, either generally or in any particular case, direct that any investment, whether made before or after the commencement of the Insurance (Amendment) Act, 1950 (47 of 1950), and whether made in or outside India, shall, subject to such conditions as may be imposed, be taken into account, in such manner as may be specified in computing the assets referred to in sub-section (1) and where any direction has been issued under this proviso copies thereof shall be laid before Parliament as soon as may be after it is issued.

(4) Where an insurer has accepted reassurance in respect of any policies of life insurance issued by another insurer and maturing for payment in India or has ceded reassurance to another insurer in respect of any such policies issued by himself, the sum referred to in subsection (1) shall be increased by the amount of the liability involved in such acceptance and decreased by the amount of the liability involved in such cession.

(5) The Government securities and other approved securities in which assets are under sub-section (1) to be invested

and kept invested shall be held by the insurer free of any encumbrance, charge, hypothecation or lien.

(6) The assets required by this section to be held invested by an insurer incorporated or domiciled outside India shall, except to the extent of any part thereof which consists of foreign assets held outside India, be held in India and all such assets shall be held in trust for the discharge of the liabilities of the nature referred to in sub-section (1) and shall be vested in trustees resident in India and approved by the Authority, and the instrument of trust under this sub-section shall be executed by the insurer with the approval of the Authority and shall define the manner in which alone the subject-matter of the trust shall be dealt with.

Explanation.—This sub-section shall apply to an insurer-incorporated India whose share capital to the extent of one-third is owned by, or the members of whose governing body to the extent of one-third consists of, members domiciled elsewhere than in India.

Power to Appoint Staff

The Authority may appoint such staff, and at such places as it or he may consider necessary, for the scrutiny of the returns, statements and information furnished by insurers under this Act and generally to ensure the efficient performance of the functions of the Authority under this Act. Registration of principal agents, chief agents and special agents

(1) The Authority or an officer authorized by it in this behalf shall in the prescribed manner and on payment of the prescribed fee, which shall not be more than twenty-five rupees for a principal agent or a chief agent and ten rupees for a special agent, register any person who makes an application to him in the prescribed manner if,—

(a) in the case of an individual, he does not suffer from any of the disqualifications mentioned in sub-section (4) of Section 42, or

(b) in the case of a company or firm, any of its directors or partners does not suffer from any of the said disqualifications, and a certificate to Act as a principal agent, chief agent or special agent, as the case may be, for the purpose of procuring insurance business shall be issued to him.

(2) A certificate issued under this section shall entitle the holder thereof to act as a principal agent, chief agent, or special agent, as the case may be, for any insurer.

(3) A certificate issued under this section shall remain in force for a period of twelve months only from the date of issue, but shall, on application made on this behalf, be renewed from year to year on production of a certificate from the insurer concerned that the provisions of clauses (2) and (3) of Part A of the Sixth Schedule in the case of a principal agent, the provisions of clauses (2) and (4) of Part B of the said Schedule in the case of a chief agent, and the provisions of clauses (2) and (3) of Part C of the said Schedule in the case of a special agent, have been complied with, and on payment of the prescribed fee, which shall not be more than twenty-five rupees, in the case of a principal agent or a chief agent, and ten rupees in the case of a special agent, and an additional fee of the prescribed amount not exceeding five rupees by way of penalty, in cases where the application for renewal of the certificate does not reach the issuing authority before the date on which the certificate ceases to remain in force: Provided that, where the applicant is an individual, he does not suffer from any of the disqualifications mentioned in clauses (b) to (d) of sub-section (4) of section 42 and where the applicant is a company or a firm, any of its directors or partners does not suffer from any of the said disqualifications.

(4) Where it is found that the principal agent, chief agent or special agent being an individual is, or being a company or firm contains a director or partner who is suffering from any of the disqualifications mentioned in

subsection (4) of section 42, without prejudice to any other penalty to which he may be liable, the Authority shall, and where a principal agent, chief agent or special agent has contravened any of the provisions of this Act may cancel the certificate issued under this section to such principal agent, chief agent or special agent.

(5) The authority which issued any certificate under this section may issue a duplicate certificate to replace a certificate lost, destroyed or mutilated on payment of the prescribed fee, which shall not be more than two rupees.

(6) Any person who acts as a principal agent, chief agent or special agent, without holding a certificate issued under this section to act as such, shall be punishable with fine which may extend to five hundred rupees, and any insurer or any person acting on behalf of an insurer, who appoints as a principal agent, chief agent or special agent any person not entitled to act as such or transacts any insurance business in India through any such person, shall be punishable with fine which may extend to one thousand rupees.

(7) Where the person contravening sub-section (6) is a company or a firm, then, without prejudice to any other proceedings which may be taken against the company or firm, every director, manager, secretary or any other officer of the company, and every partner of the firm who is knowingly a party to such contravention shall be punishable with fine which may extend to five hundred rupees.

(8) The provisions of sub-sections (6) and (7) shall not take effect until the expiry of six months from the commencement of the Insurance (Amendment) Act, 1950.

(9) No insurer shall, on or after the commencement of the Insurance (Amendment) Act, 2002, appointment or transacts any insurance business in India through any principal agent, chief agent or special agent.

Regulation of Employment of Principal Agents

(1) No insurer shall, after the expiration of seven years from the commencement of the Insurance (Amendment) Act, 1950, appoint, or transact any insurance business in India, through a principal agent.

(2) Every contract between an insurer and a principal agent shall be in writing and the terms contained in Part A of the Sixth Schedule shall be deemed to be incorporated in, and form part of, every such contract.

(3) No insurer shall, after the commencement of the Insurance (Amendment) Act, 1950 (47 of 1950), appoint any person as a principal agent except in a presidency-town unless the appointment is by way of renewal of any contract subsisting at such commencement.

(4) Within sixty days of the commencement of the Insurance (Amendment) Act, 1950 (47 of 1950), every principal agent shall file with the insurer concerned a full list of insurance agents employed by him indicating the terms of the contract between the principal agent and each of such insurance agents, and, if any principal agent fails to file such a list within the period specified, any commission payable to such principal agent on premiums received from the date of expiry of the said period of sixty days until the date of the filing of the said list shall, notwithstanding anything in any contract to the contrary, cease to be so payable.

(5) A certified copy of every contract as is referred to in sub-section (2) shall be furnished by the insurer to the Authority within thirty days of his entering into such contract, and intimation of any change in any such contract shall be furnished by the insurer with full particulars thereof to the Authority within thirty days of the making of any such change.

(6) If the commission due to any insurance agent in respect of any general insurance business procured by such agent is not paid by the principal agent for any reason, the insurer may pay the insurance agent the commission

so due and recover the amount so paid from the principal agent concerned.

(7) Every contract as is referred to in sub-section (2), subsisting at the commencement of the Insurance (Amendment) Act, 1950 (47 of 1950), shall, with respect to terms regarding remuneration, be deemed to have been so altered as to be in accordance with the provisions of sub-section (4) of section 40A.

(8) If any dispute arises as to whether a person is or was a principal agent the matter shall be referred to the Authority, whose decision shall be final.

(9) Every insurer shall maintain a register in which the name and address of every principal agent appointed by him, the date of such appointment and the date, if any, on which the appointment ceased shall be entered.

Commission, Brokerage or Fee Payable to Intermediary or Insurance Intermediary

(1) No intermediary or insurance intermediary shall be paid or contract to be paid by way of commission, fee or as remuneration in any form, an amount exceeding thirty per cent of the premium payable as may be specified by the regulations made by the Authority, in respect of any policy or policies effected through him: Provided that the Authority may specify different amounts payable by way of commission, fee or as remuneration to an intermediary or insurance intermediary or different classes of business of insurance.

(2) Without prejudice to the provisions contained in this Act, the Authority may, by the regulations made in this behalf, specify the requirements of capital, form of business and other conditions to act as an intermediary or insurance intermediary.

Register of Insurance Agents

Every insurer and every person who acting on behalf of an insurer employs insurance agents shall maintain a register showing the name and address of every insurance agent appointed by him and the date on which his appointment began and the date, if any, on which his appointment ceased.

IRDA ACT 1999

The Insurance Act, 1938 had provided for setting up of the Controller of Insurance to act as a strong and powerful supervisory and regulatory authority for insurance. Post nationalization, the role of Controller of Insurance diminished considerably in significance since the insurance companies were owned by the Government.

With the opening up of the insurance industry to the private sector, the need for a strong, independent and autonomous Insurance Regulatory Authority was felt. As the enacting of legislation would have taken time, the then Government constituted through a Government resolution an Interim Insurance Regulatory Authority pending the enactment of a comprehensive legislation. The Insurance Regulatory and Development Authority Act, 1999 is an act to provide for the establishment of an Authority to protect the interests of holders of insurance policies, to regulate, promote and ensure orderly growth of the insurance industry and for matters connected therewith or incidental thereto and further to amend the Insurance Act, 1938, the Life Insurance Corporation Act, 1956 and the General insurance Business (Nationalization) Act, 1972 to end the monopoly of the Life Insurance Corporation of India (for life insurance business) and General Insurance Corporation and its subsidiaries (for general insurance business).

Extent and Commencement

- This Act may be called the Insurance Regulatory and Development Authority Act, 1999.
- The act extends to the whole of India and will come into force on such date as the Central Government may, by notification in the Official Gazette specify. Different dates may be appointed for different provisions of this Act.
- The Act has defined certain terms, some of the most important ones are as follows:-

- Appointed day means the date on which the Authority is established under the act.
- Authority means the established under this Act.

With effect from such date as the Central Government may, by notification, appoint the Insurance Regulatory and Develop is to be constituted. The Authority shall be a body corporate, having perpetual succession and a common seal with power, subject to the provisions of this Act, to acquire, hold and dispose of property, and to contract and can be sue or be sued in its own name. The head office of the Authority shall be at such place as the Central Government may decide from time to time and it may establish offices at other places in India.

Composition of Authority

The Authority shall consist of the following members, namely

(a) a Chairperson;

(b) not more than five whole-time members;

(c) not more than four part-time members, to be appointed by the Central Government from amongst persons of ability, integrity and standing who have knowledge or experience in life insurance, general insurance, actuarial science, finance, economics, law, accountancy, administration or any other discipline which would, in the opinion of the Central Government, be useful to the Authority:

The Central Government while appointing the Chairperson and the whole-time members must ensure that at least one person each is a person having knowledge or experience in life insurance, general insurance or actuarial science respectively. Tenure of office of Chairperson and other members The Chairperson and every other whole-time member shall hold office for a term of five years from the date on which he enters upon his office and shall be eligible for reappointment: However, no person shall hold office as such Chairperson after he has attained the age of sixty-five years and no person shall hold office as such whole-time member after he has attained the age of sixty-two years. A part-time member shall hold office for a term not exceeding five years from the date on which he enters upon his office.

A member may:-

(a) relinquish his office by giving in writing to the Central Government notice of not less than three months; or be removed from his office in accordance with the following provisions.

Removal from Office

The Central Government may remove from office any member who:-

(a) is, or at any time has been, adjudged as insolvent;

(b) has become physically or mentally incapable of acting as a member;

(c) has been convicted of any offence which, in the opinion of the Central Government, involves moral turpitude;

(d) has acquired such financial or other interest as is likely to affect prejudicially his functions as a member;

(e) has so abused his position as to render his continuation in office detrimental to the public interest.

No such member shall be removed under clause (d) or clause (e) unless he has been given a reasonable opportunity of being heard in the matter. Salary and allowances of Chairperson and members

The salary and allowances payable to, and other terms and conditions of service of, the members other than part-time members shall be such as may be prescribed.

The part-time members shall receive such allowances as may be prescribed. The salary, allowances and other conditions of service of a member shall not be varied to his disadvantage after appointment.

Bar on Future Employment of Members

The Chairperson and the whole-time members shall not, for a period of two years from the date on which they cease to hold office as such, except with the previous approval of the Central Government, accept:-

(a) any employment either under the Central Government or under any State Government; or

(b) any appointment in any company in the Insurance sector.

Administrative powers of Chairperson

The Chairperson shall have the powers of general superintendence and direction in respect of all administrative matters of the Authority.

Meeting of Authority

The Authority shall meet at such times and places, and shall observe such rules and procedures in regard to transaction of business at its meetings (including quorum at such meetings) as may be determined by regulations.

The Chairperson, or if for any reason he is unable to attend a meeting of the Authority, any other member chosen by the members present from amongst themselves at the meeting shall preside at the meeting.

All questions which come up before any meeting of the Authority shall be decided by a majority vote of the members present and voting, and in the event of equality of votes, the Chairperson, or in his absence, the person presiding shall have a second or casting vote.

The Authority may make regulations for the transaction of business at its meetings.

Vacancies, etc., not to Invalidate Proceedings of Authority

No Act or proceeding of the Authority shall be invalid merely by reason of:-

(a) any vacancy in, or any defect in the constitution of, the Authority;

(b) any defect in the appointment of a person acting as a member of the Authority;

(c) any irregularity in the procedure of the Authority not affecting the merits of the case.

Officers and Employees of Authority

The Authority may appoint officers and such other employees, as it considers necessary for the efficient discharge of its functions under this Act. The terms and other conditions of service of officers and other employees of the Authority shall be governed by regulations made under this Act.

Transfer of Assets, Liabilities, etc, of the Interim Insurance Regulatory

Authority will be transferred to the Authority on the appointed day.

All suits and other legal proceedings instituted or which could have been instituted by or against the Interim Insurance Regulatory Authority immediately before that day may be continued or may be instituted by or against the Authority.

Duties, Powers and Functions of Authority

Subject to the provisions of this Act and any other law for the time being in force, the Authority has the duty to regulate, promote and ensure orderly growth of the insurance business and re-insurance business. The powers and functions of the Authority include:-

(a) to issue to the applicant a certificate of registration, to renew, modify, withdraw, suspend or cancel such registration

(b) protection of the interests of the policy-holders in matters concerning assigning of policy, nomination by policy-holders, insurable interest, settlement of insurance claim, surrender value of policy, and other terms and conditions of contracts of insurance

(c) specifying requisite qualifications code of conduct and practical training for intermediary or insurance intermediaries and agents

(d) specifying the code of conduct for surveyors and loss assessors

(e) promoting efficiency in the conduct of insurance business

(f) promoting and regulating professional organizations connected with the insurance and reinsurance business

(g) levying fees and other charges for carrying out the purposes of this Act

(h) calling for information from, undertaking inspection of, conducting enquiries and investigations including audit of the insurers, intermediaries, insurance intermediaries and other organizations connected with the insurance business

(i) control and regulation of the rates, advantages, terms and conditions that may be offered by insurers in respect of general insurance business not so controlled and regulated by the Tariff Advisory Committee under section 64U of the Insurance Act, 1938

(j) prescribing the form and manner in which books of account shall be maintained and statement of accounts will be rendered by insurers and other insurance intermediaries

(k) Regulating investment of funds by insurance companies

(l) regulating maintenance of margin of solvency

(m) adjudication of disputes between insurers and intermediaries or insurance intermediaries

(n) supervising the functioning of the Tariff Advisory Committee

(o) specifying the percentage of premium income of the insurer to finance schemes for promoting and regulating professional organizations

(p) specifying the percentage of life insurance business and general insurance business to be undertaken by the insurer in the rural or social sector

(q) exercising such other powers as may be prescribed

Finance, Accounts and Audit

Grants by Central Government

The Central Government may, after due appropriation made by the Parliament by law in this behalf, make to the Authority grants of such sums of money as the Government may think fit for being utilized for the purposes of this Act.

Fund

A Fund to be called "The Insurance Regulatory and Development Authority Fund" is to be established and the following sums will be credited thereto:-

(a) all Government grants, fees and charges received by the Authority

(b) all sums received by the Authority from such other source as may be decided upon by the Central Government

(c) the percentage of prescribed income received from the insurer.

The Fund shall be applied for meeting the following expenses:-

(a) the salaries, allowances and other remuneration of the members, officers and other employees of the Authority

(b) the other expenses of the Authority in connection with the discharge of its functions and for the purposes of this Act.

Accounts and Audit

The Authority shall maintain proper accounts and other relevant records and prepare an annual statement of accounts in such form as may be prescribed by the Central Government in consultation with the Comptroller and Auditor General of India. The accounts of the Authority shall be audited by the Comptroller and Auditor General of India at such intervals as may be specified by him and any expenditure incurred in connection with such audit shall be payable by the Authority to the Comptroller and Auditor General of India.

The Comptroller and Auditor-General of India and other person appointed by him in connection with the audit of the accounts of the Authority shall have the same rights and privileges and authority in connection with such audit as the Comptroller and Auditor General generally has in connection with the audit of the Government accounts and, in particular, shall have the right to demand the production of books, accounts, connected vouchers and other documents and papers and to inspect any of the officers of the Authority.

The accounts of the Authority as certified by the Comptroller and Auditor General of India or any other person appointed by him in this behalf together with the audit report thereon shall be forwarded annually to the Central Government and that Government shall cause the same to be laid before each House of Parliament.

Powers of Central Government

The Authority shall, in exercise of its powers or the performance of its functions under this Act, be bound by such directions on questions of policy, other than those relating to technical and administrative matters, as the Central Government may give in writing to it from time to time However, Authority must, as far as practicable, be given an opportunity to express its views before any such direction is given. The decision of the Central Government, whether a question is one of policy or not, shall be final. Power of Central Government to supersede Authority If at any time the Central Government is of the opinion:-

(a) that, on account of circumstances beyond the control of the Authority, it is unable to discharge the functions or perform the duties imposed on it by or under the provisions of this Act: or

(b) that the Authority has persistently defaulted in complying with any direction given by the Central Government under this Act or in the discharge of the functions or performance of the duties imposed on it by or under the provisions of this Act and as a result of such default the financial position of the Authority or the administration of the Authority has suffered; or

(c) that circumstances exist which render in necessary in the public interest so to do, the Central Government may, by notification and for reasons to be specified therein, supersede the Authority for such period, not exceeding six months, as may be specified in the notification and appoint a person to be the Controller of Insurance. However, before issuing any such notification, the Central Government shall give a reasonable opportunity to the Authority to make representations against the proposed supersession and shall consider the representations, if any, of the Authority.

Upon the publication of such notification superseding the Authority:-

(a) the Chairperson and other members shall, as from the date of supersession, vacate their offices as such;

(b) all the powers, functions and duties which may, by or under the provisions of this Act, be exercised or discharged by or on behalf of the Authority shall, until the Authority is reconstituted, be exercised and discharged by the Controller of Insurance; and

(c) all properties owned or controlled by the Authority shall, until the Authority is reconstituted vest in the Central Government.

On or before the expiration of the period of supersession specified in such a notification, the Central Government shall reconstitute the Authority by a fresh appointment of its Chairperson and other members and in such case any person who had vacated his office under the notification shall not be deemed disqualified for reappointment.

The Central Government shall cause a copy of the notification issued and a full report of any action taken under this section and the circumstances leading to such action to be laid before each House of Parliament at the earliest.

Furnishing of Eeturns, etc., to the Central Government

The Authority must furnish to the Central Government at such time and in such form and manner as may be prescribed, or as the Central Government may direct, such returns and statements and such particulars in regard to any proposed or existing programme for the promotion and development of the insurance industry as the Central Government may, from time to time, require.

The Authority must, within nine months after the close of each financial year, submit to the Central Government a report giving a true and full account of its activities including the activities for promotion and development of the insurance business during the previous financial year. Copies of the reports must be laid, as soon as may be after they are received, before each House of Parliament. Chairperson, members, officers and employees of Authority to be public servants. The Chairperson, members, officers and other employees of the Authority shall be deemed, when acting or purporting to act in pursuance of any of the provisions of this Act, to be public servants within the meaning of section 21 of the Indian Penal Code.

Protection of Action taken in Good Faith

No suit, prosecution or other legal proceedings shall lie against the Central Government or any officer of the Central Government or any member, officer or other employee of the Authority for anything which is in good faith done or intended to be done under this Act or the rules or regulations made there under. However, nothing in this Act exempts any person from any suit or other proceedings which might, apart from this Act, be brought against him.

Delegation of Powers

The Authority may, by general or special order in writing, delegate to the Chairperson or any other member or officer of the Authority, subject to such conditions, if any, as may be specified in the order such of its powers and functions under this Act as it may deem necessary. The Authority may, by a general or special order in writing, also form Committees of the members and delegate to them the powers and functions of the Authority as may be specified by the regulations.

Power to make Rules

The Central Government may, by notification, make rules for carrying out the purposes of this Act. Such rules may provide for all or any of the following matters, namely:-

(a) the salary and allowances payable to and other conditions of service of the members other than part-time members

(b) the allowances to be paid to the part-time members

(c) such other powers that may be performed by the Authority

(d) the form of annual statement of accounts to be prepared by the Authority

(e) the time at, the form and the manner in which returns and statements and particulars are to be furnished to the Central Government

(f) the matters on which the Insurance Advisory Committee shall advise the authority

(g) any other matter which is to be, or may be, prescribed, or in respect of which provision is to be or may be made by rules.

Establishment of Insurance Advisory Committee

The Authority may, by notification, establish with effect from such date as it may specify in such notification, a Committee to be known as the Insurance Advisory Committee.

The Insurance Advisory Committee shall consist of not more than twenty-five members excluding ex officio members to represent the interests of commerce, industry, transport, agriculture, consumer fora, surveyors, agents, intermediaries, organizations engaged in safety and loss prevention, research bodies and employees' association in the insurance sector.

The Chairperson and the members of the Authority shall be the ex officio Chairperson and ex officio members of the Insurance Advisory Committee.

The objects of the Insurance Advisory committee shall be to advise the Authority on matters relating to the making of the regulations. The Insurance Advisory Committee may advise the Authority on such other matters as may be prescribed.

Capital Requirements

Requirement as to Capital

No insurer carrying on the business of life insurance, general insurance, or reinsurance in India on or after the commencement of the Insurance Regulatory and Development Authority Act, 1999, shall be registered unless he has:-

1. a paid-up equity capital of rupees one hundred crores, in case of a person carrying on the business of life insurance or general insurance; or
2. a paid-up equity capital of rupees two hundred crores, in case of a person carrying on exclusively the business as a reinsurer:

In determining the paid-up equity capital specified under clause (i) or clause (ii), the deposit to be made under section 7 and any preliminary expenses incurred in the formation and registration of the company shall be excluded: An insurer carrying on business of life insurance, general insurance or reinsurance in India before the commencement of the Insurance Regulatory and Development Authority Act, 1999 and who is required to be registered under this Act, shall have a paid-up equity capital in accordance with clause (i) and clause (ii), as the case may be, within six months of the commencement of that Act.

Where, the nominal value of the shares intended to be transferred by any individual, firm, group, constituents of a group, or body corporate under the same management, jointly or severally exceeds one per cent. Of paid up capital of the insurer, previous approval of the Authority must be obtained for the transfer. Explanation.-For the purpose of this sub-clause, the expressions “group” and “same management”, shall have the same meanings respectively assigned to them in the Monopolies and Restrictive Trade Practices Act, 1969.

The following sections have been inserted:-

Provisions of investment of funds outside India.

No insurer shall directly or indirectly invest outside India, the funds of the policyholders.

Manner and Conditions of Investment

The Authority may, in the interests of the policyholders, specify by regulations made by the Authority, the time, manner and other conditions of investment of assets to be held by an insurer for the purposes of this Act. The Authority may, after taking into account the nature of business and to protect the interests of the policyholders, issue to an insurer the directions relating to the time, manner, and other conditions of investment of assets to be held by him. However, no directions shall be issued unless the insurer concerned has been given a reasonable opportunity of being heard.

Insurance Business in Rural or Social Sector

Every insurer shall, after the commencement of the Insurance Regulatory and Development Authority Act, 1999, undertake such percentages of life insurance business and general insurance business in the rural or social sector, as may be specified, in the Official Gazette by the Authority, in this behalf.

Miscellaneous Provisions

Penalty for default in complying with, or act in contravention of, this Act. If any person, who is required under this Act, or rules or regulations made there under,-

(a) to furnish any document, statement, account, return or report to the Authority, fail to furnish the same; or

(b) to comply with the directions, fails to comply with such directions;

(c) to maintain solvency margin, fails to maintain such solvency margin;

(d) to comply with the directions on the insurance treaties, fails to comply with sue directions on the insurance treaties, he shall be liable to a penalty not exceeding five lakhs rupees for each such failure and punishable with fine.

If a person makes a statement, or furnishes any document, statement, account, return or report which is false and which he either knows or believes to be false or does not believe to be true,-

(a) he shall be liable to a penalty not exceeding five lakhs rupees for each such failure; and

(b) he shall be punishable with imprisonment which may extend to three years or with fine for each such failure.

If any director, managing director, manager or to~ officer or employees of an insurer wrongfully obtains possession of any property or wrongfully applies to any purpose of the Act, he shall be liable to a penalty not exceeding two lakhs rupees for each such failure.

Offences by companies, Where any offence under this Act has been committed by a company, every person who, at the time the offence was committed, was in charge of, and was responsible to, the Company for the conduct of the business of the company as well as the company shall be deemed to be guilty of the offence and shall be liable to be proceeded against and punished accordingly: Nothing contained in this sub-section shall render any such person liable to any punishment, if he proves that the offence was committed without his knowledge or thathe had exercised all due diligence to prevent the commission of such offence.

Where any offence under this Act has been committed by a company and it is proved that the offence has been committed with the consent or connivance of, or is attributable to any neglect on the part of, any director, manager, secretary or other officer of the company, such director, manager, secretary or other officer shall be deemed to be guilty of that offence and shall be liable to be proceeded against and punished accordingly.

Explanation: For the purposes of this section,-

(a) "company" means any body corporate, and includes a firm, an association of person or a body of individuals whether incorporated or not; and

(b) "director", in relation to-

(i) a firm means a partner in the firm;

(ii) an association of persons or a body of individuals, means any-member controlling the affairs thereof.

Power of Authority to make regulations.

The Authority may, by notification in the Official Gazette, make regulations consistent with this Act and the rules made there under, to carry out the provisions of this Act.

AGENCY LAW

At times all of us act as principals and agents. If I my friend ask me to deposit his water bill, then he is acting as principal and I am as agent.

Agency Law is contained in Chapter X {Secs182 to 238} of the Indian Contact Act 1872. "Agent" and "principal": An "agent" is a person employed to do any act for another, or to represent another in dealings with third persons. The person for whom such act is done, or represented, is called the "principal". {sec182}.

Who may employ agent: Any person who is of the age of majority according to the law to which he is subject, and who is of sound mind, may employ an agent. Who may be an agent: As between the principal and third persons, any person may become an agent, but no person who is not of the age of majority and sound mind can become an agent, so as to be responsible to the principal according to the provisions in that behalf herein contained.

Consideration not necessary: No consideration is necessary to create an agency. Agent's authority may be express or implied: The authority of an agent may be express or implied.

Definitions of express and implied authority: An authority is said to be express when it is given by words spoken or written. An authority is said to be implied when it is to be inferred from the circumstances of the case; and things spoken or written, or the ordinary course of dealing, may be accounted circumstances of the case.

Illustration

Aman owns a shop in Serampur, living himself in Calcutta, and visiting the shop occasionally. Bharat manages the shop, and he is in the habit of ordering goods from Chaman in the name of Aman for the purposes of the shop, and of paying for them out of Aman's funds with Aman's knowledge. Bharat has an implied authority from Aman to order goods from Chaman in the name of Aman for the purpose of the shop.

Extent of agent's authority: An agent, having an authority to do an act, has authority to do every lawful thing, which is necessary in order to do such act. An agent having an authority to carry on a business has authority to do every lawful thing necessary for the purpose, or usually done in the course, of conducting such business.

Illustrations

(a) A is employed by B, residing in London, to recover at Bombay a debt due to B. A may adopt any legal process necessary for the purpose of recovering the debt, and may give a valid discharge for the same.

(b) A constitutes B his agent to carry on his business of a shipbuilder. B may purchase timber and other materials, and hire workmen, for the purpose of carrying on the business.

Agent's Authority in an Emergency: An agent has authority, in an emergency, to do all such acts for the purpose of protecting his principal from loss and would be done by a person or ordinary prudence, in his own case, under similar circumstances.

SUB AGENT

When Agent cannot Delegate

An agent cannot lawfully employ another to perform acts, which he has expressly, or impliedly undertaken to perform personally, unless by the ordinary custom of trade a sub-agent may, or, from the nature of agency, a sub-agent must, be employed.

"Sub-agent" Defined

A "sub-agent" is a person employed by, and acting under the control of, the original agent in the business of the agency.

Representation of Principal by Sub-agent Properly Appointed

Where a sub-agent is properly appointed, the principal is, so far as regards third persons, represented by the sub-agent, and is bound by and responsible for his acts, as if he were an agent originally appointed by the principal.

Agent's responsibility for sub-agents: The agent is responsible to the principal for the acts of the sub-agent.

Sub-agent's responsibility: The sub-agent is responsible for his acts to the agent, but not to the principal, except in case of fraud or willful wrong.

Agent's Responsibility for Sub-agent Appointed without Authority

Where an agent, without having authority to do so, has appointed a person to act as a sub-agent, the agent stands towards such person in the relation of a principal to an agent, and is responsible for his acts both to the principal and to third person; the principal is not represented, by or responsible for the acts of the person so employed, nor is that person responsible to the principal. Relation between principal and person duly appointed by agent to act in business of agency When an agent, holding an express or implied authority to name another person to act for the principal in the business of the agency, has named another person accordingly, such person is not a sub-agent, but an agent of the principal for such part of the business of the agency as is entrusted to him.

Agent's Duty in Naming such Person

In selecting such agent for his principal, an agent is bound to exercise the same amount of discretion as a man of ordinary prudence would exercise in his own case; and, if he does this, he is not responsible to the principal for the acts of negligence of the agent so selected.

Illustrations

A instructs B, a merchant, to buy a ship for him. B employs a ship-surveyor of good reputation to choose a ship for A. The surveyor makes the choice negligently and the ship turns out to be unseaworthy and is lost. B is not, but the surveyor is, responsible to A. Right of person as to acts done for him without his authority-effect of ratification. Where acts are done by one person on behalf of another, but without his knowledge or authority, he may elect to ratify or to disown such acts. If he ratifies them, the same effects will follow as if they had been performed by his authority. Ratification may be expressed or implied. Ratification may be expressed or may be implied in the conduct of the person on whose behalf the acts are done.

Illustrations

(a) A, without authority, buys goods, for B. Afterwards B sells them to C on his own account; B's conduct implies a ratification of the purchase made for him by A.

(b) A, without B's authority, lends B's money to C. Afterwards B accepts interest on the money from C. B's conduct implies a ratification of the loan. Knowledge requisite for valid ratification

No valid ratification can be made by a person whose knowledge of the facts of the case is materially defective. Effect of ratifying unauthorized act forming part of a transaction. A person ratifying any unauthorized act done on his behalf ratifies the whole of the transaction of which such act formed a part.

Ratification of Unauthorized act cannot Injure Third Person

An act done by one person on behalf of another, without such other person's authority, which, if done with authority would have the effect of subjecting a third person to damages, or of terminating any right to interest of a third person cannot, by ratification, be made to have such effect.

REVOCATION OF AUTHORITY

Termination of Agency

An agency is terminated by the principal revoking his authority, or by the agent renouncing the business of the agency; or by the business of the agency being completed; or by either the principal or agent dying or becoming of unsound mind; or by the principal being adjudicated an insolvent under the provisions of any Act for the time being in force for the relief of insolvent debtors.

Termination of agency, where agent has an interest in subject-matter Where the agent has himself an interest in the property, which forms the subject matter of the agency, the agency cannot, in the absence of an express contract, be terminated to the prejudice of such interest.

Illustration

A, gives authority to B to sell A's land, and to pay himself, out of the proceeds, the debts due to him from A.A cannot revoke this authority, nor can it be terminated by his insanity or death.

When principal may revoke agent's authority.

The principal may, save as is otherwise provided by the last preceding section, revoke the authority given to his agent at any time before the authority has been exercised, so as to bind the principal.

Revocation where authority has been partly exercised.

The principal cannot revoke the authority given to his agent after the authority has been partly exercised; so far as regards such acts and obligations as arise from acts already done in the agency.

Compensation for revocation by principal, or renunciation by agent. Where there is an express or implied contract that the agency should be continued for any period of time, the principal must make compensation to the agent, or the agent to the principal, as the case may be, for any previous revocation or renunciation of the agency without sufficient cause.

Notice of revocation or renunciation.

Reasonable notice must be given of such revocation or renunciation, otherwise the damage thereby resulting to the principal or the agent, as the case may be, must be made good to the one by the other. Revocation and renunciation may be expressed or implied. Revocation or renunciation may be expressed or may be implied in the conduct of that principal or agent respectively.

Illustration

A empowers B to let A's house. Afterwards A lets it himself. This is an implied revocation of B's authority. When termination of agent's authority takes effect as to agent, and as to third persons

The termination of the authority of an agent does not, so far as regards the agent, take effect before it becomes known to him, or, so far as regards third persons, before it becomes known to them.

Agent's duty on termination of agency by principal's death or insanity When an agency is terminated by the principal dying or becoming of unsound mind, the agent is bound to take on behalf of the representative, of his late principal, all reasonable steps for the protection and reservation of the interests entrusted to him.

Termination of Sub-agent's Authority

The termination of the authority of an agent causes the termination (subject to the rules herein contained regarding the termination of an agent's authority) of the authority of all sub-agents appointed by him.

AGENT'S DUTY TO PRINCIPAL

Agent's Duty in Conducting Principal's Business

An agent is bound to conduct the business of his principal according to the directions given by the principal, or in the absence of any such directions according to the customs, which prevails in doing business of the same kind at the place where the agent conducts such business. When the agent acts otherwise, if any loss be sustained, he must make it good to his principal and if any profit accrues, he must account for it.

Skill and Diligence required from Agent

An agent is bound to conduct the business of the agency with as much skill as is generally possessed by person engaged in similar business unless the principal has notice of his want of skill.

The agent is always bound to act with reasonable diligence, and to use such skill as he possesses; and to make compensation to his principal in respect of the direct consequences of his own neglect, want of skill, or misconduct, but not in respect of loss or damage which are indirectly or remotely caused by such neglect, want of skill, or misconduct.

Agent's Accounts

An agent is bound to render proper accounts to his principal on demand. Agent's, duty to communicate with principal

It is the duty of an agent in case of difficulty, to use all reasonable diligence in communicating with his principal, and in seeking to obtain his instructions. Right of principal when agent deals, on his own account, in business of agency without principal's consent. If an agent deals on his own account in the business of the agency, without first obtaining the consent of his principal and acquainting him with all material circumstances, which have come to his own knowledge on the subject, the principal may

Repudiate the transaction, if the case shows, either that any material fact has been dishonestly concealed from him by the agent, or that the dealings of the agent have been disadvantageous to him.

Illustrations

(a) A direct B to sell A's estate. B buys the estate for himself in the name of C. A, on discovering that B has bought the estate for himself, may repudiate the sale, if he can show that B has dishonestly concealed any material fact, or that the seals has been disadvantageous to him.

(b) A directs B to sell A's estate. B, on looking over the estate before selling it, finds a mine on the estate which is unknown to A. B informs A thathe wished to buy the estate for himself but conceals the discovery of the mine. A allows B to buy, in ignorance of the existence of the mine. A, on discovering that B knew of the mine at the time he bought the estate, may either repudiate or adopt the sale at his option.

Principal's right to benefit gained by agent dealing on his own account in business of agency

If an agent, without the knowledge of his principal, deals in the business of the agency on his own account instead of on account to his principal, the principal is entitled to claim from the agent any benefit which may have resulted to him from the transaction.

Agent's right of retainer out of sums received on principal's account An agent may retain, out of any sums received on account of the principal in the business of the agency, all moneys due to himself in respect of advances made or expenses properly incurred by him in conducting such business, and also such remuneration as may be payable to him for acting as agent.

Agent's Duty to Pay sums received for Principal

Subject to such deductions, the agent is bound to pay to his principal all sums received on his account.

When agent's remuneration becomes due.

In the absence of any special contract, payment for the performance of any act is not due to the agent until the completion of such act; but an agent may detain moneys received by him on account of goods sold, although the whole of the goods consigned to him for sale may not have been sold, or although the sale may not be actually complete.

Agent not entitled to remuneration for business misconduct.

An agent, who is guilty of misconduct in the business of the agency, is not entitled to any remuneration in respect of that part of the business, which he has misconducted.

Illustrations

A employs B to recover 1,000 rupees from C. Through B's misconduct the money is not recovered. B is entitled to no remuneration for his services and must make good the loss.

Agent's Lien on Principal's Property

In the absence of any contract to the contrary, an agent is entitled to retain goods, papers, and other property, whether movable or immovable of the principal received by him, until the amount due to himself for commission, disbursements and services in respect of the same has been paid or accounted for to him.

PRINCIPAL'S DUTY TO AGENT

Agent to be indemnified against consequences of lawful acts The employer of an agent is bound to indemnify him against the consequences of all lawful acts done by such agent in exercise of the authority conferred upon him.

Agent to be indemnified against consequences of acts done in good faith Where one person employs another to do an act, and the agent does the act in good faith, the employer is liable to indemnify the agent against the consequences of that act, though it may cause an injury to the rights of third persons. Non-liability of employer of agent to do a criminal act Where one person employees another to do an act which is criminal, the employer is not liable to the agent, either upon an express or an implied promise to indemnify him against the consequences of that Act.

Illustrations

A employs B to beat C, and agrees to indemnify him against all consequences of the act. B thereupon beats C, and has to pay damages to C for so doing. A is not liable to indemnify B for those damages. Compensation to agent for injury caused by principal's neglect. The principal must make compensation to his agent in respect of injury caused to such agent by the principal's neglect or want of skill.

Illustration

A employs B as a bricklayer in building a house, and put up the scaffolding himself. The scaffolding is unskillfully put up, and B is in consequence hurt. A must make compensation to B.

EFFECT OF AGENCY ON CONTRACTS WITH THIRD PERSONS

Enforcement and Consequences of Agent's Contract

Contracts entered into through an agent, and obligations arising from acts done by an agent, may be enforced in the same manner, and will have the same legal consequences as if the contracts had been entered into the acts done by the principal in person.

Illustrations

(a) A buys goods from B, knowing thathe is an agent for their sale, but not knowing who the principal is. B's principal is the person entitled to claim from A the price of the goods, and A cannot, in a suit by the principal, set-off against that claim a debt due to himself from B.

(b) A, being B's agent; with authority to receive money on his behalf, receives from C a sum of money due to B. C is discharged of his obligation to pay the sum in question to B.

Principal how far Bound, when Agent exceeds Authority

When an agent does more than he is authorized to do, and when the part of whathe does, which is within his authority, can be separated from the part, which is beyond his authority, so much only of whathe does as is within his authority is binding as between him and his principal. Principal not bound when excess of agent's authority is not separable Where an agent does more than he is authorized to do, and whathe does beyond the scope of his authority cannot be separated from what is within it, the principal is not bound to recognize the transaction.

Illustration

A authorizes B to buy 500 sheep for him. B buys 500 sheep and 200 lambs for a sum of 6,000 rupees. A may repudiate the whole transaction.

Consequences of Notice given to Agent

Any notice given to or information obtained by the agent, provided it be given or obtained in the course of the business transacted by him for the principal, shall, as between the principal and third parties, have the same legal consequences as if it had been given to or obtained by the principal.

Illustrations

A is employed by B to buy from C goods of which C is the apparent owner. A was, before he was so employed a servant of C, and then learnt that the goods really belonged to D, but B is ignorant of that fact. In spite of the knowledge of his agent, B may set-off against the price of the goods a debt owing to him from C. Agent cannot personally enforce, nor be bound by, contracts on behalf of principal.

In the absence of any contract to that effect an agent cannot personally enforce contracts entered into by him on behalf of his principal, nor is he personally bound by them.

Presumption of contract to the contrary: Such a contract shall be presumed to exit in the following cases-

(1) Where the contract is made by an agent for the sale or purchase of goods for a merchant resident abroad;

(2) Where agent does not disclose the name of his principal;

(3) Where the principal, though disclosed, cannot be sued.

Right of Parties to a Contract made by Agent not Disclosed

If an agent makes a contract with a person who neither, knows nor has reason to suspect, thathe is an agent, his principal may require the performance of the contract; but the other contracting party has, as against the principal, the same right as he would have had as against if the agent had been the principal. If the principal discloses himself before the contract is completed, the other contracting party may refuse to fulfill the contract, if he can show that, if he had known who was the principal in the contract, or if he had known that the agent was not a principal, he would not have entered into the contract.

Performance of Contract with Agent Supposed to be Principal

Where one man makes a contract with another, neither knowing nor having reasonable ground to suspect that the other is an agent, the principal, if he requires the performance of the contract, can only obtain such performance subject to the right and obligations subsisting between the agent and the other party of the contract. Liability of principal inducing belief that agent's unauthorized acts were authorized.

When an agent has, without authority, done acts or incurred obligations to third person on behalf of his principal, the principal is bound by such acts or obligations, if he has by his word or conduct induced such third person to believe that such acts and obligations were within the scope of the agent's authority.

Illustrations

(a) A consigns goods to B for sale, and gives him instructions not to sell under a fixed price. C, being ignorant of B's instruction, enters into a contract with B to buy the goods at a price lower than the reserved price. A is bound by the contract

(b) A entrusts B with negotiable instruments endorsed in blank. B sells them to C in violation of private order from A. The sale is good.

Effect, on agreement, of misrepresentation or fraud by agent.

Misrepresentation made or fraud committed, by agent acting in the course of their business for their principals, have the same effect on agreements made by such agents as if such misrepresentations of frauds had been made or committed by the principals; but misrepresentations made, or frauds committed, by agents, in matters which do not affect their authority, do not affect their principals

Illustrations

(a) A, being B's agent for the sale of goods, induces C to buy them by a misrepresentation, which he was not authorized by B to make. The contract is voidable, as between B and C, at the option of C.

(c) A, the captain of B's ship, signs bills of lading without having received on board the goods mentioned therein.

The bills of lading are void as between B and the pretended consignor.

CONSUMER PROTECTION ACT, 1986

The Consumer Protection Act was passed by the Parliament in 1986 and it came into force from 1987. Its purposes to protect consumers against defective goods, unsatisfactory services, unfair trade practices, etc.

The Act provides for three-tier machinery consisting of District Forum, State Commission and National Commission. It also provides for the formation protection councils in every state. The consumers can file their complaints at the appropriate forum for quick redressal.

The complaint may relate to defective refrigerator or TV set, nonfunctional telephone, lack of due cares in medical treatment and so on. Any service or product given free of charge is not covered by the Act.

Definitions of Important Terms

Before studying the provisions of the CPA, it is necessary to understand the terms used in the Act. Let us understand some of the more important definitions. Complainant means:-

1. A consumer; or
2. Any voluntary consumer association registered under the Companies Act, 1956 or under any other law for the time being in force; or
3. The Central Government or any State Government, who or which makes a complaint; or
4. One or more consumers where there are numerous consumers having the same interest

Complaint means any allegation in writing made by a complainant that:-

1. an unfair trade practice or a restricted trade practice has been adopted by any trader
2. the goods bought by him or agreed to be bought by him suffer from one more defects

3. the services hired or availed of or agreed to be hired or availed of by him suffer from deficiency in any respect
4. the trader has charged for the goods mentioned in the complaint a price excess of the price fixed by or under any law for the time being in force or displayed on the goods or any package containing such goods.
5. goods which will be hazardous to life and safety when used, are being offered for sale to the public in contravention of the provisions of any law for the time being in force, requiring traders to display information in regard to the contents, manner and effect of use of such goods; with a view to obtaining any relief provided by law under the CPA.

Consumer means any person who:-

1. buys any goods for a consideration which has been paid or promised or partly paid and partly promised, or under any system of deferred payment (for example hire purchase or installment sales) and includes any other user of such goods when such use is made with the approval of the buyer, but does not include a person who obtains such goods for resale or for any commercial purpose; or
2. hires or avails of any services for a consideration which has been paid or promised, or partly paid and partly promised, or under any system of deferred payment and includes any beneficiary of such services when such services are availed of with the approval of the first mentioned person For the purposes of this definition "commercial purpose" does not include use by a consumer of goods bought and used by him exclusively for the purpose of earning his livelihood by means of self-employment.

Goods mean goods as defined in the Sale of Goods Act, 1930. Under that act, goods means every kind of movable property other than actionable claims and money and includes stocks and shares, growing crops, grass and things attached to or forming part of the land which are agreed to be severed before sale or under the contract of sale. Service is defined to mean service of any description which is made available to potential users and includes the provision of facilities in connection with banking, financing, insurance, transport, processing, supply of electrical or other energy, board or lodging or both, housing construction, entertainment, amusement or the purveying of news or other information but does not include the rendering of any service free of charge or under a contract of personal service. Consumer dispute means dispute where the person against whom a complaint has been made, denies or disputes the allegation contained in the complaint. Restrictive Trade Practice means any trade practice which requires a consumer to buy, hire, or avail of any good or as the case may be, services as a condition precedent for buying, hiring or availing of any other goods or services.

Unfair Trade Practice means unfair trade practice as defined under the Monopolies and Restrictive Trade Practices Act. The MRPT act has defined certain practices to be unfair trade practices. Defect means any fault, imperfection or shortcoming in the quality, quantity, potency, purity or standard which is required to be maintained by or under any law for the time being in force or under any contract, express or implied, or as is claimed by the trade in any manner whatsoever in relation to any goods.

Deficiency means any fault, imperfection or shortcoming or inadequacy in the quality, nature and manner of performance which is required to be maintained by or under any law for the time being in force or has been undertaken to be performed by a person in pursuance of a contract or otherwise in relation to any service. A consumer is a user of goods and services. Any person paying for goods and services, which he uses, is entitled to expect that the goods and services be of a nature and quality promised to him by the seller.

The earlier principle of "Caveat Emptor" or "let the buyer beware" which was prevalent has given way to the principle of "Consumer is King". The origins of this principle lie in the fact that in today's mass production economy where there is little contact between the producer and consumer, often sellers make exaggerated claims and advertisements, which they do not intend to fulfill. This leaves the consumer in a difficult position with very few avenues for redressal. The onset on intense competition also made producers aware of the benefits of customer satisfaction and hence by and large, the principle of "consumer is king" is now accepted.

Objects of the Consumer Protection Act, 1986

The preamble to the Act states that the Act is legislated to provide for better protection of the interests of consumers and for that purpose to make provision for the establishment of consumer councils and other authorities for the settlement of consumer's disputes and for matters connected therewith. The CPA extends to the whole of India except the State of Jammu and Kashmir and applies to all goods and services unless otherwise notified by the Central Government. The basic rights of consumers as per the Consumer Protection Act (CPA) are:

1. Right to safety.
2. Right to be informed.
3. Right to choose.
4. Right to representation (or to be heard).
5. Right to seek redressal.
6. Right to consumer education.

1. Right to Safety It is the consumer right to be protected against goods and services which is hazardous to health or life.
2. Right to be Informed The consumer has the right to be informed about the quality, quantity, purity, standard and price of goods he intends to purchase. Therefore, the manufacture must mention complete information about the product, its ingredients, date of manufacture, price, precaution of use, etc. on the label and package of the product.
3. Right to Choose The consumer should be assured of freedom to choose from a variety of products at

competitive prices. Every consumer wants to buy a product on his free will. There should be free competition in the market so that the consumer may make the right choice in satisfying his needs.

4. Right to Representation (or to be Heard) The consumer has a right to register dissatisfaction with any product and get his complaintheard. Most of the reputed firms have set up consumer service cells to listen to the consumer's complaint and take appropriate steps to redress their grievances.

5. Right to Seek Redressal. It is the right to seek redressal against any defect in goods or unfair trade suffered by the consumer. If the quality and performance of a product falls short of seller's claims, the consumer has a right to certain remedies. The Consumer Protection Act requires that the product must be repaired, replaced or taken back by the seller as provided under the contract between the buyer and the seller.

6. Right to Consumer Education. It means right of acquiring knowledge and being a well-informed consumer throughout his life. He should also be made aware of his rights and the remedies available through publicity in the mass media.

Consumer Responsibilities

(i) To provide adequate information to the seller The consumer has the responsibility to provide adequate information about his needs and expectation to the sellers.

(ii) To exercise caution in purchasing The consumer must try to get full information on the quality, design, utility, quantity, price, etc. of the product before purchasing it.

(iii) To insist on cash memo or receipt The consumer must get a cash memo or receipt as a proof of purchase of goods from the seller. This would help him in making a complaint to the seller in case of any defect in the goods.

(iv) To file complaint against genuine grievance The consumer must file a complaint with the seller or manufacturer about any defects or shortcoming in the products and services.

(v) To be quality conscious The consumer should never compromise on the quality of goods. While making purchases, the consumers must look for standard quality certification marks such as ISI, Agmark, Woolmark, FPO, etc. For example, electric iron must carry ISI mark.

Redressal Machinery under the Act

Consumer Protection Councils

The interests of consumers are enforced through various authorities set up under the CPA. The CPA provides for the setting up of the Central Consumer Protection Council, the State Consumer Protection Council and the District Forum.

Central Consumer Protection Council

The Central Government has set up the Central Consumer Protection Council, which consists of the following members:-

(a) The Minister in charge of Consumer Affairs in the Central Government who is its Chairman, and

(b) Other official and non-official members representing varied interests

The Central council consists of 150 members and its term is 3 years. The Council meets as and when necessary but at least one meeting is held in a year.

State Consumer Protection Council

The State Council consists of:-

(a) The Minister in charge of Consumer Affairs in the State Government who is its Chairman, and

(b) Other official and non-official members representing varied interests The State Council meets as and when necessary but not less than two meetings must be held every year.

Redressal Machinery under the Act

The CPA provides for a 3-tier approach in resolving consumer disputes. The District Forum has jurisdiction to entertain complaints where the value of goods / services complained against and the compensation claimed is less than Rs. 20 lakhs, the State Commission for claims exceeding Rs. 20 lakhs but not exceeding Rs. 1 crore and the National Commission for claims exceeding Rs.1 crore.

District Forum

Under the CPA, the State Government has to set up a district Forum in each district of the State. The government may establish more than one District Forum in a district if it deems fit. Each District Forum consists of:-

(a) A person who is, or who has been, or is qualified to be, a District Judge who shall be its President

(b) Two other members who shall be persons of ability, integrity and standing and have adequate knowledge or experience of or have shown capacity in dealing with problems relating to economics, law, commerce, accountancy, industry, public affairs or administration, one of whom shall be a woman.

Appointments to the State Commission shall be made by the State Government on the recommendation of a Selection Committee consisting of the President of the State Committee, the Secretary-Law Department of the State and the secretary in charge of Consumer Affairs Every member of the District Forum holds office for 5 years or up to the age of 65 years, whichever is earlier and is not eligible for re-appointment. A member may resign by giving notice in writing to the State Government whereupon the vacancy will be filled up by the State Government.

The District Forum can entertain complaints where the value of goods or services and the compensation, if any, claimed is less than rupees twenty lakhs. However, in addition to jurisdiction over consumer goods services valued upto Rs.20 lakhs, the District Forum also may pass orders against traders indulging in unfair trade practices, sale of defective goods or render deficient services provided the turnover of goods or value of services does not exceed rupees twenty lakhs. A complaint shall be instituted in the District Forum within the local limits of whose jurisdiction-

(a) The opposite party or the defendant actually and voluntarily resides or carries on business or has a branch office or personally works for gain at the time of institution of the complaint; or

(b) Any one of the opposite parties (where there are more than one) actually and voluntarily resides or carries on business or has a branch office or personally works for gain, at the time of institution of the complaint provided that the other opposite party/parties acquiescence in such institution or the permission of the Forum is obtained in respect of such opposite parties; or

(c) The cause of action arises, wholly or in part.

State Commission

The Act provides for the establishment of the State Consumer Disputes Redressal Commission by the State Government in the State by notification. Each State Commission shall consist of:-

(a) A person who is or has been a judge of a High Court appointed by State Government (in consultation with the Chief Justice of the High Court) who shall be its President;

(b) Two other members who shall be persons of ability, integrity, and standing and have adequate knowledge or experience of, or have shown capacity in dealing with, problems relating to economics, law, commerce, accountancy, industry, public affairs or administration, one of whom must be a woman.

Every appointment made under this is made by the State Government on the recommendation of a Selection Committee consisting of the President of the State Commission, Secretary-Law Department of the State and Secretary in charge of

Consumer Affairs in the State. Every member of the District Forum holds office for 5 years or upto the age of 65 years, whichever is earlier and is not eligible for re-appointment. A member may resign by giving notice in writing to the State Government whereupon the vacancy will be filled up by the State Government. The State Commission can entertain complaints where the value of goods or services and the compensation, if any, exceeds Rs. 20 lakhs but does not exceed Rs. 1crore. The State Commission also has the jurisdiction to entertain appeal against the orders of any District Forum within the State The State Commission also has the power to call for the records and appropriate orders in any consumer dispute which is pending before or has been decided by any District Forum within the State if it appears that such District Forum has exercised any power not vested in it by law or has failed to exercise a power rightfully vested in it by law or has acted illegally or with material irregularity.

National Commission

The Central Government provides for the establishment of the National Consumer Disputes Redressal Commission The National Commission shall consist of:-

(a) A person who is or has been a judge of the Supreme Court, to be appoint by the Central Government (in consultation with the Chief Justice of India) who be its President;

(b) Four other members who shall be persons of ability, integrity and standing and have adequate knowledge or experience of, or have shown capacity in dealing with, problems relating to economics, law, commerce, accountancy, industry, public affairs or administration, one of whom shall be a woman

Appointments shall be by the Central Government on the recommendation of a Selection Committee consisting of a Judge of the Supreme Court to be nominated by the Chief Justice of India, the Secretary in the Department of Legal Affairs and the Secretary in charge of Consumer Affairs in the Government of India. Every member of the National Commission shall hold office for a term of five years or upto seventy years of age, whichever is earlier and shall not be eligible for reappointment.

The National Commission shall have jurisdiction:-

a. to entertain complaints where the value of the goods or services and the compensation, if any, claimed exceeds rupees one crores:

b. to entertain appeals against the orders of any State Commission; and

c. to call for the records and pass appropriate orders in any consumer dispute which is pending before, or has been decided by any State Commission where it appears to the National Commission that such Commission has exercised a jurisdiction not vested in it by law, or has failed to exercise a jurisdiction so vested, or has acted in the exercise of its jurisdiction illegally or with material irregularity.

Complaints may be filed with the District Forum by:-

1. The consumer to whom such goods are sold or delivered or agreed to be sold or delivered or such service provided or agreed to be provided
2. Any recognized consumer association, whether the consumer to whom goods sold or delivered or agreed to be sold or delivered or service provided or agreed to be provided, is a member of such association or not
3. One or more consumers, where there are numerous consumers having the same interest with the permission of the District Forum, on behalf of or for the benefit of, all consumers so interested
4. The Central or the State Government.

On receipt of a complaint, a copy of the complaint is to be referred to the opposite party, directing him to give his version of the case within 30 days. This period may be extended by another 15 days. If the opposite party admits the allegations contained in the complaint, the complaint will be decided on the basis of materials on the record. Where the opposite party denies or disputes the allegations or omits or fails to take any action to represent his case within the time provided, the dispute will be settled in the following manner:

In case of dispute relating to any goods: Where the complaint alleges a defect in the goods which cannot be determined without proper analysis or test of the goods, a sample of the goods shall be obtained from the complainant, sealed and authenticated in the manner prescribed for referring to the appropriate laboratory for the purpose of any analysis or test whichever may be necessary, so as to find out whether such goods suffer from any other defect. The appropriate laboratory' would be required to report its finding to the referring authority, i.e. the District Forum or the State Commission within a period of forty-five days from the receipt of the reference or within such extended period as may be granted by these agencies.

Limitation Period for Filing of Complaint

The District Forum, the State Commission, or the National Commission shall not admit a complaint unless it is filed within two years from the date on which the cause of action has arisen. However, where the complainant satisfies the District Forum / State Commission, thathe had sufficient cause for not filing the complaint within two years, such complaint may be entertained by it after recording the reasons for condoning the delay.

Powers of the Redressal Agencies

The District Forum, State Commission and the National Commission are vested with the powers of a civil court under the Code of Civil Procedure while trying a suit in respect of the following matters:-

1. The summoning and enforcing attendance of any defendant or witness examining the witness on oath;
2. The discovery and production of any document or other material producible as evidence;
3. The reception of evidence on affidavits:
4. The requisitioning of the report of the concerned analysis or test from the appropriate laboratory or from any other relevant source;

5. Issuing of any commission for the examination of any witness; and
6. Any other matter which may be prescribed.

Under the Consumer Protection Rules, 1987, the District Forum, Commission and the National Commission have the power to require any person:-

(i) To produce before, and allow to be examined by an officer of any authorities, such books of accounts, documents or commodities as may be required and to keep such book, documents etc. under its custody for the purposes of the Act;

(ii) To furnish such information which may be required for the purposes to any officer so specified.

They have the power to:-

(i) To pass written orders authorizing any officer to exercise power of entry and search of any premises where these books, papers, commodities, or documents are kept if there is any ground to believe that these may be destroyed, altered, falsified or secreted. Such authorized officer may also seize books, papers, documents or commodities if they are required for the purposes of the Act, provided the seizure is communicated to the District Forum / State Commission / National commission within 72 hours. On examination of such documents or commodities, the agency concerned may order the retention thereof or may return it to the party concerned.

(ii) to issue remedial orders to the opposite party.

(iii) to dismiss frivolous and vexatious complaints and to order the complainant to make payment of costs, not exceeding Rs. 10,000 to the opposite party.

Remedies Granted under the Act

The District Forum / State Commission / National Commission may pass one or more of the following orders to grant relief to the aggrieved consumer:-

1. To remove the defects pointed out by the appropriate laboratory from goods in question;

2. To replace the goods with new goods of similar description, which shall be free from any defect;
3. To return to the complainant the price, or, as the case may be, the charges paid by the complainant;
4. To pay such amount as may be awarded by it as compensation to the consumer for any loss or injury suffered by the consumer due to negligence of the opposite party;
5. To remove the defects or deficiencies in the services in question;
6. To discontinue the unfair trade practice or the restrictive trade practice or not to repeat them;
7. Not to offer the hazardous goods for sale:
8. To withdraw the hazardous goods from being offered for sale:
9. To provide for adequate costs to parties.

Appeals

Any person aggrieved by an order made by the Forum may prefer an appeal to the State Commission in the prescribed form and manner. Similarly, any person aggrieved by any original order of the State Commission may prefer an appeal to the National Commission in the prescribed form and manner. Any person aggrieved by any original order of the National Commission may prefer an appeal to the Supreme Court.

All such appeals are to be made within thirty days from the date of the order provided that the concerned Appellate authority may entertain an appeal after the said period of thirty days if it is satisfied that there was sufficient cause for not filling it within that period. The period of 30 days is to be computed from the date of receipt of the order by the appellant.

Where no appeal has been preferred against any of the orders of the authorities, such orders would be final. The District Forum, State Commission or National Commission may enforce respective orders as if it was a decree or order made by a Court and in the event of their inability to execute the same; they may send the order to the Court for execution by it as if it were a Court decree or order.

Penalties

Failure or omission by a trader or other person against whom a complaint is made or the complainant to comply with any order of the State Commission or the National Commission shall be punishable with imprisonment for a term which shall not be less than one month but which may extend to 3 years, or with fine of not less than Rs. 2,000 but which may to Rs. 10000 or with both.

However, if it is satisfied that the circumstances of any case so requires, then the District Forum or the State Commission or the National Commission may impose a lower fine or a shorter term of imprisonment.

SUMMARY

During the mushrooming of insurance companies many financially unsound concerns were also floated which failed miserably. The Insurance Act 1938 was the first legislation governing not only life insurance but also non-life insurance to provide strict state control over insurance business. The demand for nationalization of life insurance industry was made repeatedly in the past but it gathered momentum in 1944 when a bill to amend the Life Insurance Act 1938 was introduced in the Legislative Assembly.

However, it was much later on the 19th of January, 1956, that life insurance in India was nationalized. About 154 Indian insurance companies, 16 non-Indian companies and 75 provident were operating in India at the time of nationalization. Nationalization was accomplished in two stages; initially the management of the companies was taken over by means of an Ordinance, and later, the ownership too by means of a comprehensive bill.

The Parliament of India passed the Life Insurance Corporation Act on the 19th of June 1956, and the Life Insurance Corporation of India was created on 1st September, 1956, with the objective of spreading life insurance much more widely and in particular to the rural areas with a view to reach all insurable persons in the country, providing them adequate financial cover at a reasonable cost.

The IRDA Bill provides for the establishment of an authority to protect the interests of the holders of insurance policies, to regulate, promote and insure orderly growth of the insurance industry and amend the Insurance Act, 1938, the Life Insurance Act, 1956 and the General Insurance Business (Nationalization) Act, 1972. The bill allows foreign equity stake in domestic private insurance companies to a maximum of 26 per cent of the total paid-up capital and seeks to provide statutory status to the insurance regulator. The insurance business in India is pegged at $ 6.6 Billion whereas industry leaders feel privatization will increase it to $ 40 Billion within next 3-5 years.

5

RISK MANAGEMENT AND GENERAL INSURANCE

A non-life insurance contract is different from a life insurance contract. A life insurance contract is a long term contract, while general insurance contract is a one-year renewable contract. The risk namely 'death' is certain in life insurance. The only uncertainty is as to when it will take place, whereas in general insurance, the insured event may or may not take place. It is difficult to determine the economic value of life, whereas the financial value of any asset to be insured under a general insurance policy can be determined. Because of these peculiar features, a non life insurance contract is different from a life insurance contract. In this lesson we will learn in detail the treatment of each type of non-life insurance.

Section 2(6B) of the Insurance Act 1938, defines general insurance business. According to this general insurance business means fire, marine, or miscellaneous insurance whether carried separately or in combination. General Insurance Corporation of India (GIC) was set up with exclusive privilege for transacting General Insurance business. After the passage of IRDA Act 1999, GIC has been delinked from its subsidiaries and has been assigned the role of Indian reinsurer.

MEANING AND IMPORTANCE OF NON-LIFE INSURANCE

Non-life insurance refers to the property and liability insurance. Fire insurance covers stationary property. Marine insurance covers mobile property. Bonding is a special coverage that guarantees the performance of the contract by one party to another. Casualty coverage includes accident and health insurance besides the above mentioned categories. Miscellaneous Insurance business means all other general insurance contracts including therein motor insurance.

The role of insurance is two fold. Insurance achieves both risk transfer and risk reduction. The insurer collects the premium from a group of business firms who wants to protect their property against the damage caused by fire. Insurer will then indemnify the firm that suffers a loss to property due to fire out of the premium so collected.

So the collective contributions of this entire group of the insured have been utilized to pay for the losses of the unfortunate few who sustain losses.

Insurance also acts as a risk reduction mechanism in various senses. Firstly, the individual risks have been shifted to the insurance company by way of pooling. Secondly, firm's risk exposure is well spread out because insurer has an access to the reinsurance market making possible a further spread of risk. If an aircraft is destroyed, the airline company will have a big hole in its financials. If the aircraft is insured, the loss would be spread out among a large number of insurance companies throughout the world.

Every business enterprise is exposed to a large number of risks and uncertainties to its premises, plant and machinery, raw materials, finished stock and other things. Goods may be damaged or lost in the process of transportation and may be destroyed due to fire or flood while in storage. As a matter of fact, business means risk and uncertainties.

Some of the risks can be avoided by timely precautions but some are unavoidable and are beyond the control of a businessman. For those types of risks, Insurance is the best protection. By providing protection against at least some of these risks, the insurance industry helps him better manage his risks and contributes to capital formation in the economy. After transferring risks and uncertainties of the business to the insurance company, the entrepreneur can focus on his core activity-of running the business.

Also, the insurance companies bring their experience and expertise to the field of risk management. Thus, they are able to add value to the customer's business processes.

Objectives

After going through this lesson you should be able to:

- Define the contract of fire insurance.
- Explain the characteristics of fire insurance contract.
- Understand the meaning of the term 'fire'.
- Describe the special policies under fire insurance.
- Write about fire claims and the procedures followed to settle a fire claim.
- Define the contract of marine insurance.
- Explain different types of perils that can affect a marine adventure.
- How to assign a marine policy.
- What are various clauses of a marine policy.
- Explain the difference between express and implied warranties.
- Describe different types of marine policy.
- Know the claim procedure to be followed for marine insurance.
- Define the contract of health insurance.
- Describe the various health insurance policies.
- The future of health insurance in India.
- Define the contract of Motor insurance.
- Explain the basic principles of motor insurance.
- Describe the motor insurance policies.
- Mention the classification of motor vehicles.

- Understand the operation of motor accident claims tribunal.
- Explain various types of insurances under miscellaneous insurances like personal accident insurance, Fidelity Insurance, Travel Insurance, Workmen's Compensation Insurance, Wedding Insurance, Employee State Insurance Scheme, Unemployment Insurance, Personal Liability Insurance, Credit Insurance, Burglary Insurance etc.

Fire Insurance

Fire is hazardous to human life as well as property. Loss of life by fire is covered under Life insurance and loss of property by fire is covered under fire insurance. Fire causes enormous damage by physically reducing the materials to ashes.

A fire insurance policy provides protection strictly against fire. There could be enormous reasons for fire. In practice certain other related perils are also covered by the fire insurance policy. The General Insurance Act (Tariff) recommends the form of the contract in which a fire insurance is to be written. The policy form contains a preamble and operative clause, general exclusions and general conditions.

Fire Insurance comes under tariff class of business. All India Fire Tariff is the revised fire insurance tariff, which came into force on May 1, 2001. Now a single policy was introduced to cover all property risks called standard fire and special peril policy in the place of three standard policies i.e. A, B&C.

Definition

A contract of fire insurance can be defined as a contract under which one party (the insurer) agrees for consideration (premium) to indemnify the other party (The insured) for the financial loss which the latter may suffer due to damage to the property insured by fire during a specified period of time and up to an agreed amount.

The document containing the terms and conditions of the contract is known as 'Fire Insurance Policy'. A fire policy contains the name of the parties, description of the insured property, the sum for which the property is insured, amount of premium payable and the period insured against. The premium may be paid either in single instalment or by way of instalments. The insurer is liable to make good the loss only when loss is caused by actual fire. The phrase 'loss or damage by fire' also includes the loss or damage caused by efforts to extinguish fire.

Scope of Cover

Standard Fire and special perils policy usually cover loss due to the following perils:

1. Fire: Destruction or damage to the property insured by its own fermentation, natural heating or spontaneous combustion or drying process can not be treated as damage due to fire.
2. Lightning: It may result in fire damage or other type of damage, such as cracks in a building due to a lightning strike.
3. Explosion: An explosion is caused inside a vessel when the pressure within the vessel exceeds the atmospheric pressure acting externally on its surface. This policy, however, does not cover destruction or damage caused to the boilers or other vessels where heat is generated.
4. Storm, cyclone, typhoon, hurricane, tornado, landslide: These are all various types of violent natural disturbances accompanied by thunder or strong winds or heavy rain fall. Loss or damage directly caused by these disturbances are covered excluding those resulting from earthquake, volcanic eruption etc.
5. Bush fire: This covers damage caused by burning of bush and jungles but excluding destruction or damage caused by forest fire.
6. Riot, strike, malicious, and terrorism damages: Any loss or physical damage to the property insured directly caused by such activity or by the action of any lawful authorities in suppressing such disturbance is covered.
7. Aircraft damage: Loss, destruction or damage caused by Aircraft, other aerial or space devices and articles

dropped there from excluding those caused by pressure waves.

8. Overflowing of water tanks and pipes etc.: Loss or damage to property by water or otherwise on account of bursting or accidental overflowing of water tanks, apparatus and pipes is covered.

General Exclusions

Policy does not Cover

1. The first 5% of each and every claim subject to a minimum of Rs. 10,000 in respect of loss arising out of "Act of god perils" such as Lightning, Landslide etc.
2. Loss, destruction or damage caused by war, invasion, act of foreign enemy, mutiny, war like operations, civil war, military rising etc.
3. Loss, destruction or damage caused to the insured property by pollution or contamination.
4. Loss, destruction or damage to the stocks in cold storage premises caused by change of temperature.
5. Loss of earnings, loss by delay, loss of market or other indirect loss or damage of any kind whatsoever.
6. Any loss or damage caused by or through or in consequence directly or indirectly due to earthquake, volcanic eruption etc.
7. Loss by theft during or after the occurrence of any insured peril except as provided under Riot, Strike and Terrorism Damage cover.
8. Loss, destruction or damage to any electrical machine, apparatus, fixture, or fitting arising from or occasioned by over-running, excessive pressure, short circuiting etc.
9. Expenses necessarily incurred on (i) Architect's, surveyor's and consulting engineer's fees and (ii) Debris removed by the insured following the loss to the property insured by an peril insured in excess of 3% and 1% of the claim amount respectively.

Add-on Covers

The insurer can issue the standard fire policy with added benefits at the option of the policyholders by charging additional premium.

These added benefits are as follows:

1. Architects, Surveyors and Consulting engineer's fees (in excess of 3% claim amount)
2. Debris removal (in excess of 1% of claim amount)
3. Deterioration of stocks in cold storage due to power failure
4. Forest fire
5. Spontaneous combustion
6. Earthquake as per minimum rates and excess applicable as specified in the tariff.
7. Omission to insure additions, alterations or extensions.

On the basis of judicial decisions, the following losses are also covered by fire insurance.

(a) Goods spoiled or property damaged by water used to extinguish the fire.

(b) Pulling down of adjacent buildings by the fire brigade in order to prevent the spread of fire.

(c) Breakage of goods in the process of removal from the building where fire is raging.

(d) Wages paid to persons employed for extinguishing fire.

The following types of losses, however, are not covered by a fire policy:

(i) Loss by theft during and after the occurrence of fire.

(ii) Loss caused by burning of property by order of any public authority.

(iii) Loss caused by underground fire.

(iv) Loss or damage to property occasioned by its own fermentation or spontaneous combustion.

(v) Loss happening by fire which is caused by earthquake, invasion, act of foreign enemy, warlike operations, civil wars, riot etc.

In all the above cases the insurer is not liable, unless specifically provided for in the fire insurance policy. The insurer can issue the standard fire policy as per the New Fire Tariff along with added benefits at the option of the policyholders by charging additional premium.

Meaning of Fire

Fire is not described in the policy. It should therefore, be taken in the general sense as an ignition of some kind. Damage by lightening or explosion is not covered unless these cause actual ignition which spread into fire. A claim for loss by fire must satisfy the following conditions;

(A) The loss must be caused by actual fire or ignition and not just by high temperature. There should be rapid combustion that produces ignition and may result in flames. Hence, chemical action producing heat but not actual fire and damage caused by an acid is not considered as fire damage.

(B) The proximate cause of loss should be fire.

(C) The loss or damage must relate to subject matter of the policy.

(D) The fire must be accidental, not incidental. If the fire is caused through a deliberate act of the insured or his agents, the insurer will not be liable for the loss. Fire due to the negligence of the insured or his servant is however, covered by the policy. If a third party willfully sets fire to the insured's property, the loss is by fire and the insurer is liable.

(E) The ignition must be either of the goods or of the premises where goods are kept.

The essential features of a contract of fire insurance are as under:

(1) It is a contract under Indian Contract Act, 1872. Like other insurance contracts, fire insurance contracts are

also governed by general provisions of Indian Contract Act, 1872. It implies that fire insurance also has to satisfy the essentials of a valid contract.

(2) It is a contract of indemnity. The principal of indemnity implies that the insurer restores the insured to his position before incurring the loss caused by the fire. The insured can not claim anything more than the amount of actual loss. He can be indemnified only to the extent of damage incurred, not the entire value of the property insured.

(3) It is a contract of utmost faith. It is a contract of 'uberrimae fidei', i.e. utmost good faith. Both the insured and the insurer must disclose everything which is in their knowledge and can affect the contract of insurance.

(4) Existence of insurable interest. Insurable interest arises out of a pecuniary relationship between the insured and the subject matter of the insurance. The destruction or damage to the latter involves the insured in financial loss. Insurable interest should exist at the time of taking a fire insurance policy and continue throughout the policy term. Claim can be made for the loss due to fire only when the insurable interest exists. The insurable interest in goods may arise out of ownership, possession or contract.

The following persons have insurable interest in the subject matter of insurance in case of fire policy:

(1) A person has insurable interest in the property he owns.

(2) Partner has insurable interest in the property of partnership.

(3) A businessman has insurable interest in his stock, plant, machinery and building.

(4) Agent has insurable interest in the property of his principle.

(5) Mortgagee has insurable interest in the property which is mortgaged.

(6) It is a yearly contract.

Generally, a contract of fire insurance is a contract from year to year only and the insurance automatically comes to an end after the expiry of the year. However, the contract can be renewed before the expiry of the contract.

Types of Fire Policies

The important fire insurance policies are discussed below:

1. *Valued Policy*. They are the exception in fire insurance. Under valued policy, the value declared in the policy is the amount the insurer will have to pay to the insured in the event of a total loss irrespective of the actual value of loss. The policy violates the principle of indemnity. The insurer has to pay a specified amount quite independent of the market or actual value of the property at the time of loss. So such a policy is very rarely issued. It may be issued only on artistic work, antiques and similar rare articles whose value cannot be determined easily.

2. *Specific Policy*. Under this policy, the insurer undertakes to make good the loss to the insured upto the amount specified in the policy. Supposing, a building worth Rs.2,00,000 is insured against fire for Rs. 1,00,000. If the damage to the property is Rs.75,000 the insurer will get the full compensation. Even if the loss is Rs.1,00,000 the insurer will get the full amount. But if the loss is more than Rs. 1, 00,000 the insured will get Rs. 1,00,000 only. Hence, the value of property is not relevant in determining the amount of indemnity in case of a specific policy.

3. *Average Policy*. Under a fire insurance policy containing the 'average clause' the insured is liable for such proportion of the loss as the value of the uncovered property bears to the whole property. e.g. if a person gets his house insured for Rs. 4,00,000 though its actual value is Rs. 6,00,000, if a part of the house is damaged in fire and the insured suffers a loss of Rs. 3,00,000, the amount of compensation to be paid by the insurer comes out to Rs. 2,00,000 calculated as follows:

Amount of claim= Insured amount * Actual loss

Actual value of property

4,00,000 * 3,00,000 =2,00,000

6, 00,000

4. *Floating policy*. A floating policy is used for covering fluctuating stocks of goods held in different lots for one premium. With every transaction of sale or purchase, the quantities of goods kept at different places fluctuate. It is difficult for the owner to take a policy for a specific amount. The best way is to take out a floating policy for all the stocks of goods.
5. *Reinstatement Policy*. In such a policy, the insurer has the right to reinstate or replenish the property destroyed instead of paying compensation to the insured in cash. It may be granted on building, machinery, furniture, fixture and fittings only.
6. *Consequential loss Policy*. Sometimes the insured has to suffer a greater financial loss on account of dislocation of business caused by fire e.g. close down business after fire for repair, to meet fixed expenses such as rent, salaries, taxes and other expenses as usual. Such considerable loss to the insured is not covered by the ordinary fire policy. In order to cover such loss by fire, the 'Consequential Loss Policy' has been introduced. The loss so suffered is separately calculated from the loss actually suffered.
7. *Comprehensive policy*. This policy covers the risks of the fire arising out of any cause that is civil commotion, lightening, riots, thefts, labor disturbances and strikes etc. It is also known as 'all insurance policy'.
8. *A Blanket policy*. This policy is issued to cover all the fixed and current assets of an enterprise by one insurance.
9. *Declaration policy*. In this policy, trader takes out a policy for the maximum value of stock which may be expected to hold during the year. At a fixed date each

month, the insured has to make a declaration regarding the actual value of stock at risk on that date. On the basis of such declaration, the average amount of stock at risk in the year is calculated and this amount becomes the sum assured.

10. *Sprinklers leakage policy.* It covers the loss arising out of water leakage from sprinklers which are setup to extinguish fire.

Claim Procedure for Fire Insurance

In the event of fire the insured must immediately give the insurer a notice about the loss caused by fire. A written claim should be delivered with in 15 days from the date of loss. The insured is required to furnish all plans, invoices, documents, proofs and other relevant informations required by the insurer.

If the insured failed to submit these documents with in 6 months from the date of loss, the insurer has the right to consider it as no claim. On receipt of the claim the insurer verifies whether the essentials of a valid claim are satisfied or not. e.g. The cause of fire should be an insured peril. The insured completes the form, signs the declaration given in the form as to the truthfulness and accuracy of the information and returns the same. An official employed by the insurer investigates small and simple claims. For large claims, the insurance company employs independent loss surveyor. On the basis of the claim form and the investigation report, the company then settles the claim.

MARINE INSURANCE

Insurance on the risks of transportation of goods is one of the oldest and most vital forms of insurance. The value of goods shipped by business firms each year cost millions of rupees. These goods are exposed to damage or loss from numerous transportation perils. The goods can be protected by marine insurance contracts. It is an important element of general insurance. It essentially provides cover from loss suffered due to marine perils. In India the marine insurance is regulated by the Indian Maritime Insurance Act 1963, which is based on the original English Act. Marine insurance as we know it today can be described as mother of all insurances. It is believed to have originated in England owing to the frequent movement of ships over high seas for trade. In India, insurance has been in vogue for several centuries. History holds proof that these people had a system of pooling their contributions, if any one of their clan were to meet a tragedy in their voyages.

Today marine insurance has assumed a vast canvas due to the expanding trade across the globe, which involves large shipping companies that require protection for their fleet against the perils of the sea.

Marine insurance is a contract under which, the insurer undertakes to indemnify the insured in the manner and to the extent thereby agreed, against marine losses, incidental to marine adventures. It may be defined as a form of insurance covering loss or damage to vessels or to cargo during transportation to the high seas.

It follows from the above discussion the marine insurance is a contract between the insured and the insurer. The insured may be a cargo owner or a ship owner or a freight receiver. The insurer is known as the underwriter. The document in which the contract is incorporated is called "Marine policy". The insured pays a particular sum, which is called premium, in exchange for an undertaking from the insurer to indemnify the insured against loss or damage caused by certain specified perils.

The salient features of a contract of marine insurance are as follows:

1. It is based on utmost good faith. Both the insured and the insurer must disclose everything which is in their knowledge and can affect the contract of insurance.
2. It is a contract of indemnity. The insured is entitled to recover only the actual amount of loss from the insurer.
3. Insurable interest in the subject-matter insured must exist at the time of the loss. It need not exist when the insurance policy is taken. Under marine insurance, the following persons are deemed to have insurable interest:

(a) The owner of the ship.

(b) The owner of the cargo.

(c) A creditor who has advanced money on the security of the ship or cargo.

(d) The mortgagor and mortgagee.

(e) The master and crew of the ship have insurable interest in respect of their wages.

(f) In case of advance freight, the person advancing the freight has an insurable interest if such freight is not repayable in case of loss.

4. It is subject to the doctrine of causa proxima. Where a loss is brought by several causes in succession to one another, the proximate or nearest cause of loss must be taken into account. If the proximate cause is covered by the policy, only then the insurance company will be liable to compensate the insured.

5. It must contain all the essential requirements of a valid contract, e.g. lawful consideration, free consent, capacity of the parties, etc.

Meaning of Marine Perils

Maritime perils can be defined as the fortuitous (an element of chance or ill luck) accidents or casualties of the sea caused without the willful intervention of human agency. The perils are incidental to the sea journey that arises in consequence of the sea journey. There are different forms of perils, of which only a few are covered by insurance while others are not. Accordingly we have insured and uninsured perils.

Insured perils are storm, collision of one ship with another ship, against rocks, burning and sinking of the ship, spoilage of cargo from sea water, mutiny, piracy or willful destruction of the ship and cargo by the master (captain) of the ship or the crew, jettison etc. Uninsured perils are regular wear and tear of the vessel, leakage (unless it is caused by an accident), breakage of goods due to bad movement of the ship, damage by rats and loss by delay. All losses and damages caused due to reasons not considered as perils of the sea are not provided insurance cover..

Subject Matter of Marine Insurance

The insured may be the owner of the ship, owner of the cargo or the person interested in freight. In case the ship carrying the cargo sinks, the ship will be lost along with the cargo.

The income that the cargo would have generated would also be lost. Based on this we can classify the marine insurance into three categories:

(a) Hull Insurance: Hull refers to the ocean going vessels (ships trawlers etc.) as well as its machinery. The hull insurance also covers the construction risk when the vessel is under construction. A vessel is exposed to many dangers or risks at sea during the voyage. An insurance effected to indemnify the insured for such losses is known as Hull insurance.

(b) Cargo Insurance: Cargo refers to the goods and commodities carried in the ship from one place to another. The cargo transported by sea is also subject to manifold risks at the port and during the voyage. Cargo insurance covers the shipper of the goods if the goods are damaged or lost. The cargo policy covers the risks associated with the transshipment of goods. The policy can be written to cover a single shipment. If regular shipments are made, an open cargo policy can be used that insures the goods automatically when a shipment is made.

(c) Freight Insurance: Freight refers to the fee received for the carriage of goods in the ship. Usually the ship owner and the freight receiver are the same person. Freight can be received in two ways-in advance or after the goods reach the destination. In the former case, freight is secure. In the latter the marine laws say that the freight is payable only when the goods reach the destination port safely. Hence if the ship is destroyed on the way the ship owner will loose the freight along with the ship. That is why, the ship owners purchase freight insurance policy along with the hull policy.

(d) Liability Insurance: It is usually written as a separate contract that provides comprehensive liability insurance for property damage or bodily injury to third parties. It is also known as protection and indemnity insurance which protects the ship owner for damage caused by the ship to docks, cargo, illness or injury to the passengers or crew, and fines and penalties.

Types of Marine Policy

There are different types of marine policies known by different names according to the manner of their execution or the risk they cover. They are:

1. Voyage Policy: Under the policy, the subject matter is insured against risk in respect of a particular voyage from a port of departure to the port of destination, e.g. Mumbai to New York. The risk starts from the departure of ship from the port and it ends on its arrival at the port of destination. This policy covers the subject matter irrespective of the time factor. This policy is not suitable for hull insurance as a ship usually does not operate over a particular route only. The policy is used mostly in case of cargo insurance.
2. Time Policy: It is one under which the insurance is affected for a specified period of time, usually not exceeded twelve months. Time policies are generally used in connection with the insurance of ship. Thus if the voyage is not completed with in the specified period, the risk shall be covered until the voyage is completed or till the arrival of the ship at the port of call.
3. Mixed Policies: It is one under which insurance contract is entered into for a certain time period and for a certain voyage or voyages, e.g., Kolkata to New York, for a period of one year. Mixed Policies are generally issued to ships operating on particular routes. It is a mixture of voyage and time policies.

4. Valued Policies: It is one under which the value of subject matter insured is specified on the face of the policy itself. This kind of policy specifies the settled value of the subject matter that is being provided cover for. The value which is agreed upon is called the insured value. It forms the measure of indemnity in the event of loss. Insured value is not necessarily the actual value. It includes (a) invoice price of goods (b) freight, insurance and other charges (c) ten to fifteen percent margin to cover expected profits.

5. Unvalued policy: It is the policy under which the value of subject matter insured is not fixed at the time of effecting insurance but has to be ascertained wherever the subject matter is lost or damaged.

6. Open policy: An open policy is issued for a period of 12 months and all consignments cleared during the period are covered by the insurer. This form of insurance Policy is suitable for big companies that have regular shipments. It saves them the tedious and expensive process of acquiring an insurance policy for each shipment. The rates are fixed in advance, without taking the total value of the cargo being shipped into consideration. The assured has to declare the nature of each shipment, and the cover is provided to all the shipments. The assured also deposits a premium for the estimated value of the consignment during the policy period..

6. Floating Policy: A merchant who is a regular shipper of goods can take out a 'floating policy' to avoid botheration and waste of time involved in taking a new policy for every shipment. This policy stands for the contract of insurance in general terms. It does not include the name of the ship and other details. The other details are required to be furnished through subsequent declarations. Thus, the insured takes a policy for a huge amount and he informs the underwriter as and when he makes shipment of goods. The underwriter goes on recording the entries in the policy. When the sum assured

is exhausted, the policy is said to be "fully declared" or "run off".

7. Block Policy: This policy covers other risks also in addition to marine risks. When goods are to be transported by ship to the place of destination, a single policy known as block policy may be taken to cover all risks. E.g. when the goods are dispatched by rail or road transport for shipment, a single policy may cover all the risks from the point of origin to the point of destination.

Assignment of Marine Policy

A marine insurance policy may be transferred by assignment unless the terms of the policy expressly prohibit the same. The policy may be assigned either before or after loss. The assignment may be made either by endorsement on the policy itself or on a separate document. The insured need not give a notice or information to the insurer or underwriter about assignment. In case of death of the insured, a marine policy is automatically assigned to his heirs.

At the time of assignment, the assignor must possess an insurable interest in the subject matter insured. An insured who has parted with or lost interest in the subject matter insured can not make a valid assignment. After the occurrence of the loss, the policy can be assigned freely to any person. The assignor merely transfers his own right to claim to the assignee.

Clauses in a Marine Policy

A policy of marine insurance may contain several clauses. Some of the clauses are common to all marine policies while others are included to meet special requirements of the insured. Hull, cargo and freight policies have different standard clauses. There are standard clauses which are invariably used in marine insurance.

Firstly, policies are constructed in general, ordinary and popular sense, and, later on, specific clauses are added to them according to terms and conditions of the contract. Some of the important clauses in a marine policy are described below:

1. Valuation Clause. This clause states the value of the subject matter insured as agreed upon between both the parties.
2. Sue and Labour clause. This clause authorizes the insured to take all possible steps to avert or minimize the loss or to protect the subject matter insured in case of danger. The insurer is liable to pay the expenses, if any, incurred by the insured for this purpose.
3. Waiver Clause. This clause is an extension of the above clause. The clause states that any act of the insured or the insurer to protect, recover or preserve the subject matter of insurance shall not be taken to mean that the insured wants to forgo the compensation, nor will it mean that the insurer accepts the act as abandonment of the policy.
4. Touch and Stay Clause. This clause requires the ship to touch and stay at such ports and in such order as specified in the policy. Any departure from the route mentioned in the policy or the ordinary trade route followed will be considered as deviation unless such departure is essential to save the ship or the lives on board in an emergency.
5. Warehouse to warehouse clause. This clause is inserted to cover the risks to goods from the time they are dispatched from the consignor's warehouse until their delivery at the consignee's warehouse at the port of destination.
6. Inchmaree Clause. This clause covers the loss or damage caused to the ship or machinery by the negligence of the master of the ship as well as by explosives or latent defect in the machinery or the hull.
7. F.P.A. and F.A.A. Clause. The F.P.A. (Free of Particular Average) clause relieves the insurer from particular average liability. The F.A.A. (free of all average) clause relieves the insurer from liability arising from both particular average and general average.

8. Lost or Not Lost Clause. Under this clause, the insurer is liable even if the ship insured is found not to be lost prior to the contact of insurance, provided the insurer had no knowledge of such loss and does not commit any fraud. This clause covers the risks between the issue of the policy and the shipment of the goods.
9. Running down Clause. This clause covers the risk arising out of collision between two ships. The insurer is liable to pay compensation to the owner of the damaged ship. This clause is used in hull insurance.
10. Free of Capture and Seizure Clause. This clause relieves the insurer from the liability of making compensation for the capture and seizure of the vessel by enemy countries. The insured can insure such abnormal risks by taking an extra 'war risks' policy.
11. Continuation Clause. This clause authorizes the vessel to continue and complete her voyage even if the time of the policy has expired. This clause is used in a time policy. The insured has to give prior notice for this and deposit a monthly prorate premium.
12. Barratry Clause. This clause covers losses sustained by the ship owner or the cargo owner due to willful conduct of the master or crew of the ship.
13. Jettison Clause. Jettison means throwing overboard a part of the ship's cargo so as to reduce her weight or to save other goods. This clause covers the loss arising out of such throwing of goods. The owner of jettisoned goods is compensated by all interested parties.
14. At and From Clause. This clause covers the subject matter while it is lying at the port of departure and until it reaches the port of destination. It is used in voyage policies. If the policy consists of the word 'from' only instead of 'at and from', the risk is covered only from the time of departure of the ship.

Warranties

Besides the three important principles i.e. good faith, indemnity, and insurable interest, it is necessary that all the marine insurance contracts must fulfil the warranties also. Warrantee means a condition which is basic to the contract of insurance.

The breach of which entitles the insurer to avoid the policy altogether. If the warranty is not complied with by the insured, the contract comes to an end. There are two exceptions where the breach of warranty is excused and does not affect that insurer's liability:

(i) Where owning to change in the circumstance the warranty is inapplicable and

(ii) Where due to enactment of a subsequent law the warranty becomes unlawful.

Kinds of Warranties

Warranties are of two types:

(i) Express, and

(ii) Implied.

An express warranty is one which is expressed or clearly stated in the contract and it can be easily ascertained whether it has been fulfilled or not. For instance a marine policy usually contains the following express warranties:

(i) The ship will sail on a specified day.

(ii) The ship is safe on a particular day.

(iii) The ship will proceed to the port of destination without any deviation.

(iv) The ship is neutral and will remain so during the voyage.

The implied warranty, on the other hand, is not expressly mentioned in the contract but the law takes it for granted that such warranty exists. An express warranty does not exclude implied warranty unless it is inconsistent therewith. Implied warranties do not appear in the policy documents at all, but are understood without being put into words, and as such, are automatically applicable. These are included in the policy by law, general practice, long established custom or usage. The important implied warranties are discussed below:

(a) *Sea-Worthiness of the ship.*: A ship is sea worthy when it is in a fit condition as to repair, equipment, crew, etc. to encounter the ordinary perils of the voyage. This implies that the ship must be suitably constructed, properly equipped and manned, sufficiently fuelled and provisioned and capable of withstanding the ordinary strain and stress of the voyage. It must not be overloaded.

(b) *Legality of Voyage.*: The journey undertaken by the ship must be for legal purposes. Carrying prohibited or smuggled goods is illegal and therefore, the insurer shall not be liable for the loss.

(c) *Non-deviation of the ship route.*: It is assumed that the ship will maintain the same route as stated in the policy in ordinary course, but in case of peril it is permitted to deviate. If the ship does not follow the usual route, the insurer will not be liable even if the ship regains her route before any loss takes place. However, the insurer remains liable for any loss which might have occurred prior to the deviation.

Types of Marine Losses

A loss arising in a marine adventure due to perils of the sea is a marine loss. Marine loss may be classified into two categories:

(1) *Total loss*: A total loss implies that the subject matter insured is fully destroyed and is totally lost to its owner. It can be Actual total loss or Constructive total loss. In actual total loss subject matter is completely destroyed or so damaged that it ceases to be a thing of the kind insured. e.g. sinking of ship, complete destruction of cargo by fire, etc.

In case of constructive total loss the ship or cargo insured is not completely destroyed but is so badly damaged that the cost of repair or recovery would be greater than the value of the property saved. e.g. a ship dashed against the rock and is stranded in a badly damaged position. If the expenses of bringing it back and repairing it would be more than the actual value of the damaged ship, it is abandoned.

(2) *Partial loss*: A partial loss occurs when the subject matter is partially destroyed or damaged. Partial loss can be general average or particular average. General average refers to the sacrifice made during extreme circumstances for the safety of the ship and the cargo. This loss has to be borne by all the parties who have an interest in the marine adventure. e.g. A loss caused by throwing overboard of goods is a general average and must be shared by various parties.

Particular average may be defined as a loss arising from damage accidentally caused by the perils insured against. Such a loss is borne by the underwriter who insured the object damaged. e.g. If a ship is damaged due to bad weather the loss incurred is a particular average loss.

Marine Insurance in India

There is evidence that marine insurance was practiced in India since long time. In earlier days travellers by sea and land were exposed to risk of losing their vessels and merchandise because of piracy on the open seas. It was the British insurers who introduced general insurance in India, in its modern form. The first company known as the Sun Insurance Office Ltd. was set up in Calcutta in the year 1710.

This followed by several insurance companies of different parts of the world, in the field of marine insurance. In India marine insurance is transacted by the subsidiaries of the General Insurance Corporation of India-New India Assurance, National Insurance, Oriental Insurance and United India Insurance. Marine and hull insurance contribute 20% to the total premium of the general insurance industry in India.

HEALTH INSURANCE

A systematic plan for financing medical expenses is an important and integral part of a risk management plan. With rising health care costs, it was no longer possible for an individual to meet the heavy cost of treatment involving hospitalization. The reasons for rise in health care costs are:

(a) Increase in medical treatment costs.

(b) Technological advancements in medical equipment.

(c) High labour costs.

Definition

"Health insurance is an insurance, which covers the financial loss arising out of poor health condition or due to permanent disability, which results in loss of income."

A health insurance policy is a contract between an insurer and an individual or group, in which the insurer agrees to provide specified health insurance at an agreed upon price (premium). It usually provides either direct payment or reimbursement for expenses associated with illness and injuries. The cost and range of protection provided by health insurance depends on the insurance provider and the policy purchased..

Health Insurance Policies

The health insurance policies available in India are:

(a) Mediclaim policy (individuals and groups)

(b) Overseas mediclaim policy

(c) Raj Rajeshwari Mahila Kalyan Yojna

(d) Bhagyashree Child Welfare Policy

(e) Cancer Insurance Policy

(f) Jan Arogya Bima Policy

Mediclaim Policy (individuals and groups)

Mediclaim policy is offered to individuals and groups exceeding 50 members. It covers the hospitalization for diseases or sickness and for injuries. Under group mediclaim policy, group discount is allowed to groups exceeding 101 people. The medical expenses will be reimbursed only if the insured is admitted in the hospital for a minimum duration of 24 hours. Cost of treatment includes consultation fee of doctors, cost of medicines and hospitalization charges.

Health insurance in India is available at very economical rates. It is very popular among professionals like Chartered accountants, Advocates, Engineers etc. It is very suitable for self-employed persons because it covers risks against several general and serious diseases.

Overseas Mediclaim Policy

In 1984, the Overseas Mediclaim Policy was developed. This policy will reimburse the medical expenses incurred by Indians upto 70 years of age while traveling abroad. The premium will be charged based on their age, purpose of travel, duration and plan selected by the insured under the policy. This policy is provided is provided to businessmen, people going on holiday tour, traveling for educational professional and official purposes.

Raj Rajeshwari Mahila Kalyan Yojna

It is a personal accident policy offered by an insurance company for the welfare of women. It is offered to women residing in rural and urban areas. Women between 10-75 years of age are eligible for this policy irrespective of their occupation and income level.

Bhagyashree Child Welfare Policy

It is offered to girls between 0-18 years. The age of the parents of the girls shouldn't be more than 60 years. It provides coverage to one girl child in a family who loses her father or mother in an accident.

Cancer Insurance Policy

It is designed for cancer patients aid association members. The persons insured under this policy will pay premium to their association along with the membership fee. This policy will offer coverage to the insured in case he develops cancer. All the expenses incurred for treatment of cancer not exceeding the sum insured will be paid directly to the insured person.

Jan Arogya Bima Policy

This policy provides medical insurance to poorer section of the people. This policy covers illness like heart attack, jaundice, food poisoning, and accidents etc. that requires immediate hospitalization.

Future of Health Insurance

During the last 50 years, India has made considerable progress in improving its health status. Still it is in a developing stage. The increasing health care costs in the country are likely to contribute to the development of more health insurance products.

Health insurance is not at the present recognized as a separate segment in Indian insurance industry. Privatization of insurance industry is likely to encourage the development of this segment. Health insurance in India has indeed a long way to go.

MOTOR INSURANCE

There has been a sudden rise in the motor accidents in the last few years. Much of these are attributable to increase in the number of vehicles. Every vehicle before being driven on roads has to be compulsorily insured. The motor insurance policy represents a combined coverage of the vehicles including accessories, loss or damage to his property or life and the third party coverage. Persons driving vehicles may cause losses and injuries to other persons. Every individual who owns a motor vehicle is also exposed to certain other risks. These include damage to his vehicle due to accidents, theft, fire, collision and natural disasters and also injuries to himself.

In 1939, motor vehicle act came into force in India. Compulsory insurance was introduced by motor vehicle act to protect the pedestrians and other third parties. Claims for damages may arise due to possession of car, usage and maintenance of car. Motor insurance policy will pay the financial liability arising out of these risks to the insured person.

Motor insurance policy is a contract between the insured and the insurer in which the insurer promises to indemnify the financial liability in event of loss to the insured. Motor Vehicles Act in 1939 was passed to mainly safeguard the interests of pedestrians. According to the Act, a vehicle cannot be used in a public place without insuring the third part liability. According to Section 24 of Motor Vehicles Act, "No person shall use or allow any other person to use a motor vehicle in a public place, unless the vehicle is covered by a policy of insurance."

Classification of Motor

Vehicles As per the Motor Vehicles Act for the purpose of insurance the vehicles are classified into three broad categories such as.

Private Cars

(a) Private Cars-vehicles used only for social, domestic and pleasure purposes

(b) Private vehicles-Two wheeled

1. Motorcycle / Scooters
2. Auto cycles
3. Mechanically assisted pedal cycles Commercial vehicles

    (1) Goods carrying vehicles

    (2) Passengers carrying vehicles

    (3) Miscellaneous & Special types of vehicles

The risks under motor insurance are of two types:

(1) Legal liability due to bodily injury, death or damage caused to the property of others.

(2) Loss or damage to one's own vehicle\ injury to or death of self and other occupants of the vehicle.

Basic Principles of Motor Insurance

Motor insurance being a contract like any other contract has to fulfill the requirements of a valid contract as laid down in the Indian Contract Act 1872. In addition it has certain special features common to other insurance contracts. They are:

- Utmost good faith
- Insurable interest

- Indemnity
- Subrogation and contribution
- Proximate cause

Utmost good Faith

The principle of Utmost good faith casts an obligation on the insured to disclose all the material tracts. These material facts must be disclosed to the insurer at the time of entering into the contract. All the information given in the proposal form should be true and complete.e.g. the driving history, physical health of the driver, type of vehicle etc. If any of the mentioned material facts declared by the insured in the proposal form are found inappropriate by the insurer at the time of claim it may result in the claim being repudiated.

Insurable Interest

In a valid insurance contract it is necessary on the part of the insured to have an insurable interest in the subject matter of insurance. The presence of insurable interest in the subject matter of insurance gives the person the right to insure. The interest should be pecuniary and must be present at inception and throughout the term of the policy. Thus the insured must be either benefited by the safety of the property or must suffer a loss on account of damage to it.

Indemnity

Insurance contracts are contracts of indemnity. Indemnity means making good of the loss by reimbursing the exact monetary loss. It aims at keeping the insured in the same position he was before the loss occurred and thus prevent him from making profit from insurance policy.

Subrogation and Contribution

Subrogation refers to transfer of insured's right of action against a third party who caused the loss to the insurer. Thus, the insurer who pays the loss can take up the assured's place and sue the party that caused the loss in order to minimise his loss for which he has already indemnified the assured. Subrogation comes in the picture only in case of damage or loss due to a third party. The insurer derives this right only after the payment of damages to the insured. Contribution ensures that the indemnity provided is proportionately borne by other insurers in case of double insurance.

Types of Motor Insurance Policies

The All India Motor Tariff governs motor insurance business in India. According to the Tariff all classes of vehicles can use two types of policy forms. They are form A and form B. Form A which is known as Act Policy is a compulsory requirement of the motor vehicle act. Use without such insurance is a penal offence. Form B which is also known as Comprehensive Policy is an optional cover.

1. *Liability only policy* – This covers third party liability and or death and property damage. Compulsory personal accident covers for the owner in respect of owner driven vehicles is also included.
2. *Package policy* – This covers loss or damage to the vehicle insured in addition to 1 above.
3. *Comprehensive policy*-Apart from the above-mentioned coverage, it is permissible to cover private cars against the risk of fine and / or theft and third party/ theft risks.

Every owner of motor vehicle has to take out a policy covering third party risks but insurance against other two risks is optional. When insurance policy covers third party risks, third party who has suffered any damages, can sue the Insurance company even though he was not a party to the contract of insurance. Insurance policies for the vehicles subject to the purchase agreements, lease agreements and hypothecation are to be issued in the joint names of the hirer and owner, lease and lessor, owner and pledge respectively. In case of policy renewal a notice of one month in advance before the date of expiry is issued by the insurers. The notice gives the details of premium payable for renewal.

Transfer of Ownership

In case of any sale of vehicle involving transfer of policy, the insured should apply to the insurer for consent to such transfer. The transfer is allowed, if within 15 days of receipt of application, the insurer does not reject the plea. The transferee shall apply within fourteen days from the date of transfer in writing to the insurer who has insured the vehicle, with the details of the registration of the vehicle, the date of transfer of the vehicle, the previous owner of the vehicle and the number and date of the insurance policy so that the insurer may make the necessary changes in his record and issue fresh

Certificate of Insurance

Insurer's Duty to Third Party

It is obligatory on the part of the insurer to pay the third party since, the insurer has no rights to avoid or reject the payment of liability to a third party. The duties of the insurer towards a third party are provided in section 96(1). The court determines the third party liability and accordingly compensation is paid. The liability is unlimited.

Cancellation of Insurance

The insurer may cancel a policy by sending to the insured seven days notice of cancellation by recorded delivery to the insured's last known address and the insurer will refund to the insured the pro-rata premium for the balance period of the policy. A policy may be cancelled at the option of the insured with seven days notice of cancellation and the insurer will be entitled to retain premium on short period scale of rates for the period for which the cover has been in existence prior to the cancellation of the policy. The balance premium, if any, will be refundable to the insured.

Double Insurance

When two policies are in existence on the same vehicle with identical cover, one of the policies many be cancelled. Where one of the policies commences at a date later than the other policy, the policy commencing later is to be cancelled by the insurer concerned.

If a vehicle is insured at any time with two different offices of the same insurer, 100% refund of premium of one policy may be allowed by canceling the later of the two policies. However, if the two policies are issued by two different insurers, the policy commencing later is to be cancelled by the insurer concerned and pro-rata refund of premium thereon is to be allowed.

Calculation of Premiums

In the case of Comprehensive Insurance Cover, for the purpose of premium, vehicles are categorized as follows:

Private Car

This is used for personal purposes. Private cars are lesser exposed than taxis, as the latter is used extensively for maximum revenue. The premium is computed on the following basis

1. Geographical area of use: Large cities have higher average claim costs followed by suburban areas, smaller cities, and small towns or rural areas. In India, the geographical areas have been classified into Group A and Group B.
2. Cubic capacity: The more the cubic capacity, the higher the premium rate.
3. Value of the vehicle.: The premium rate is applied on the value of the vehicle. Owner has to declare the correct value of the vehicle to the insurer. This value is known as the Insured's Estimated Value (IEV) in motor insurance and represents the sum insured. Two-wheeler

It is used for personal purpose only. Premium is calculated on cubic capacity and value of vehicle. Theft of accessories is not covered, unless the vehicle is stolen at the same time.

Commercial Vehicle

This is the vehicle used for hire. For goods carrying commercial vehicle, premium is calculated on the basis of carrying capacity i.e. gross vehicle weight and value of the vehicle. For passenger carrying commercial vehicles, premium is calculated on the basis of again carrying capacity i.e. number of passengers and value of the vehicle.

Accessories extra, as specified. Heavier vehicles are more exposed to accidents since the resultant damages they incur are more. Similarly, vehicles with higher carrying capacity expose more passengers to risk. Therefore heavier vehicles attract higher premium rate.

Claim Settlement

Claim Arise When

1) The insured's vehicle is damaged or any loss incurred.
2) Any legal liability is incurred for death of or bodily injury
3) Or damage to the third party's property.

The claim settlement in India is done by opting for any of the following by the insurance company

- o Replacement or reinstatement of vehicle
- o Payment of repair charges

In case, the motor vehicle is damaged due to accident it can be repaired and brought back to working condition. If the repair is beyond repair then the insured can claim for total loss or for a new vehicle. It is based on the market value of the vehicle at the time of loss.

Motor insurance claims are settled in three stages. In the first stage the insured will inform the insurer about loss. The loss is registered in claim register. In the second stage, the automobile surveyor will assess the causes of loss and extent of loss.

He will submit the claim report showing the cost of repairs and replacement charges etc. In the third stage, the claim is examined based on the report submitted by the surveyor and his recommendations. The insurance company may then authorize the repairs. After the vehicle is repaired, insurance company pays the charges directly to the repairer or to the insured if he had paid the repair charges.

Section 110 of Motor Vehicle Act, 1939 empowers the State Government in establishing motor claim tribunals. These tribunals will help in settling the third party claims for the minimum amount.

CLAIMS AND COMPLIANCES

Insurer's obligations

The insurer's obligation to pay a claim is perhaps the most common issue in insurance disputes. The insurer's obligation to pay a claim depends on certain factors, like the circumstances surrounding the loss and the precise coverage of the insurance policy. Normally a court chooses the most acceptable interpretation of the obligation if a disagreement arises over the words of the policy document. In fact to protect the insured, an incontestability clause is included in many insurance contracts. This clause denies the insurer the right to contest the validity of the contract after a specified period of time.

Insured's compliance

If the insured party had hidden or distorted a material fact in the policy application the insurance company is within its rights to deny or cancel coverage. On the other hand if an application appears to have the potential for high risk of loss for the insurance company, it may reject the application or alternately offer a very high premium.

If an insured defaults in paying his premiums, the insurer may cancel the policy. Also if the insured intentionally caused the loss or damage the insurer can refuse to pay any claim for the same. It may so happen that the insurer may knows that it can withdraw a policy or deny a claim, but conveys to the insured that it has willingly given up this right. In such circumstances the insured could maintain that the insurer had waived its right to contest a claim.

Subrogation

The coverage of a liability policy may induce an insurer to defend the insured in a lawsuit filed against him by a third party. Also the insurer can sue the third party in place of the insured if the said third party causes a loss covered by the policy held by the insured. This right is called subrogation and it is aimed at the party that is responsible for the loss, to bear the burden of the loss. This process also prevents an insured from recovering his losses twice, once each from the insurer and the responsible party. However an insurer can subrogate claims only on certain specific policies. For instance, property and liability insurance policies allow subrogation because the basis for the payment of claims is indemnification or reimbursement of the insured for losses suffered. But life insurance policies do not allow subrogation. In life insurance an insured is not indemnified for losses that could be measured in dollars because it is a policy for the insured and his nominee. A life insurance policy does not cover any liability to a third party. It pays a fixed sum of money to the beneficiary and consequently the insured does not stand any chance of making two recoveries, from the insurer and the third party. As far as the insurer is concerned the question of suing a third party does not arise in the event of a claim.

Insurance Claim Management

Most insurance companies are identified by their efficiency in handling claims as it is one of the most important parts of the business if not the most important. It has been observed that the credit rating of many insurance companies took a beating due to poor claims handling. Many insurance companies in their stubbornness to dispute a claim had to take heavy losses after damaging litigation. But the best insurance companies take this aspect of their business seriously and have tried to improve their claims handling with more resources and technology.

AUTO INSURANCE

Auto Insurance or Automobile Insurance (also known as Vehicle Insurance, Motor Insurance, or Car Insurance) refers to the insurance which can be bought for trucks, cars, and other types of vehicles. The principal objective of an Auto Insurance Policy is to offer safeguards against adverse financial consequences resulting from motor vehicle accidents (MVAs). The Automobile Insurance Company has the discretion to adjudge that a car is wholly destructed (write-off or totaled) if it seems that the replacement cost would be lower compared to repairing costs. In case of Auto Insurance, coverage is available for some or all the parties given below:

- The party insured
- The insured car
- Third parties In a large number of countries, buying Auto Insurance is mandatory to drive on public or state highways.

The basis of charging the premium is dependent on the following factors: the coverage, the age, gender, and driving history of the driver, and the distance covered by the car. The different types of coverage that are available in Automobile Insurance include the following:

- Liability Coverage (Combined Single Limit & Split Limits)
- Collision Coverage
- Comprehensive Coverage
- Loss of Use Coverage
- Underinsured/Uninsured Coverage
- Loan/Lease Payoff Coverage (GAP Coverage or GAP Insurance)
- Car Towing Insurance (Roadside Assistance Coverage)

LIFE INSURANCE COUNCIL OF INDIA

Structure

- The Life Insurance Council will have an Executive Committee of 21 members of which 2 will be from the IRDA and the rest from licensed life insurers
- The Committee will set up standards of conduct and practices for efficient customer service, advise IRDA on controlling insurers' expenses and serve as a forum that helps maintain healthy market conduct
- It will create and manage a process for agent examination and certification
- The Life Insurance Council is funded by the Life Insurers in India

The Purpose

- The Life Insurance Council seeks to play a significant and complementary role in transforming India's life insurance industry into a vibrant, trustworthy and profitable service, helping the people of India on their journey to prosperity.

Its Mission

- To function as an active forum to aid, advise and assist insurers in maintaining high standards of conduct and service to policyholders
- Advise the supervisory authority in the matter of controlling expenses
- Interact with the Government and other bodies on policy matters
- Actively participate in spreading insurance awareness in India
- Take steps to develop education and research insurance
- Help bring to India the benefit of the best practices in the world

The Council Will

- Strive for a positive image of the industry through media, forums and opinion- makers and enhance consumer confidence in the industry
- Assist the industry in maintaining high standards of ethics and governance
- Promote awareness regarding the role and benefits of life insurance
- Organize structured, regular and proactive discussions with Government, lawmakers and Regulators on matters relevant to the contribution by the life insurance industry and act as an effective liaison between them
- Conduct research on operational, economic, legislative, regulatory and customer-oriented issues in life

insurance, publish monographs on current developments in life insurance and contribute to the development of the sector

- Set up the Mortality and Morbidity Information Bureau (MMIB) and take an active role in its functioning
- Set up similar organizations for the benefit of the life insurance industry
- Act as a forum of interaction with organizations in other segments of the financial services sector
- Play a leading role in insurance education, research, training, discussion forums and conferences
- Provide help and guidance to members when necessary
- Be an active link between the Indian life insurance industry and the global markets

Legislations & Control

- Address common issues in legislation and practice. Interface with the various other regulatory bodies on behalf of the insurance industry.
- Identify regularly the important issues to be taken up with Government and/or IRDA & PFRDA and make presentations on behalf of the industry
- Prepare benchmarks for the industry in all areas of operation and help maintain high standards of conduct, ethics and governance
- Take measures to prevent practices that are detrimental to the interests of the policyholders

Training & Certification

- Take up the work relating to the training, examination and certification of Agents as provided in the Insurance Act
- Play a positive role in establishing standards, training of officials and intermediaries not only in products and sales but also other aspects relevant to the life insurance industry and lift the level of professionalism

- Conduct professional development programs in collaboration with international councils and life insurance institutes

ESTABLISH A CONSUMER RELATIONS CELL

The Promise

- Strengthening the role of the insurance sector in India and creating wealth for its people... The Life Insurance Council. A three way interaction among the insurer, the insured and Regulatory body. A convergence of interests... and the collective voice of life insurance.

In Perspective

- Indian Life Insurance Industry
- More than a century in India
- Large mobilisation of savings next only to banks
- Significant participant in the Capital Markets
- Constitutes 15% of Gross Domestic Savings
- Assets under management- more than Rs. 4,00,000 Crores
- Invested in Infrastructure- Rs. 40,000 Crores

Employment

- Employs close to 2,00,000. Retail customers: 92%

Agency Force

- 1.5 million

Policies in Force

- Nearly 20 crores

Offices

- Nearly 3000 offices across India and growing

Growth

- Penetration grew from 1.2% to 2.2% of GDP
- Insurance Density grew from Rs. 280 to Rs. 600 (per capita premium)
- Premium grown from Rs. 28,000 Crores to Rs. 63, 000 Crores.

6

SIGNIFICANCE OF INSURANCE

The story of insurance is probably as old as the story of mankind. The same instinct that prompts modern businessmen today to secure themselves against loss and disaster existed in primitive men also. They too sought to avert the evil consequences of fire and flood and loss of life and were willing to make some sort of sacrifice in order to achieve security. Though the concept of insurance is largely a development of the recent past, particularly after the industrial era – past few centuries – yet its beginnings date back almost 6000 years.

Life Insurance in its modern form came to India from England in the year 1818. Oriental Life Insurance Company started by Europeans in Calcutta was the first life insurance company on Indian Soil. All the insurance companies established during that period were brought up with the purpose of looking after the needs of European community and Indian natives were not being insured by these companies. However, later with the efforts of eminent people like Babu Muttylal Seal, the foreign life insurance companies started insuring Indian lives. But Indian lives were being treated as sub-standard lives and heavy extra premiums were being charged on them. Bombay Mutual Life Assurance Society heralded the birth of first Indian life insurance company in the year 1870, and covered Indian lives at normal rates.

Starting as Indian enterprise with highly patriotic motives, insurance companies came into existence to carry the message of insurance and social security through insurance to various sectors of society. Bharat Insurance Company (1896) was also one of such companies inspired by nationalism. The Swadeshi movement of 1905-1907 gave rise to more insurance companies. The United India in Madras, National Indian and National Insurance in Calcutta and the Co-operative Assurance at Lahore were established in 1906. In 1907, Hindustan Co-operative Insurance Company took its birth in one of the rooms of the Jorasanko, house of the great poet Rabindranath Tagore, in Calcutta.

The Indian Mercantile, General Assurance and Swadeshi Life (later Bombay Life) were some of the companies established during the same period. Prior to 1912 India had no legislation to regulate insurance business. In the year 1912, the Life Insurance Companies Act, and the Provident Fund Act were passed.

The Life Insurance Companies Act, 1912 made it necessary that the premium rate tables and periodical valuations of companies should be certified by an actuary. But the Act discriminated between foreign and Indian companies on many accounts, putting the Indian companies at a disadvantage.

The first two decades of the twentieth century saw lot of growth in insurance business. From 44 companies with total business-in-force as Rs.22.44 crore, it rose to 176 companies with total business-in-force as Rs.298 crore in 1938. During the mushrooming of insurance companies many financially unsound concerns were also floated which failed miserably. The Insurance Act 1938 was the first legislation governing not only life insurance but also non-life insurance to provide strict state control over insurance business. The demand for nationalization of life insurance industry was made repeatedly in the past but it gathered momentum in 1944 when a bill to amend the Life Insurance Act 1938 was introduced in the Legislative Assembly.

However, it was much later on the 19th of January, 1956, that life insurance in India was nationalized. About 154 Indian insurance companies, 16 non-Indian companies and 75 provident were operating in India at the time of nationalization. Nationalization was accomplished in two stages; initially the management of the companies was taken over by means of an Ordinance, and later, the ownership too by means of a comprehensive bill.

The Parliament of India passed the Life Insurance Corporation Act on the 19th of June 1956, and the Life Insurance Corporation of India was created on 1st September, 1956, with the objective of spreading life insurance much more widely and in particular to the rural areas with a view to reach all insurable persons in the country, providing them adequate financial cover at a reasonable cost.

LIC had 5 zonal offices, 33 divisional offices and 212 branch offices, apart from its corporate office in the year 1956. Since life insurance contracts are long term contracts and during the currency of the policy it requires a variety of services need was felt in the later years to expand the operations and place a branch office at each district headquarter. re-organization of LIC took place and large numbers of new branch offices were opened. As a result of re-organisation servicing functions were transferred to the branches, and branches were made accounting units.

It worked wonders with the performance of the corporation. It may be seen that from about 200.00 crores of New Business in 1957 the corporation crossed 1000.00 crores only in the year 1969-70, and it took another 10 years for LIC to cross 2000.00 crore mark of new business. But with re-organisation happening in the early eighties, by 1985-86 LIC had already crossed 7000.00 crore Sum Assured on new policies.

Today LIC functions with 2048 fully computerized branch offices, 100 divisional offices, 7 zonal offices and the Corporate office. LIC's Wide Area Network covers 100 divisional offices and connects all the branches through a Metro Area Network. LIC has tied up with some Banks and Service providers to offer on-line premium collection facility in selected cities. LIC's ECS and ATM premium payment facility is an addition to customer convenience. Apart from on-line Kiosks and IVRS, Info Centres have been commissioned at Mumbai, Ahmedabad, Bangalore, Chennai, Hyderabad, Kolkata, New Delhi, Pune and many other cities. With a vision of providing easy access to its policyholders, LIC has launched its SATELLITE SAMPARK offices.

The satellite offices are smaller, leaner and closer to the customer. The digitalized records of the satellite offices will facilitate anywhere servicing and many other conveniences in the future. LIC continues to be the dominant life insurer even in the liberalized scenario of Indian insurance and is moving fast on a new growth trajectory surpassing its own past records. LIC has issued over one crore policies during the current year. It has crossed the milestone of issuing 1,01,32,955 new policies by 15th Oct, 2005, posting a healthy growth rate of 16.67% over the corresponding period of the previous year.

From then to now, LIC has crossed many milestones and has set unprecedented performance records in various aspects of life insurance business. The same motives which inspired our forefathers to bring insurance into existence in this country inspire us at LIC to take this message of protection to light the lamps of security in as many homes as possible and to help the people in providing security to their families.

Some of the important milestones in the life insurance business in India are:

1818: Oriental Life Insurance Company, the first life insurance company on Indian soil started functioning.

1870: Bombay Mutual Life Assurance Society, the first Indian life insurance company started its business.

1912: The Indian Life Assurance Companies Act enacted as the first statute to regulate the life insurance business.

1928: The Indian Insurance Companies Act enacted to enable the government to collect statistical information about both life and non-life insurance businesses.

1938: Earlier legislation consolidated and amended to by the Insurance Act with the objective of protecting the interests of the insuring public.

1956: 245 Indian and foreign insurers and provident societies are taken over by the central government and nationalised.

LIC formed by an Act of Parliament, viz. LIC Act, 1956, with a capital contribution of Rs. 5 crore from the Government of India. The General insurance business in India, on the other hand, can trace its roots to the Triton Insurance Company Ltd., the first general insurance company established in the year 1850 in Calcutta by the British. Some of the important milestones in the general insurance business in India are:

1907: The Indian Mercantile Insurance Ltd. set up, the first company to transact all classes of general insurance business.

1957: General Insurance Council, a wing of the Insurance Association of India, frames a code of conduct for ensuring fair conduct and sound business practices.

1968: The Insurance Act amended to regulate investments and set minimum solvency margins and the Tariff Advisory Committee set up.

1972: The General Insurance Business (Nationalisation) Act, 1972 nationalised the general insurance business in India with effect from 1st January 1973.

107 insurers amalgamated and grouped into four companies viz. the National Insurance Company Ltd., the New India Assurance Company Ltd., the Oriental Insurance Company Ltd. and the United India Insurance Company Ltd. GIC incorporated as a company.

OBJECTIVES

- Spread Life Insurance widely and in particular to the rural areas and to the socially and economically backward classes with a view to reaching all insurable persons in the country and providing them adequate financial cover against death at a reasonable cost.
- Maximize mobilization of people's savings by making insurance-linked savings adequately attractive.
- Bear in mind, in the investment of funds, the primary obligation to its policyholders, whose money it holds in trust, without losing sight of the interest of the community as a whole; the funds to be deployed to the

best advantage of the investors as well as the community as a whole, keeping in view national priorities and obligations of attractive return.

- Conduct business with utmost economy and with the full realization that the moneys belong to the policyholders.
- Act as trustees of the insured public in their individual and collective capacities.
- Meet the various life insurance needs of the community that would arise in the changing social and economic environment.
- Involve all people working in the Corporation to the best of their capability in furthering the interests of the insured public by providing efficient service with courtesy.
- Promote amongst all agents and employees of the Corporation a sense of participation, pride and job satisfaction through discharge of their duties with dedication towards achievement of Corporate Objective.

Mission

"Explore and enhance the quality of life of people through financial security by providing products and services of aspired attributes with competitive returns, and by rendering resources for economic development."

Vision

"A trans-nationally competitive financial conglomerate of significance to societies and Pride of India."

Life insurance in India made its debut well over 100 years ago. In our country, which is one of the most populated in the world, the prominence of insurance is not as widely understood, as it ought to be. What follows is an attempt to acquaint readers with some of the concepts of life insurance, with special reference to LIC. It should, however, be clearly understood that the following content is by no means an exhaustive description of the terms and conditions of an LIC policy or its benefits or privileges. For more details, please contact our branch or divisional office. Any LIC Agent will be glad to help you choose the life insurance plan to meet your needs and render policy servicing.

WHAT IS LIFE INSURANCE?

Life insurance is a contract that pledges payment of an amount to the person assured (or his nominee) on the happening of the event insured against.

The contract is valid for payment of the insured amount during:

- The date of maturity, or
- Specified dates at periodic intervals, or
- Unfortunate death, if it occurs earlier.

Among other things, the contract also provides for the payment of premium periodically to the Corporation by the policyholder. Life insurance is universally acknowledged to be an institution, which eliminates 'risk', substituting certainty for uncertainty and comes to the timely aid of the family in the unfortunate event of death of the breadwinner.

By and large, life insurance is civilisation's partial solution to the problems caused by death. Life insurance, in short, is concerned with two hazards that stand across the life-path of every person:

1. That of dying prematurely leaving a dependent family to fend for itself.
2. That of living till old age without visible means of support.

LIFE INSURANCE VS. OTHER SAVINGS

Contract Of Insurance: A contract of insurance is a contract of utmost good faith technically known as uberrima fides. The doctrine of disclosing all material facts is embodied in this important principle, which applies to all forms of insurance. At the time of taking a policy, policyholder should ensure that all questions in the proposal form are correctly answered. Any misrepresentation, non-disclosure or fraud in any document leading to the acceptance of the risk would render the insurance contract null and void.

Protection: Savings through life insurance guarantee full protection against risk of death of the saver. Also, in case of demise, life insurance assures payment of the entire amount assured (with bonuses wherever applicable) whereas in other savings schemes, only the amount saved (with interest) is payable.

Aid To Thrift: Life insurance encourages 'thrift'. It allows long-term savings since payments can be made effortlessly because of the 'easy instalment' facility built into the scheme. (Premium payment for insurance is either monthly, quarterly, half yearly or yearly).

For example: The Salary Saving Scheme popularly known as SSS, provides a convenient method of paying premium each month by deduction from one's salary.

In this case the employer directly pays the deducted premium to LIC. The Salary Saving Scheme is ideal for any institution or establishment subject to specified terms and conditions.

Liquidity: In case of insurance, it is easy to acquire loans on the sole security of any policy that has acquired loan value. Besides, a life insurance policy is also generally accepted as security, even for a commercial loan.

Tax Relief: Life Insurance is the best way to enjoy tax deductions on income tax and wealth tax. This is available for amounts paid by way of premium for life insurance subject to income tax rates in force.

Assessees can also avail of provisions in the law for tax relief. In such cases the assured in effect pays a lower premium for insurance than otherwise.

Money When You Need It: A policy that has a suitable insurance plan or a combination of different plans can be effectively used to meet certain monetary needs that may arise from time-to-time. Children's education, start-in-life or marriage provision or even periodical needs for cash over a stretch of time can be less stressful with the help of these policies. Alternatively, policy money can be made available at the time of one's retirement from service and used for any specific purpose, such as, purchase of a house or for other investments. Also, loans are granted to policyholders for house building or for purchase of flats (subject to certain conditions).

WHO CAN BUY A POLICY?

Any person who has attained majority and is eligible to enter into a valid contract can insure himself/herself and those in whom he/she has insurable interest. Policies can also be taken, subject to certain conditions, on the life of one's spouse or children. While underwriting proposals, certain factors such as the policyholder's state of health, the proponent's income and other relevant factors are considered by the Corporation.

Insurance for Women

Prior to nationalisation (1956), many private insurance companies would offer insurance to female lives with some extra premium or on restrictive conditions. However, after nationalisation of life insurance, the terms under which life insurance is granted to female lives have been reviewed from time-to-time.

At present, women who work and earn an income are treated at par with men. In other cases, a restrictive clause is imposed, only if the age of the femalc is up to 30 years and if she does not have an income attracting Income Tax.

Medical And Non-Medical Schemes

Life insurance is normally offered after a medical examination of the life to be assured. However, to facilitate greater spread of insurance and also to avoid inconvenience, LIC has been extending insurance cover without any medical examination, subject to certain conditions.

With Profit And Without Profit Plans

An insurance policy can be 'with' or 'without' profit. In the former, bonuses disclosed, if any, after periodical valuations are allotted to the policy and are payable along with the contracted amount. In 'without' profit plan the contracted amount is paid without any addition. The premium rate charged for a 'with' profit policy is therefore higher than for a 'without' profit policy.

Keyman Insurance

Keyman insurance is taken by a business firm on the life of key employee(s) to protect the firm against financial losses, which may occur due to the premature demise of the Keyman.

LIC has been one of the pioneering organizations in India who introduced the leverage of Information Technology in servicing and in their business. Data pertaining to almost 10 crore policies is being held on computers in LIC. We have gone in for relevant and appropriate technology over the years.

1964 saw the introduction of computers in LIC. Unit Record Machines introduced in late 1950's were phased out in 1980's and replaced by Microprocessors based computers in Branch and Divisional Offices for Back Office Computerization. Standardization of Hardware and Software commenced in 1990's. Standard Computer Packages were developed and implemented for Ordinary and Salary Savings Scheme (SSS) Policies.

FRONT END OPERATIONS

With a view to enhancing customer responsiveness and services , in July 1995, LIC started a drive of On Line Service to Policyholders and Agents through Computer. This on line service enabled policyholders to receive immediate policy status report , prompt acceptance of their premium and get Revival Quotation, Loan Quotation on demand. Incorporating change of address can be done on line. Quicker completion of proposals and dispatch of policy documents have become a reality. All our 2048 branches across the country have been covered under front-end operations.

Thus all our 100 divisional offices have achieved the distinction of 100% branch computerisation. New payment related Modules pertaining to both ordinary & SSS policies have been added to the Front End Package catering to Loan, Claims and Development Officers' Appraisal. All these modules help to reduce time-lag and ensure accuracy.

METRO AREA NETWORK

A Metropolitan Area Network, connecting 74 branches in Mumbai was commissioned in November, 1997, enabling policyholders in Mumbai to pay their Premium or get their Status Report, Surrender Value Quotation, Loan Quotation etc. from ANY Branch in the city. The System has been working successfully. More than 10,000 transactions are carried out over this Network on any given working day. Such Networks have been implemented in other cities also.

WIDE AREA NETWORK

All 7 Zonal Offices and all the MAN centres are connected through a Wide Area Network (WAN). This will enable a customer to view his policy data and pay premium from any branch of any MAN city. As at November 2005, we have 91 centers in India with more than 2035 branches networked under WAN.

INTERACTIVE VOICE RESPONSE SYSTEMS (IVRS)

IVRS has already been made functional in 59 centers all over the country. This would enable customers to ring up LIC and receive information (e.g. next premium due, Status, Loan Amount, Maturity payment due, Accumulated Bonus etc.) about their policies on the telephone. This information could also be faxed on demand to the customer.

LIC ON THE INTERNET

Our Internet site is an information bank. We have displayed information about LIC & its offices . Efforts are on to upgrade our web site to make it dynamic and interactive.

The addresses/e-mail Ids of ur Zonal Offices, Zonal Training Centers, Management Development Center, Overseas Branches, Divisional Offices and also all Branch Offices with a view to speed up the communication process.

PAYMENT OF PREMIUM AND POLICY STATUS ON INTERNET

(You have to register for these services)

LIC has given its policyholders a unique facility to pay premiums through Internet absolutely free and also view their policy details on Internet premium payments. There are 11 service providers with whom L I C has signed the agreement to provide this service.

INFORMATION KIOSKS

We have set up 150 Interactive Touch screen based Multimedia KIOSKS in prime locations in metros and some major cities for dissemination information to general public on our products and services. These KIOSKS are enable to provide policy details and accept premium payments.

INFO CENTRES

We have also set up 8 call centres, manned by skilled employees to provide you with information about our Products, Policy Services, Branch addresses and other organizational information.

Overview

With largest number of life insurance policies in force in the world, Insurance happens to be a mega opportunity in India. It's a business growing at the rate of 15-20 per cent annually and presently is of the order of Rs 450 billion. Together with banking services, it adds about 7 per cent to the country's GDP. Gross premium collection is nearly 2 per cent of GDP and funds available with LIC for investments are 8 per cent of GDP.

Yet, nearly 80 per cent of Indian population is without life insurance cover while health insurance and non-life insurance continues to be below international standards. And this part of the population is also subject to weak social security and pension systems with hardly any old age income security. This itself is an indicator that growth potential for the insurance sector is immense.

A well-developed and evolved insurance sector is needed for economic development as it provides long term funds for infrastructure development and at the same time strengthens the risk taking ability.

It is estimated that over the next ten years India would require investments of the order of one trillion US dollar. The Insurance sector, to some extent, can enable investments in infrastructure development to sustain economic growth of the country.

Insurance is a federal subject in India. There are two legislations that govern the sector- The Insurance Act- 1938 and the IRDA Act- 1999. The insurance sector in India has come a full circle from being an open competitive market to nationalisation and back to a liberalised market again. Tracing the developments in the Indian insurance sector reveals the 360 degree turn witnessed over a period of almost two centuries.

Historical Perspective

The history of life insurance in India dates back to 1818 when it was conceived as a means to provide for English Widows. Interestingly in those days a higher premium was charged for Indian lives than the non-Indian lives as Indian lives were considered more riskier for coverage.

The Bombay Mutual Life Insurance Society started its business in 1870. It was the first company to charge same premium for both Indian and non-Indian lives. The Oriental Assurance Company was established in 1880.

The General insurance business in India, on the other hand, can trace its roots to the Triton (Tital) Insurance Company Limited, the first general insurance company established in the year 1850 in Calcutta by the British. Till the end of nineteenth century insurance business was almost entirely in the hands of overseas companies. Insurance regulation formally began in India with the passing of the Life Insurance Companies Act of 1912 and the provident fund Act of 1912. Several frauds during 20's and 30's sullied insurance business in India. By 1938 there were 176 insurance companies.

The first comprehensive legislation was introduced with the Insurance Act of 1938 that provided strict State Control over insurance business. The insurance business grew at a faster pace after independence. Indian companies strengthened their hold on this business but despite the growth that was witnessed, insurance remained an urban phenomenon.

The Government of India in 1956, brought together over 240 private life insurers and provident societies under one nationalised monopoly corporation and Life Insurance Corporation (LIC) was born. Nationalisation was justified on the grounds that it would create much needed funds for rapid industrialization. This was in conformity with the Government's chosen path of State lead planning and development.

The (non-life) insurance business continued to thrive with the private sector till 1972. Their operations were restricted to organised trade and industry in large cities.

The general insurance industry was nationalised in 1972. With this, nearly 107 insurers were amalgamated and grouped into four companies- National Insurance Company, New India Assurance Company, Oriental Insurance Company and United India Insurance Company. These were subsidiaries of the General Insurance Company (GIC).

Important milestones in the life insurance business in India:

1912: The Indian Life Assurance Companies Act enacted as the first statute to regulate the life insurance business.

1928: The Indian Insurance Companies Act enacted to enable the government to collect statistical information about both life and non-life insurance businesses.

1938: Earlier legislation consolidated and amended to by the Insurance Act with the objective of protecting the interests of the insuring public.

1956: 245 Indian and foreign insurers and provident societies taken over by the central government and nationalised. LIC formed by an Act of Parliament- LIC Act 1956- with a capital contribution of Rs. 5 crore from the Government of India.

Important milestones in the general insurance business in India are:

1907: The Indian Mercantile Insurance Ltd. set up- the first company to transact all classes of general insurance business.

1957: General Insurance Council, a wing of the Insurance Association of India, frames a code of conduct for ensuring fair conduct and sound business practices.

1968: The Insurance Act amended to regulate investments and set minimum solvency margins and the Tariff Advisory Committee set up.

1972: The general insurance business in India nationalised through The General Insurance Business (Nationalisation) Act, 1972 with effect from 1st January 1973. 107 insurers amalgamated and grouped into four companies- the National Insurance Company Limited, the New India Assurance Company Limited, the Oriental Insurance Company Ltd. and the United India Insurance Company Ltd. GIC incorporated as a company.

Insurance Sector Reforms

In 1993, Malhotra Committee- headed by former Finance Secretary and RBI Governor R.N. Malhotra- was formed to evaluate the Indian insurance industry and recommend its future direction.The Malhotra committee was set up with the objective of complementing the reforms initiated in the financial sector. The reforms were aimed at creating a more efficient and competitive financial system suitable for the requirements of the economy keeping in mind the structural changes currently underway and recognising that insurance is an important part of the overall financial system where it was necessary to address the need for similar reforms. In 1994, the committee submitted the report and some of the key recommendations included:

Structure

Government stake in the insurance Companies to be brought down to 50%. Government should take over the holdings of GIC and its subsidiaries so that these subsidiaries can act as independent corporations. All the insurance companies should be given greater freedom to operate.

Competition

Private Companies with a minimum paid up capital of Rs.1bn should be allowed to enter the sector. No Company should deal in both Life and General Insurance through a single entity. Foreign companies may be allowed to enter the industry in collaboration with the domestic companies.

Postal Life Insurance should be allowed to operate in the rural market. Only one State Level Life Insurance Company should be allowed to operate in each state.

Regulatory Body

The Insurance Act should be changed. An Insurance Regulatory body should be set up. Controller of Insurance- a part of the Finance Ministry- should be made independent

Investments

Mandatory Investments of LIC Life Fund in government securities to be reduced from 75% to 50%. GIC and its subsidiaries are not to hold more than 5% in any company (there current holdings to be brought down to this level over a period of time)

Customer Service

LIC should pay interest on delays in payments beyond 30 days. Insurance companies must be encouraged to set up unit linked pension plans. Computerisation of operations and updating of technology to be carried out in the insurance industry.

The committee emphasised that in order to improve the customer services and increase the coverage of insurance policies, industry should be opened up to competition. But at the same time, the committee felt the need to exercise caution as any failure on the part of new players could ruin the public confidence in the industry. Hence, it was decided to allow competition in a limited way by stipulating the minimum capital requirement of Rs.100 crores. The committee felt the need to provide greater autonomy to insurance companies in order to improve their performance and enable them to act as independent companies with economic motives. For this purpose, it had proposed setting up an independent regulatory body-The Insurance Regulatory and Development Authority.

Reforms in the Insurance sector were initiated with the passage of the IRDA Bill in Parliament in December 1999. The IRDA since its incorporation as a statutory body in April 2000 has fastidiously stuck to its schedule of framing regulations and registering the private sector insurance companies.

Since being set up as an independent statutory body the IRDA has put in a framework of globally compatible regulations. The other decision taken simultaneously to provide the supporting systems to the insurance sector and in particular the life insurance companies was the launch of the IRDA online service for issue and renewal of licenses to agents. The approval of institutions for imparting training to agents has also ensured that the insurance companies would have a trained workforce of insurance agents in place to sell their products.

Present Scenario

The Government of India liberalised the insurance sector in March 2000 with the passage of the Insurance Regulatory and Development Authority (IRDA) Bill, lifting all entry restrictions for private players and allowing foreign players to enter the market with some limits on direct foreign ownership. Under the current guidelines, there is a 26 percent equity cap for foreign partners in an insurance company. There is a proposal to increase this limit to 49 percent.

The opening up of the sector is likely to lead to greater spread and deepening of insurance in India and this may also include restructuring and revitalizing of the public sector companies.

In the private sector 12 life insurance and 8 general insurance companies have been registered. A host of private Insurance companies operating in both life and non-life segments have started selling their insurance policies since 2001.

Non-Life Insurance Market

In December 2000, the GIC subsidiaries were restructured as independent insurance companies. At the same time, GIC was converted into a national re-insurer. In July 2002, Parliamant passed a bill, delinking the four subsidiaries from GIC.

Presently there are 12 general insurance companies with 4 public sector companies and 8 private insurers. Although the public sector companies still dominate the general insurance business, the private players are slowly gaining a foothold. According to estimates, private insurance companies have a 10 percent share of the market, up from 4 percent in 2001. In the first half of 2002, the private companies booked premiums worth Rs 6.34 billion. Most of the new entrants reported losses in the first year of their operation in 2001.

With a large capital outlay and long gestation periods, infrastructure projects are fraught with a multitude of risks throughout the development, construction and operation stages. These include risks associated with project implementaion, including geological risks, maintenance, commercial and political risks. Without covering these risks the financial institutions are not willing to commit funds to the sector, especially because the financing of most private projects is on a limited or non-recourse basis.

Insurance companies not only provide risk cover to infrastructure projects, they also contribute long-term funds. In fact, insurance companies are an ideal source of long term debt and equity for infrastructure projects. With long term liability, they get a good asset- liability match by investing their funds in such projects. IRDA regulations require insurance companies to invest not less than 15 percent of their funds in infrastructure and social sectors. International Insurance companies also invest their funds in such projects. Insurance costs constitute roughly around 1.2- 2 percent of the total project costs. Under the existing norms, insurance premium payments are treated as part of the fixed costs. Consequently they are treated as pass-through costs for tariff calculations.

Premium rates of most general insurance policies come under the purview of the government appointed Tariff Advisory Commitee. For Projects costing up to Rs 1 Billion, the Tariff Advisory Committee sets the premium rates, for Projects between Rs 1 billion and Rs 15 billion, the rates are set in keeping with the committee's guidelines; and projects above Rs 15 billion are subjected to re-insurance pricing. It is the last segment that has a number of additional products and competitive pricing.

Insurance, like project finance, is extended by a consortium. Normally one insurer takes the lead, shouldering about 40-50 per cent of the risk and receiving a proportionate percentage of the premium. The other companies share the remaining risk and premium. The policies are renewed usually on an annual basis through the invitation of bids.

Of late, with IPP projects fizzling out, the insurance companies are turning once again to old hands such as NTPC, NHPC and BSES for business.

Re-insurance Business

Insurance companies retain only a part of the risk (less than 10 per cent) assumed by them, which can be safely borne from their own funds. The balance risk is re-insured with other insurers. In effect, therefore, re-insurance is insurer's insurance. It forms the backbone of the insurance business. It helps to provide a better spread of risk in the international market, allows primary insurers to accept risks beyond their capacity, settle accumulated losses arising from catastrophic events and still maintain their financial stability.

While GIC's subsidiaries look after general insurance, GIC itself has been the major reinsurer. Currently, all insurance companies have to give 20 per cent of their reinsurance business to GIC. The aim is to ensure that GIC's role as the national reinsurer remains unhindered. However, GIC reinsures the amount further with international companies such as Swissre (Switzerland), Munichre (Germany), and Royale (UK). Reinsurance premiums have seen an exorbitant increase in recent years, following the rise in threat perceptions globally.

Life Insurance Market

The Life Insurance market in India is an underdeveloped market that was only tapped by the state owned LIC till the entry of private insurers. The penetration of life insurance products was 19 percent of the total 400 million of the insurable population. The state owned LIC sold insurance as a tax instrument, not as a product giving protection. Most customers were under- insured with no flexibility or transparency in the products. With the entry of the private insurers the rules of the game have changed.

The 12 private insurers in the life insurance market have already grabbed nearly 9 percent of the market in terms of premium income. The new business premiums of the 12 private players has tripled to Rs 1000 crore in 2002- 03 over last year. Meanwhile, state owned LIC's new premium business has fallen. Innovative products, smart marketing and aggressive distribution. That's the triple whammy combination that has enabled fledgling private insurance companies to sign up Indian customers faster than anyone ever expected. Indians, who have always seen life insurance as a tax saving device, are now suddenly turning to the private sector and snapping up the new innovative products on offer.

The growing popularity of the private insurers shows in other ways. They are coining money in new niches that they have introduced. The state owned companies still dominate segments like endowments and money back policies. But in the annuity or pension products business, the private insurers have already wrested over 33 percent of the market. And in the popular unit-linked insurance schemes they have a virtual monopoly, with over 90 percent of the customers.

The private insurers also seem to be scoring big in other ways- they are persuading people to take out bigger policies. For instance, the average size of a life insurance policy before privatisation was around Rs 50,000. That has risen to about Rs 80,000. But the private insurers are ahead in this game and the average size of their policies is around Rs 1.1 lakh to Rs 1.2 lakh- way bigger than the industry average.

Buoyed by their quicker than expected success, nearly all private insurers are fast- forwarding the second phase of their expansion plans. No doubt the aggressive stance of private insurers is already paying rich dividends. But a rejuvenated LIC is also trying to fight back to woo new customers. The insurance industry is set to see more of its capital freed, with the Insurance Regulatory Development Authority (IRDA) recommending transition to a risk-based capital framework for insurers. The proposed framework envisages assessing the capital requirement of insurers based on the underlying risk and volatility of their business. The companies will have to earmark capital for different line of businesses.

This model, known as Solvency II, has been adopted in most developed economies. If Indian insurers were to replicate this, they would have to set aside much less capital than they do now for unit linked insurance plans (ULIPs) compared to traditional insurance products. The recommendation to adopt the new framework was made last week to a high-level panel on the financial sector assessment programme. The panel, comprising senior government officials and regulators, is set to recommend further course of reforms in the financial sector.

Unlike traditional insurance products, the investment risk in ULIPs is borne by the policy holder. The solvency margin requirement for ULIPs is just one third of that for traditional insurance products. Solvency margin is the excess of assets over liabilities that an insurer has to maintain as a prudential measure. Simply put, the risk-based capital framework factors in a lower risk on policy holders' liabilities. But companies will have to set aside higher capital if there is an asset liability mismatch in their portfolio.

Industry analysts say that IRDA has so far been hesitant to suggest the new framework mainly due to the uncertainty over investor behaviour in a choppy market. Besides, the transition would also require inputs from the actuarial side, both from insurance companies and the regulator. But there is a shortage of such talent now which needs to be addressed. "Even countries that have adopted this model have done so cautiously and over a long span", said former chairman of

IRDA C S Rao in an interview to ET last month. Fact is the risk-based model gives a clear picture of the financial strength of the insurer and also allows for regulatory intervention, if required. It also helps in making comparisons across companies.

Currently, the minimum capital requirement for a private insurer is Rs 100 crore. Companies need capital to grow. It is also required to meet unexpected claims, expense over-runs and investment losses. The minimum capital prescribed under the new framework will act as a buffer to cushion losses, reckon experts. The IRDA has also made out a case for putting in place corporate governance norms for insurers and greater supervisory powers for the regulator.

The latter would require amendments to the insurance legislation. An empowered group of ministers is vetting these proposed amendments along with other changes including a hike in the FDI cap from 26% to 49%. Meanwhile, the IRDA has also looked at the status of India's compliance with the insurance core principles (ICP) enunciated by the International Association of Insurance Supervisors (IAIS), a body of regulators and supervisors of over 190 jurisdictions.

The principles include, among others, conditions for effective supervision, supervisory system, supervised entity, ongoing supervision, prudential requirements, markets and consumers and anti money laundering. The score card: India has observed or largely observed around 17 out of the 28 odd core principles. But there are a few gaps. The conditions for effective supervision may not be fully in sync with global standards till changes are made in the legislation. The regulator also does not have complete control either over public sector insurance companies. Comprehensive internal controls are yet to be in place. There is also a case for beefing up on-site supervision.

More importantly, there is a case for enhancing disclosures to the public and having a proper mechanism in place for risk assessment. The IRDA has now set the ball rolling to usher in these reform measures. The insurance regulator does not want to take any chances on complaints over misselling of unit linked insurance plans (Ulips) to investors. Following concerns raised in several quarters on misselling by agents and companies, it has undertaken a special audit of over half a dozen companies selling Ulips.

As per the audit, companies are adhering to the norms laid down by the regulator to ensure more transparency to investors. "The Insurance Regulatory Development Authority (IRDA) inspected the sample brochures of life insurance companies to check if they were in sync with the norms laid down in the benefit illustration. We did not find any major deviations," said a senior official. LIC, Bajaj Allianz Life Insurance, SBI Life, ICICI Prudential Life, HDFC Standard Life and Tata AIG Life Insurance featured in the list of companies that were audited by the IRDA, he added. Ulips are popular savings instruments as they offer protection in terms of life cover and flexibility in investments to the policyholder. A part of the premium is invested in equities or government bonds, depending on the choice of the policyholder. While the investments are akin to a mutual fund, the returns are reflected in the increase in the value of the unit, mirrored in the net asset value (market value) declared by the company.

Bajaj Allianz Life Insurance's marketing head, Sanjay Jain confirmed that IRDA did conduct an audit to check if the company was maintaining its records as per the prescribed norms. He added that this was in line with the inspections conducted on other life insurance companies as well. Currently, there are around 70-75 Ulips offered by life insurers. In most cases, cost structure is front-loaded — bulk of the agents' commission is paid in the first year.

Policy holders are often unaware of the fact that of every Rs 100 invested in the first year, a substantial portion goes towards commissions and other charges. Hence, if a Ulip were to be sold to an individual with an investment horizon of only three years, most schemes are likely to result in generating returns lower than expected because of the front-end charges. The insurance regulator had received several complaints on misselling of Ulips during the tenure of CS Rao, former chairman of IRDA. To begin with, it banned the sale of actuarially-funded products. The regulator then came out with a benefit illustration to ensure greater transparency for investors buying Ulips.

Going by IRDA's benefit illustration, insurers have to give policyholders a break-up of all the charges they need to pay and the exact amount that will be available for investment during the premium payment period. This is aimed at ensuring that investors buying Ulips are fully aware of the cost structure and investment risks.

Normally, charges at the beginning of the year include premium allocation charge, policy administration charge, mortality charge, rider charge, among others. The difference between premium payable each year and total charges is the amount available for investment. Insurers also have to list out charges at the end of each policy year, factoring in the interest rates approved by the IRDA in the file and use application. These charges include fund management charge and surrender charges.

The policy holder and the marketing official selling the product need to be signatories to the premium-cum charges statement. Any change in the charges while under-writing or finalising the deal will also have to be approved by the policy holder. Officials admit that a lot more needs to be done on investor education, given that the investment risk is borne by the policy holder.

7

BASICS OF INSURANCE

INDEMNITY

A contract of insurance contained in a fire, marine, burglary or any other policy (excepting life assurance and personal accident and sickness insurance) is a contract of indemnity. This means that the insured, in case of loss against which the policy has been issued, shall be paid the actual amount of loss not exceeding the amount of the policy, i.e. he shall be fully indemnified. The object of every contract of insurance is to place the insured in the same financial position, as nearly as possible, after the loss, as if he loss had not taken place at all. It would be against public policy to allow an insured to make a profit out of his loss or damage.

UTMOST GOOD FAITH

Since insurance shifts risk from one party to another, it is essential that there must be utmost good faith and mutual confidence between the insured and the insurer. In a contract of insurance the insured knows more about the subject matter of the contract than the insurer.

Consequently, he is duty bound to disclose accurately all material facts and nothing should be withheld or concealed. Any fact is material, which goes to the root of the contract of insurance and has a bearing on the risk involved. It is only when the insurer knows the whole truth thathe is in a position to judge (a) whether he should accept the risk and (b) what premium he should charge. If that were so, the insured might be tempted to bring about the event insured against in order to get money.

INSURABLE INTEREST

A contract of insurance effected without insurable interest is void. It means that the insured must have an actual pecuniary interest and not a mere anxiety or sentimental interest in the subject matter of the insurance. The insured must be so situated with regard to the thing insured thathe would have benefit by its existence and loss from its destruction. The owner of a ship run a risk of losing his ship, the charterer of the ship runs a risk of losing his freight and the owner of the cargo incurs the risk of losing his goods and profit. So, all these persons have something at stake and all of them have insurable interest. It is the existence of insurable interest in a contract of insurance, which distinguishes it from a mere watering agreement.

CAUSA PROXIMA

The rule of causa proxima means that the cause of the loss must be proximate or immediate and not remote. If the proximate cause of the loss is a peril insured against, the insured can recover. When a loss has been brought about by two or more causes, the question arises as to which is the causa proxima, although the result could not have happened without the remote cause. But if the loss is brought about by any cause attributable to the misconduct of the insured, the insurer is not liable.

RISK

In a contract of insurance the insurer undertakes to protect the insured from a specified loss and the insurer receive a premium for running the risk of such loss. Thus, risk must attach to a policy.

MITIGATION OF LOSS

In the event of some mishap to the insured property, the insured must take all necessary steps to mitigate or minimize the loss, just as any prudent person would do in those circumstances. If he does not do so, the insurer can avoid the payment of loss attributable to his negligence. But it must be remembered that though the insured is bound to do his best for his insurer, he is, not bound to do so at the risk of his life.

SUBROGATION

The doctrine of subrogation is a corollary to the principle of indemnity and applies only to fire and marine insurance. According to it, when an insured has received full indemnity in respect of his loss, all rights and remedies which he has against third person will pass on to the insurer and will be exercised for his benefit until he (the insurer) recoups the amounthe has paid under the policy. It must be clarified here that the insurer's right of subrogation arises only when he has paid for the loss for which he is liable under the policy and this right extend only to the rights and remedies available to the insured in respect of the thing to which the contract of insurance relates.

CONTRIBUTION

Where there are two or more insurance on one risk, the principle of contribution comes into play. The aim of contribution is to distribute the actual amount of loss among the different insurers who are liable for the same risk under different policies in respect of the same subject matter. Any one insurer may pay to the insured the full amount of the loss covered by the policy and then become entitled to contribution from his co-insurers in proportion to the amount which each has undertaken to pay in case of loss of the same subject-matter. In other words, the right of contribution arises when (i) there are different policies which relate to the same subject-matter (ii) the policies cover the same peril which caused the loss, and (iii) all the policies are in force at the time of the loss, and (iv) one of the insurers has paid to the insured more than his share of the loss.

INSURANCE LAW & REGULATIONS IN INDIA

The concept of insurance has been prevalent in India since ancient times amongst Hindus. Overseas traders practised a system of marine insurance. The joint family system, peculiar to India, was a method of social insurance of every member of the family on his life. The law relating to insurance has gradually developed, undergoing several phases from nationalisation of the insurance industry to the recent reforms permitting entry of private players and foreign investment in the insurance industry. The Constitution of India is federal in nature in as much there is division of powers between the Centre and the States. Insurance is included in the Union List, wherein the subjects included in this list are of the exclusive legislative competence of the Centre. The Central Legislature is empowered to regulate the insurance industry in India and hence the law in this regard is uniform throughout the territories of India. The development and growth of the insurance industry in India has gone through three distinct stages.

Insurance law in India had its origins in the United Kingdom with the establishment of a British firm, the Oriental Life Insurance Company in 1818 in Calcutta, followed by the Bombay Life Assurance Company in 1823, the Madras Equitable Life Insurance Society in 1829 and the Oriental Life Assurance Company in 1874. However, till the establishment of the Bombay Mutual Life Assurance Society in 1871, Indians were charged an extra premium of up to 20% as compared to the Brit ish. The first statutory measure in India to regulate the life insurance business was in 1912 with the passing of the Indian Life Assurance Companies Act, 1912 ("Act of 1912") (which was based on the English Act of 1909). Other classes of insurance business were left out of the scope of the Act of 1912, as such kinds of insurance were still in rudimentary form and legislative controls were not considered necessary.

General insurance on the other hand also has its origins in the United Kingdom. The first general insurance company Triton Insurance Company Ltd. was promoted in 1850 by British nationals in Calcutta. The first general insurance company established by an Indian was Indian Mercantile Insurance Company Ltd. in Bombay in 1907. Eventually, with the growth of fire, accident and marine insurance, the need was felt to bring such kinds of insurance within the purview of the Act of 1912. While there were a number of attempts to introduce such legislation over the years, non-life insurance was finally regulated in 1938 through the passing of the Insurance Act, 1938 ("Act of 1938"). The Act of 1938 along with various amendments over the years continues till date to be the definitive piece of legislation on insurance and controls both life insurance and general insurance. General insurance, in turn, has been defined to include "fire insurance business", "marine insurance business" and "miscellaneous insurance business", whether singly or in combination with any of them.

On January 19, 1956, the management of life insurance business of two hundred and forty five Indian and foreign insurers and provident societies then operating in India was taken over by the Central Government. The Life Insurance Corporation ("LIC") was formed in September 1956 by the Life Insurance Corporation Act, 1956 ("LIC Act") which granted LIC the exclusive privilege to conduct life insurance business in India. However, an exception was made in the case of any company, firm or persons intending to carry on life insurance business in India in respect of the lives of "persons ordinarily resident outside India", provided the approval of the Central Government was obtained. The exception was however not absolute and a curious prohibition existed. Such company, firm or person would not be permitted to insure the life of any "person ordinarily resident outside India", during any period of their temporary residence in India. However, the LIC Act, 1956 left outside its purview the Post Office Life Insurance Fund, any Family Pension Scheme framed under the Coal Mines Provident Fund, Family Pension and Bonus Schemes Act, 1948 or the Employees' Provident Funds and the Family Pension Fund Act, 1952.

The general insurance business was also nationalised with effect from January 1, 1973, through the introduction of the General Insurance Business (Nationalisation) Act, 1972 ("GIC Act"). Under the provisions of the GIC Act, the shares of the existing Indian general insurance companies and undertakings of other existing insurers were transferred to the General Insurance Corporation ("GIC") to secure the development of the general insurance business in India and for the regulation and control of such business. The GIC was established by the Central Government in accordance with the provisions of the Companies Act, 1956 ("Companies Act") in November 1972 and it commenced business on January 1, 1973. Prior to 1973, there were a hundred and seven companies, including foreign companies, offering general insurance in India.

These companies were amalgamated and grouped into four subsidiary companies of GIC viz. the National Insurance Company Ltd. ("National Co."), the New India Assurance Company Ltd. ("New India Co."), the Oriental Insurance Company Ltd. ("Oriental Co."), and the United India Assurance Company Ltd. ("United Co."). GIC undertakes mainly re-insurance business apart from aviation insurance. The bulk of the general insurance business of fire, marine, motor and miscellaneous insurance business is under taken by the four subsidiaries.

Since 1956, with the nationalization of insurance industry, the LIC held the monopoly in India's life insurance sector. GIC, with its four subsidiaries, enjoyed the monopoly for general insurance business. Both LIC and GIC have played a significant role in the development of the insurance market in India and in providing insurance coverage in India through an extensive network. For example, currently, the LIC has a network of 7 zones, 100 divisions and over 2,000 branches. LIC has over 550,000 agents and over 100 million lives are covered.

From 1991 onwards, the Indian Government introduced various reforms in the financial sector paving the way for the liberalization of the Indian economy. It was a matter of time before this liberalization affected the insurance sector. A huge gap in the funds required for infrastructure was felt particularly since much of these funds could be filled by life insurance funds, being long tenure funds.

Consequently, in 1993, the Government of India set up an eight-member committee chaired by Mr. R. N. Malhotra, a former Governor of India's apex bank, the Reserve Bank of India to review the prevailing structure of regulation and supervision of the insurance sector and to make recommendations for strengthening and modernizing the regulatory system. The Committee submitted its report to the Indian Government in January 1994. Two of the key recommendations of the Committee included the privatization of the insurance sector by permitting the entry of private players to enter the business of life and general insurance and the establishment of an Insurance Regulatory Authority.

It took a number of years for the Indian Government to implement the recommendations of the Malhotra Committee. The Indian Parliament passed the Insurance Regulatory and Development Act, 1999 ("IRD Act") on December 2, 1999 with the aim "to provide for the establishment of an Authority, to protect the interests of the policy holders, to regulate, promote and ensure orderly growth of the insurance industry and to amend the Insurance Act, 1938, the Life Insurance Corporation Act, 1956 and the General Insurance Business (Nationalization) Act, 1972". The IRD Act has established the Insurance Regulatory and Development Authority ("IRDA" or "Authority") as a statutory regulator to regulate and promote the insurance industry in India and to protect the interests of holders of insurance policies. The IRD Act also carried out a series of amendments to the Act of 1938 and conferred the powers of the Controller of Insurance on the IRDA.

The members of the IRDA are appointed by the Central Government from amongst persons of ability, integrity and standing who have knowledge or experience in life insurance, general insurance, actuarial science, finance, economics, law, accountancy, administration etc. The Authority consists of a chairperson, not more than five whole-time members and not more than four part-time members.

The Authority has been entrusted with the duty to regulate, promote and ensure the orderly growth of the insurance and re-insurance business in India.

In furtherance of this responsibility, it has been conferred with numerous powers and functions which include prescribing regulations on the investments of funds by insurance companies, regulating maintenance of the margin of solvency, adjudication of disputes between insurers and intermediaries, supervising the functioning of the Tariff Advisory Committee, specifying the percentage of premium income of the insurer to finance schemes for promoting and regulating professional organizations and specifying the percentage of life insurance business and general insurance business to be undertaken by the insurer in the rural or social sector.

The Tariff Advisory Committee ("Advisory Committee") is a body corporate, which controls and regulates the rates, advantages, terms and conditions offered by insurers in the general insurance business.

The Advisory Committee has the authority to require any insurer to supply such information or statements necessary for discharge of its functions. Any insurer f ailing to comply with such provisions shall be deemed to have contravened the provisions of the Insurance Act. Every insurer is required to make an annual payment of fees to the Advisory Committee of an amount not exceeding in case of reinsurance business in India, one percent of the total premiums in respect of facultative insurance accepted by him in India; and in case of any other insurance business, one percent of the total gross premium written direct by him in India.

All insurers and provident societies incorporated or domiciled in India are members of the Insurance Association of India ("Insurance Association") and all insurers and provident societies incorporated or domiciled elsewhere than in India are associate members of the Insurance Association. There are two councils of the Insurance Association, namely the Life Insurance Council and the General Insurance Council. The Life Insurance Council, through its Executive Committee, conducts examinations for individuals wising to qualify themselves as insurance agents. It also fixes the limits for actual expenses by which the insurer carrying on life insurance business or any group of insurers can exceed from the prescribed limits under the Insurance Act. Likewise, the General Insurance Council, through its Executive Committee, may fix the limits by which the actual expenses of management incurred by an insurer carrying on general insurance business may exceed the limits as prescribed in the Insurance Act.

The Ombudsmen are appointed in accordance with the Redressal of Public Grievances Rules, 1998, to resolve all complaints relating to settlement of claims on the part of insurance companies in a cost-effective, efficient and effective manner. Any person who has a grievance against an insurer may make a complaint to an Ombudsman within his jurisdiction, in the manner specified. However, prior to making a complaint, such person should have made a representation to the insurer and either the insurer has rejected the complaint or has not replied to it. Further, the complaint should be made not later than a year from the date of rejection of the complaint by the insurer and should not be any other proceedings pending in any other court, Consumer Forum or arbitrator pending on the same subject matter. The Ombudsmen are also empowered to receive and consider any partial or total repudiation of claims by an insurer, any dispute in regard to the premium paid in terms of the policy, any dispute on the legal construction of the policies in as much such a dispute relates to claims, delay in settlement of claims and the non-issue of any insurance document to customers after receipt of premium.

The Ombudsmen act as a counsellor and mediator and make recommendations to both par ties in the event that the complaint is settled by agreement between both the parties. However, if the complaint is not settled by agreement, the Ombudsman may pass an award of compensation within three months of the complaint, which shall not be in excess of which is necessary to cover the loss suffered by the complainant as a direct consequence of the insured peril, or for an amount not exceeding rupees two million (including ex gratia and other expenses), whichever is lower. Ombudsman within his jurisdiction, in the manner specified. However, prior to making a complaint, such person should have made a representation to the insurer and either the insurer has rejected the complaint or has not replied to it.

Further, the complaint should be made not later than a year from the date of rejection of the complaint by the insurer and should not be any other proceedings pending in any other court, Consumer Forum or arbitrator pending on the same subject matter. The Ombudsmen are also empowered to receive and consider any partial or total repudiation of claims by an insurer, any dispute in regard to the premium paid in terms of the policy, any dispute on the legal construction of the policies in as much such a dispute relates to claims, delay in settlement of claims and the non-issue of any insurance document to customers after receipt of premium. The Ombudsmen act as a counsellor and mediator and make recommendations to both par ties in the event that the complaint is settled by agreement between both the parties. However, if the complaint is not settled by agreement, the Ombudsman may pass an award of compensation within three months of the complaint, which shall not be in excess of which is necessary to cover the loss suffered by the complainant as a direct consequence of the insured peril, or for an amount not exceeding rupees two million (including exgratia and other expenses), whichever is lower.

Every insurer seeking to carry out the business of insurance in India is required to obtain a certificate of registration from the IRDA prior to commencement of business. The pre-conditions for applying for such registration have been set out under the Act of 1938, the IRD Act and the various regulations prescribed by the Authority.

The following are some of the import ant general registration requirements that an applicant would need to fulfil:

(a) The applicant would need to be a company registered under the provisions of the Indian Companies Act, 1956. Consequently, any person intending to carry on insurance business in India would need to set up a separate entity in India.

(b) The aggregate equity participation of a foreign company (either by itself or through its subsidiary companies or its nominees) in the applicant company cannot not exceed twenty six per cent of the paid up capital of the insurance company. However, the Insurance Act and the regulations there under provide for the manner of computation of such twenty-six per cent.

(c) The applicant can carry on any one of life insurance business, general insurance business or reinsurance business. Separate companies would be needed if the intent were to conduct more than one business.

(d) The name of the applicant needs to contain the words "insurance company" or "assurance company".

The applicant would need to meet with the following capital structure requirements:

(a) A minimum paid up equity capital of rupees one billion in case of an applicant which seeks to carry on the business of life insurance or general insurance.

(b) A minimum paid-up equity capital of rupees two billion, in case of a person carrying on exclusively the business of reinsurance.

In determining the aforesaid capital requirement, the deposits to be made and any preliminary expenses incurred in the formation and registration of the company would be included. A "promoter" of the company is not permitted to hold, at any time, more than twenty-six per cent of the paid-up capital in any Indian insurance company. However, an interim measure has been permitted percentages higher than twenty six percent are permitted if the promoters divest, in a phased manner, over a period of ten years from the date of commencement of business, the share capital held by them in excess of twenty six per cent.

An applicant desiring to carry on insurance business in India is required to make a requisition for a registration application to the IRDA in a prescribed format along with all the relevant documents. The applicant is required to make a separate requisition for registration for each class of business i.e. life insurance business consisting of linked business, non-linked business or both, or general insurance business including health insurance business.

The IRDA may accept the requisition on being satisfied of the bonafides of the applicant, the completeness of the application and that the applicant will carry on all the functions in respect of the insurance business including management of investments *etc*. In the event that the aforesaid requirements are not met with, the Authority may after giving the applicant a reasonable opportunity of being heard, reject the requisition. Thereafter, the applicant may apply to the Authority within thirty days of such rejection for re-consideration of its decision. Additionally, an applicant whose requisition for registration has been rejected, may approach the Authority with a fresh request for registration application after a period of two years from the date of rejection, with a new set of promoters and for a class of insurance business different than the one originally applied for.

In the event that the Authority accepts the requisition for registration application, it shall direct supply of the application for registration to the applicant. An applicant, whose requisition has been accepted, may make an application along with the relevant documents evidencing deposit, capital and other requirements in the prescribed form for grant of a certificate of registration. If, when considering an application, it appears to the Authority that the assured rates, advantages, terms and conditions offered or to be offered in connection with life insurance business are in any respect not workable or sound, he may require that a statement thereof to be submitted to an actuary appointed by the insurer and the Authority shall order the insurer to make such modifications as reported by the actuary. After consideration of the matters *inter alia* capital structure, record of performance of each promoters and directors and planned infrastructure of the company, the Authority may grant the certificate of registration. The Authority would, however, give preference in grant of certificate of registration to those applicants who propose to carry on the business of providing health covers to individuals or groups of individuals. An applicant granted a certificate of registration may commence the insurance business within twelve months from the date of registration. In the event that the Authority rejects the application for registration, the applicant aggrieved by the decision of the Authority may within a period of thirty days from the date of communication of such rejection, appeal to the Central Government for reconsideration of the decision and the decision of the Central Government in this regard would be final.

An insurer who has been granted a certificate of registration should renew the registration before 1st the 31 day of December each year, and such application should be accompanied by evidence of fees that should be the higher of-

- fifty thousand rupees for each class of insurance business, and
- one fifth of one per cent of total gross premium writ ten direct by an insurer in India during the financial year preceding the year in which the application for renewal of certificate is required to be made, or the application for renewal of certificate is required to be made, or rupees fifty million whichever is less; (and in case of an insurer carrying on solely re-insurance business, instead of the total gross premium written direct in India, the total premium in respect of facultative re-insurance accepted by him in India shall be taken into account).

This fee may vary according to the total gross premium writ ten direct in India, during the year preceding the year in which the application is required to be made by the insurer in the class of insurance business to which the registration relates but shall not exceed one-fourth of one percent of such premium income or rupees fifty million, whichever is less, or be less, in any case than fifty thousand rupees for each class of insurance business.

However, in the case of an insurer carrying on solely re-insurance business, the total premiums in respect of facultative re-insurance accepted by him in India shall be taken into account.

The registration of an Indian insurance company or insurer may be suspended for a class or classes of insurance business, in addition to any penalty that may be imposed or any action that may be taken, for such period as may be specified by the Authority, in the following cases:

- conducts its business in a manner prejudicial to the interests of the policy-holders;
- fails to furnish any information as required by the Authority relating to its insurance business;
- does not submit periodical returns as required under the Act or by the Authority;
- does not co-operate in any inquiry conducted by the Authority;
- indulges in manipulating the insurance business;
- fails to make investment in the infrastructure or social sector as specified under the Insurance Act.

The Authority, in case of repeated defaults of the grounds for suspension of a certificate of registration, may impose a penalty in the form of cancellation of the certificate. The Authority is compulsorily required to cancel the registration of an insurer either wholly or in so far as it relates to a particular class of insurance business, as the case may be:

- if the insurer fails to comply with the provisions relating to deposits; or
- if the insurer fails, at any time, to comply wit h the provisions relating to the excess of the value of his assets over the amount of his liabilities; or
- if the insurer is in liquidation or is adjudged an insolvent; or
- if the business or a class of the business of the insurer has been transferred to any person or has been transferred to or amalgamated with the business of any other insurer; or
- if the whole of the deposit made in respect of the insurance business has been returned to the insurer;
- if, in the case of an insurer, the standing contract is cancelled or is suspended and continues to be suspended for a period of six months, or
- if the Central Government of India so directs.

In addition to the above, the Authority has the discretion to cancel the registration of an insurer · if the insurer makes default in complying with, or acts in contravention of, any requirement of the Insurance Act or of any rule or any regulation or order made or, any direction issued thereunder, or

- if the Authority has reason to believe that nay claim upon the insurer arising in India under any policy of insurance remains unpaid for three months after final judgment in regular course of law, or
- if the insurer carries on any business other than insurance business or any prescribed business, or
- if the insurer makes a default in complying with any direct ion issued or order made, as the case may be, by the Authority under the IRDA Act, 1999.
- If the insurer makes a default in complying with, or acts in contravention of, any requirement of the Companies Act, or the LIC Act, or the GIC Act or the Foreign Exchange Management Act, 2000.

The order of cancellation shall take effect on the date on which notice of the order of cancellation is served on the insurer. Thereafter, the insurer would be prohibited from entering into any new contracts of insurance, but all rights and liabilities in respect of contracts of insurance entered into by him before the cancellation takes effect shall continue as if the cancellation had not taken place. The Authority may, aft er the expiry of six months from the date on which the cancellation order takes effect, apply to the Court for an order to wind up the insurance company, or to wind up the affairs of the company in respect of a class of insurance business, unless the registration of the insurance company has been revived or an application for winding up has already been presented to the Court.

The Authority has a discretion, where the registration of an insurer has been cancelled, to revive the registration, if the insurer within six months from the date on which the cancellation took effect:

- makes the deposits, or

- complies with the provisions as to the excess of the value of his assets over the amount of his liabilities, or
- has his standing contract restored, or
- has the application accepted, or
- satisfies the Authority that no claim upon him remains unpaid, or
- has complied with any requirements of the Insurance Act or the IRDA Act, or any rule or regulation, or any order made thereunder or any direct ion issued under these Acts, or
- tha the has ceased to carry on any business other than insurance business or any prescribed business.

The main regulations that regulate the insurance business are the Insurance Act, 1938, the Life Insurance Corporation Act, 1956, the General Insurance Business (Nationalisation) Act, 1982, the Marine Insurance Act, 1963 and the Motor Vehicles Act, 1988. The Indian Contract Act, 1872, governs most of the aspects of the insurance contract. Additionally, the Foreign Exchange Management Act, 2000, Income Tax Act, 1961, Indian Stamp Act and the Hindu and Indian Succession Act govern some aspects involved in insurance. Every insurer should, in respect of the insurance business carried on by him in India, deposit with the Reserve Bank of India ("RBI") for and on behalf of the Central Government of India the following amounts, either in cash or in approved securities estimated at the market value of the securities on the day of deposit, or partly in cash and partly in approved securities:

- in the case of life insurance business, a sum equivalent to one per cent of his total gross premiumst written in India in any financial year commencing after the 31 day of March, 2000, not exceeding rupees hundred million;
- in the case of general insurance business, a sum equivalent to three per cent of his total gross stpremium written in India, in any financial year commencing after the 31 day of March, 2000, not exceeding rupees hundred million;

- in the case of re-insurance business, a sum of rupees two hundred million.

If business done or to be done is marine insurance only and relates exclusively to country craft or its cargo or both, only rupees one hundred thousand should be deposited with the RBI.

These deposits will be held by the RBI though for the credit of the insurer and are returnable to the insurer in the event the provisions of the Insurance Act mandate such return. Interest accruing, due and collected on deposited securities will be paid to the insurer, subject to any deductions of the normal commission chargeable for the realization of interest. In addition, it is import ant to note that the deposits will:

- not be susceptible to any assignment or charge; or
- not be available for the discharge of any liability of the insurer other than liabilities arising out of policies of insurance issued by the insurer so long as any such liabilities remain undischarged, or
- not be liable to attachment in execution of any decree except a decree obtained by a policy-holder of the insurer in respect of a debt due upon a policy which debt the policy-holder has failed to realize in any other way.

Where the insurer has ceased to carry on all classes of insurance business in India, the deposit made with the RBI shall, on an application being made to the Court, be returned to the insurer after satisfaction of all his liabilities in India in respect of all classes of insurance business. Every insurer is required to invest and keep invested certain amount of assets as determined under the Insurance Act. The funds of the policyholders cannot be invested (directly or indirectly) outside India.

An insurer involved in the business of life insurance is required to invest and keep invested at all times assets, the value of which is not less than the sum of the amount of its liabilities to holders of life insurance policies in India on account of matured claims and the amount required to meet the liability on policies of life insurance maturing for payment in India, reduced by the amount of premiums which have fallen due to the insurer on such policies but have not been paid and the days of grace for payment of which have not expired and any amount due to the insurer for loans granted on and within the surrender values of policies of life insurance maturing for payment in India issued by him or by an insurer whose business he has acquired and in respect of which he has assumed liability.

Every insurer carrying on the business of life insurance is required to invest and at all times keep invested his controlled fund (other than funds relating to pensions and general annuity business and unit linked life insurance business) in the following manner, free of any encumbrance, charge, hypothecation or lien:

For the purposes of calculating the investments, the amount of deposits made with the RBI by the insurer in respect of his life insurance business shall be deemed to be assets invested in Government securities. In computing the assets to be invested by the insurer, any investment made with reference to the currency other than the Indian rupee which is in excess of the amount required to meet the liabilities of the insurer in India with reference to that currency to the extent of such excess and any investment made in purchase of any immovable property outside India or on account of any such property shall not be taken into account.

Further, an insurer should not out of his controlled fund invest any sum in the shares or debentures of any private limited company. Where an insurer has accepted reassurance in respect of any policies of life insurance issued by another insurer and maturing for payment in India or has ceded reassurance to another insurer in respect of any such policies issued by himself, the assets to be invested by the insurer shall be increased by the amount of the liability involved in such acceptance and decreased by the amount of the liability involved in such cession.

In case of an insurer incorporated or domiciled outside India or an insurer incorporated in India whose share capital to the extent of one-third is owned by, or the members of whose governing body to the extent of one-third consists of members domiciled elsewhere than in India, the assets required to be invested should, (except to the extent of any part which consists of foreign assets held outside India) be held in India by way of a trust for the discharge of the liabilities.

Every Insurer shall invest and at all times keep invested his segregated fund of unit linked life insurance business as per pattern of investment offered to and approved by the policy-holders. The insurer is permitted to offer unit linked policies only where the units are linked to categories of assets that are both marketable and easily realizable. However, the total investment in other approved category of investments should at not time exceed twenty five per cent of the fund. An insurer carrying on general insurance business is required to invest and keep invested at all times his total assets in approved securities in the following manner:

Every insurer is required to invest and at all times keep invested assets of pension business, general annuity business and group business in the following manner:

Every re-insurer carrying on re-insurance business in India is required to invest and at all times keep invested his total assets in the same manner as specified for the general insurance business. An insurer should maintain, at all times, an excess of the value of his assets over the amount of his liabilities of not less than the relevant amount arrived at in the following manner ("required solvency margin"):

(a) in the case of an insurer carrying on life insurance business, the required solvency margin shall be the higher of rupees five hundred million (one billion in case of re-insurers) or the aggregate sum arrived at based on the calculations specified in the Insurance Act.

(b) in the case of an insurer carrying on general insurance business, the required solvency margin, shall be the highest of the following amounts:-

(i) rupees five hundred million (rupees one billion in case of a re-insurer); or

(ii) a sum equivalent to twenty per cent of net premium income; or

(iii) a sum equivalent to thirty per cent of net incurred claims.

This shall be subject to credit for re-insurance in computing net premiums and net incurred claims being actual but a percentage, determined by the regulations, not exceeding fifty per cent.

An insurer who fails to maintain the required solvency margin will be deemed to be insolvent and may be wound up by the court. An insurer is required under the IRDA (Assets, Liabilities and Solvency Margin of Insurers) Regulations, 2000, to prepare a statement of solvency margin in accordance with Schedule III-A, in respect of life insurance business, and in Form KG in accordance with Schedule III-B, in respect of general insurance business, as the case may be.

Every insurer is required to prepare a statement of the value of assets in accordance with the provisions of the aforesaid regulations. Every insurer should prepare a statement of the amount of liabilities in accordance with the provisions of Schedule II-A of the aforesaid regulations, in respect of the life insurance business, and in Form HG in accordance with Schedule II-B, in respect of the general insurance business. The aforesaid forms should be furnished separately for business within India and the total business transacted by the insurer.

In the event that an insurer transacts insurance business in a country outside India and submits the statements or returns or any such particulars to a public Authority of that country, he is required to enclose such particulars along with the Forms specified in the aforesaid regulations and the IRDA (Actuarial Report and Abstract) Regulations, 2000.

Every insurer should submit to the Authority the following returns, showing that as of 31 day of December of the preceding year the assets held and invested, investments made out of the controlled fund and all other particulars necessary to establish that the requirements of the Insurance Act have been complied with.

An insurer carrying on the business of insurance or reinsurance in India is required, under the IRDA (Appointed Actuary) Regulations, 2000, to appoint a person fulfilling the eligibility requirements, to act as an appointed actuary, after seeking the approval of the Authority in this regard.

It is mandatory for an insurer carrying on the business of life insurance in India to appoint any actuary. An appointed actuary has access to all such information and documents of an insurer for the performance of his duties and obligations. An appointed actuary may also attend the meetings of the insurer and discuss matters related to the actuarial advice and solvency of margin.

An appointed actuary, in addition to rendering actuarial advice to insurer (in particular in the areas of product design and pricing, insurance contract wording, investments and reinsurance), is also required *inter alia* to ensure the solvency of the insurer at all times, certify the assets and liabilities that have been valued and maintain the solvency margin.

In case the insurer is carrying on life insurance business, an appointed actuary should also *inter alia*-

- certify the actuarial report, abstract and other returns required under the Insurance Act,
- comply with the provisions wit h respect to the bases of premium,
- comply with the provisions with respect to recommendation of interim bonus or bonuses payable by the life insurer to policyholders whose policies mature for payment by reason of death or otherwise during the inter-valuation period, and
- ensure that the policyholders' reasonable expectations have been considered in the matter of valuation of liabilities and distribution of surplus to the participating policyholders who are entitled for a share of surplus.

In case of an insurer carrying on general insurance business in India, the appointed actuary is required to ensure that the rates are fair in respect of those contracts that are governed by the insurer's in-house tariff and that the actuarial principles, in the determination of liabilities, have been used in the calculation of reserves for incurred but not reported claims and other reserves where actuarial advice is sought by the Authority.

Every insurer carrying on life insurance business should every year cause an investigation to be carried out by an actuary with respect to financial condition of the life insurance business, including a valuation of his liabilities and should cause an abstract of the report to be made. This provision shall apply in the event that an investigation into the financial condition of the insurer is made with a view to the distribution of profits or an investigation is made of which the results are made public.

The IRDA (Insurance Advertisements) Regulations, 2000, seeks to regulate and control every insurance advertisement issued by the insurer, intermediary or insurance agent. For this purpose, every insurer, intermediary or insurance agent is required to establish and maintain a system of control over the content, form and method of dissemination of all advertisements concerning its policies and such advertisement should be filed with the Authority as soon as it is first issued.

An advertisement issued by an insurer should not fall in the category of an unfair or misleading advertisement. An '*unfair or misleading advertisement*' means and includes any advertisement:

- that fails to clearly identify the product as insurance;
- makes claims beyond the ability of the policy to deliver or beyond the reasonable expectation of performance;
- describes benefits that do not match the policy provisions;
- uses words or phrases in a way which hides or minimizes the costs of the hazard insured against or the risks inherent in the policy;
- omits to disclose or discloses insufficiently, important exclusions, limitations and conditions of the contract;
- gives information in a misleading way;

- illustrates future benefits on assumptions which are not realistic nor realizable in the light of the insurer's current performance;
- where the benefits are not guaranteed, does not explicitly say so as prominently as the benefits are stated or says so in manner or form that it could remain unnoticed;
- implies a group or other relationship like sponsorship, affiliation or approval, that does not exist;
- makes unfair or incomplete comparisons with products which are not comparable or disparages competitors.

Every advertisement should disclose the full particulars and identity of the insurer, and that insurance is the subject matter of solicitation. In the event that such advertisement describes any benefits, the form number of the policy and the type of coverage should be fully disclosed. In case of Internet advertisements, the website or portal of the insurer or intermediary should contain disclosure statements which outline the site's specific policies vis-à-vis the privacy of personal information for the protection of both their own businesses and the consumers they serve and should also display the registration or license numbers.

In addition to these requirements, every insurer or intermediary is also required to follow recognized standards of professional conduct as prescribed by the Advertisement Standards Council of India.

If an advertisement is not in compliance with the aforesaid regulations, the Authority may take action in one or more of the following ways:

- issue a letter to the advertiser seeking information within a specific time, not being more than ten days from the date of issue of the letter;
- direct the advertiser to correct or modify the advertisement already issued in a manner suggested by the Authority with a stipulation that the corrected or modified advertisement shall receive the same type of publicity as the one sought to be corrected or modified;

- direct the advertiser to discontinue the advertisement;
- any other action deemed fit by the Authority, keeping in view the circumstances of the case, to ensure that the interests of the public are protected.

Every insurer who begins to carry on the business of insurance in India should ensure that he undertakes the following obligations to provide life insurance or general insurance policies, during the first five financial years, to the persons residing in the rural sector or social sector, workers in the unorganised or informal sector or for economically vulnerable or backward classes of the society and other categories of persons and such insurance policies shall include insurance for crops.

A policy of insurance is a contract of a personal nature and hence cannot be transferred by the insured without the consent of the insurer. In the case of life and personal accident insurances, the subject matter of the insurance is a life and is not amenable to transfer. An assignment of the policy in such cases is just an assignment of the right to receive the proceeds of the policy. The Insurance Act lays down the mode of assignment and transfer of a life insurance policy. An assignment or transfer may be made only on satisfaction of the following conditions:

(i) an endorsement upon the policy itself or by a separate instrument;

(ii) the endorsement or instrument should be signed by the transferor or his agent and should be attested by at least one witness;

(iii) it should specifically set forth the fact of transfer or assignment.

The aforesaid conditions need to be complied with irrespective whether the transfer or assignment is made without consideration or not. The insurer, on being given notice of the assignment or transfer, shall recognize the assignee or transferee as the only person entitled to the benefit of the policy and such a person shall also be subject to all the liabilities and equities to which the transferor or assignor was subject to.Additionally, an assignment may be (a) absolute, or (b) conditional that it shall be inoperative or that the interest shall pass to some other person on the happening of a specific event during the lifetime of the person insured, or (c) in favour of the survivor or survivors of a number of persons. However, the term "policy holder" does not include an assignee whose inter est in the policy is defeasible or is for the time being subject to any condition. Hence, an assignee of a policy subject to any condition shall not be entitled to the rights of a policy holder.

A policy holder of a life insurance policy on his own life has the right, either while effecting the policy or before it matures, to nominate a person to whom the money secured by the policy should be paid in the event of the death of the policy holder. An insurer is not bound by such nomination unless it is brought to his notice, endorsed on the policy and registered in the records of the policy. It is pertinent to not e that a transfer of assignment of a policy automatically leads to cancellation of a nomination. Additionally, these provisions relating to nomination under the Insurance Act do not 16 apply to any policies under the Married Women's Property Act, 1874. The Reserve Bank of India ("**RBI**") is the apex bank of India established in 1935 under the Reserve Bank of India Act, 1934.

The Exchange Control Department within the RBI is responsible for the regulation and enforcement of exchange controls. Prior to 1999, India had stringent exchange control regulations under the Foreign Exchange Regulation Act, 1973 ("FERA"). The Foreign Direct Investment ("FDI") regime in India has been progressively liberalized in the nineties with the passage of the Foreign Exchange Management Act, 1999 ("FEMA"), which replaced FERA. Most restrictions on foreign investment have been removed and the procedures have been simplified. Non-residents can invest directly in India, either wholly or as a joint venture. Foreign investment is allowed in virtually all sectors including the services sect or, subject to Government permission in certain cases. Insurance companies that are registered with the IRDA, are permitted to issue general insurance policies denominated in foreign currency and are also permitted to receive premiums in foreign currency without the prior approval of the RBI. However, this is permitted only for certain kinds of cases such as marine insurance for vessels owned by foreign shipping companies and chartered by Indian companies, aviation insurance for aircrafts imported from outside India on lease/hire basis for the purpose of air taxi operations *etc.*

Authorised dealers are also permitted to settle claims in foreign currency on general insurance policies subject to certain conditions such as the claim has been made for the loss occurred during the policy period, the claim has been settled as per the surveyors report and other substantiating documents, claims on account of reinsurance are being lodged with the reinsurers and will be received as per the reinsurance agreement, the remittance is being made to the non-resident beneficiary under the policy *etc.* However, in the case of resident beneficiaries, the claim is required to be settled in rupee equivalent of the foreign currency due and under no circumstances can payment be made in foreign currency to a resident beneficiary.

As per the provisions of the Foreign Exchange Management (Insurance) Regulations, 2000, no person resident in India is permitted to take any general or life insurance policy issued by an insurer outside India. However, the RBI may permit, for sufficient reasons, a resident in India to take any life insurance policy issued by an insurer outside India. However, an exemption has recently been made only for units located in Special Economic Zones ("**SEZs**") for general insurance policies taken by such units. Therefore, remittances towards premium for general insurance policies taken out by units located in SEZs from insurers outside India are permitted provided that the premiums are paid out of the foreign exchange balances.

A person resident in India but not permanently resident therein is permitted to continue holding any insurance policy issued to him by an insurer outside India, if the premium on such policy is paid out of foreign currency resources outside India. A person resident in India may take a general insurance policy issued by an insurer outside India, provided that, before taking the policy he has obtained a no objection certificate from the Central Government of India. Further, a person resident in India is also permitted to continue to hold any insurance policy issued by an insurer outside India when such person was resident outside India, subject to fulfilment of certain conditions. A foreign company may enter the insurance business in India in either of the following ways:

- FDI is permitted in India primarily either under the 'automatic route', or with prior government approval. Where FDI does not fall under the 'automatic route', the foreign invest or would require the approval from the Foreign Investment Promotion Board ("FIPB"). Indian companies are generally permitted to accept FDI without prior approval, provided certain sectoral policies and investment limits are met. In the insurance sector there is 26% sectoral cap on FDI, subject to obtaining license from the IRDA, which means that a foreign company can invest up to only 26% in an Indian insurance company (calculated in the manner specified in the Insurance Act and regulations thereunder), while 74% would have to be invested by an Indian company.
- In the event that a foreign insurance company is not desirous of directly investing in an Indian insurance company, it may, in the beginning, set up a branch or liaison office, subject to the approval of the RBI and/or the Government of India in this regard. The branch office in India is permitted to under take only a certain set of activities such as carrying our research work for the parent company, representing the parent company in India etc. A liaison office is also permitted to under take only a certain set of activities such as acting as a communication channel between the parent company and Indian companies. Insurance companies and insurance agents, in India, are subject to tax for the premiums and the commissions received by them respectively, under the Indian Income Tax Act, 1963 ("Income Tax Act").

The Income Tax Act deals with the computation of the income of the following insurance companies:

- Companies carrying on life insurance business which are resident in India;
- Companies carrying on any other kind of insurance business, which are resident in India; and
- Non-resident persons carrying on the business of insurance in India through a branch.

There is no recognized business method of ascertaining the profits derived from life insurance business. This would depend on the actuarial calculations and valuations. The Income Tax Act lays down provisions with respect to the income received by an assessee from the business of insurance, whether the company which receives such business income is resident in India or not. These special provisions exclude the operation of other sections under the Income Tax Act dealing with computation of income. Therefore, the profits and gains from the insurance business are to be computed artificially in accordance with these rules. The First Schedule of the Income Tax Act overrides the other provisions relating to computation of income under separate and distinctheads of income.

The income is therefore, not to be computed under the different heads and in accordance with the provisions of the Income Tax Act, but the income from all the sources should be computed as one figure on the basis laid down in this schedule.

The profits and loss of a person carrying on the business of insurance are to be computed separately from the profits and gains from any other business. Though the profits of life insurance business are to be computed separately from the profits of non-life insurance business or other business carried on by the assessee, any loss incurred in life insurance business can be set off against profits of non-life insurance business or other business. In computing the profits of life insurance business, the profits and gains of the business is taken to be the annual average of the "surplus".

This surplus is arrived at by adjusting the surplus or deficit disclosed by the actuarial valuation made in respect of the last inter-valuation period ending before the commencement of the assessment year. The tax payable, computed in the manner stated above, will be reduced by tax withheld at source for income from interest on securities in respect of annual average of income tax. In computing the profits of any business other than life insurance, the profits and gains is taken to be the balance of the profits disclosed in the annual accounts. In case of non-resident companies carrying on the business of insurance in India, in the absence of reliable data, the profits and gains is taken to be that proportion of the world income which corresponds to the proportion of the premium income derived from India. A branch of a foreign insurance company is subject to income tax at the rate of 42% (including 5% surcharge on tax) while a subsidiary of a foreign insurance company is subject to tax at the rate of 38.75% (including 5% surcharge on tax).

The Finance Act, 2002 has brought insurance within the service tax net. The insured is thus liable to pay service tax at the rate of 5%. The Income Tax Act provides that the income tax payable on the profits and gains arising from the life insurance business will be calculated at the rate of 12.5% of such profits and gains. An insurance company is required to deposit an amount equal to one-third of the tax, in a Social Security Fund as notified by the Central Government.

Further, the insurance company is required to deposit an amount of not less than 2.5% of the profits and gains of the insurance business in such a Security Fund. Where the insurance company has deposited such an amount, the income tax payable by the insurance company will be reduced by that amount and the amount to be deposited in the Security Fund would also be calculated on the income tax so reduced. The Income Tax Act has laid down provisions for the taxation of insurance commissions. 'Insurance Commission' has been defined to mean any income (remuneration or reward) by way of commission or otherwise for soliciting or procuring insurance business. The effect of the provision is that any person responsible for paying any such income to a resident individual will be required to deduct income tax at the prescribed rates. The provision applies only in the event that the individual is a resident of India. This provision is not applicable for an individual who is not a resident of India. Tax for such payments made to a non-resident will have to be deducted under in accordance with the provisions of Section 195 of the Income Tax Act.

An insurance policy needs to be duly stamped in accordance with the stamp duty prescribed for each kind of policy under the Indian Stamp Act, 1899 ("Stamp Act"). The rates of stamp duty on insurance policies are the same throughout the territories of India. Generally, the stamp duty on a life insurance policy or group insurance is borne by the person effecting the insurance. In the case of a fire insurance policy, the insurer is liable to bear the stamp duty. Non-payment of stamp duty, is a punishable offence with a fine which may extend up to rupees two hundred if an insurer receives the premium for an insurance policy and does not execute a policy or executes a policy which is not stamped. All persons who desire to act as an insurance agent for any insurer would have to be registered as such under the provisions of the Insurance Act and the IRDA (Licensing of Agents) Regulations, 2000. A license issued under the provisions of the Insurance Act entitles the holder to act as an insurance agent for any insurer.

Any person ("applicant"), desirous of being an insurance agent or a composite insurance agent, may make an application for a license to act as an insurance agent to the Authority. The applicant should possess the minimum qualifications of twelfth standard or equivalent examination conducted by any recognized Board or institution, in cases where the applicant resides in a place with a population of five thousand or more as per the last census; and passed the tenth standard or equivalent examination from a recognized Board or institution if the applicant resides in any other place. Such an applicant should also not suffer from any of the following disqualifications:

- that the person is a minor;
- that he is found to be of unsound mind by a Court of competent jurisdiction;
- that he is found guilty of criminal misappropriation or criminal breach of trust or cheating or forgery or an abetment of or attempt to commit any such offence by a Court of competent jurisdiction.

- Provided that where at least five years have elapsed since the completion of the sentence imposed on any person in respect of such person that his conviction shall cease to operate as a disqualification;
- that in the course of any judicial proceeding relating to any policy of insurance or the winding up of an insurance company or in the course of an investigation of the affairs of an insurer it has been found that he has been guilty of or has knowingly participated in or connived at any fraud, dishonesty or misrepresentation against an insurer or an insured;
- that he does not possess the requisite qualifications and practical training for a period not exceeding twelve months;
- that he has not passed the examination;
- that he violates the code of conduct.

However, any license that had been issued prior to the commencement of the IRDA Act, 1999 shall be deemed to have been issued in accordance with the IRDA (Licensing of Agents) Regulations, 2000 and the provisions of the regulation in relation to the practical training, qualifications and examination shall not be applicable to such existing insurance agents. No insurance agent can be paid by way of commission or as remuneration, in any form, an amount exceeding,-

- in case of life insurance business, forty per cent of the first year's premium payable on any policy or policies effected through him and five per cent of a renewal premium payable on such a policy. However, the insurer may, during the first ten years of their business, pay fifty-five per cent of the first years' premium payable on any policy or policies effected through them and six per cent of the renewal premiums payable on such policies.
- in the case of business of any other class, fifteen per cent of the premium. An insurance surveyor is a technical expert who inspects the damage or loss of an insurance

company. The insurer, based on the estimation of damage of the surveyor, arrives at the amount of compensation payable to the assured.

Every individual, who intends to act as a surveyor and loss assessor in respect of the general insurance business, may make an application to the Authority for a license. The Authority may grant a license (which shall be valid for a period of five years) after he is satisfied that the applicant:

(i) satisfies all the applicable requirements of the Insurance Act and rules thereunder;

(ii) has furnished evidence of payment of fees for grant of license, depending upon the categorization;

(iii) has undergone a period of practical training, not exceeding twelve months; and

(iv) any other information that may be required by the Authority.

A surveyor and loss assessor is required to spend a major part of his time in investigating and managing losses arising from any contingency and prepare reports. He is required to carry out his duties in compliance with the code of conduct.

A surveyor and loss assessor has inter alia the duty and responsibility to ensure that he discloses whether he has any interest in the subject matter in question or whether it pertains to any of his relatives, business partners or through material shareholding; or maintaining confidentiality and neutrality without jeopardizing the liability of the insurer and claim of the insured; or conducting inspection and re-inspection of the property in question suffering a loss; or recommending applicability of depreciation, or the percentage and quantum of depreciation etc. Under the provisions of the IRDA (Third Party Administrators Health services) Regulations, 2001, ("TPA Regulations") the Third Party Administrator ("TPA") means a third party administrator, who has obtained a license from the Authority, and is engaged for a fee or remuneration, as specified in the agreement with the insurance company, for the provision of health services.

An insurance company may engage more than one TPA and similarly, one TPA may serve more than one insurance company. The TPA is required to maintain professional confidentiality of records, books, evidence etc. of all transactions that it carries out. In addition, the TPA is required to furnish to the insurance company and the Authority, an annual report and any other return as may be required by the Authority.

The TPA is prohibited from charging the policyholders with any separate fees. Only a company, with a share capital and registered under the Companies Act, 1956, can function as a TPA. In addition, the company is also required to fulfil the following conditions to be eligible to act as a TPA:

- The main or primary object of the company should be to carry on business in India as a TPA in the health services, and on being licensed by the Authority.
- The minimum paid up capital of the company shall be in equity shares amounting to rupees ten million.
- The TPA should, at no point of time, have a working capital of less than rupees ten million.
- At least one of the directors of the TPA should be qualified medical doctor registered with the Medical Council of India;
- The aggregate holdings of equity shares by a foreign company shall not at any time exceed twenty-six per cent of the paid-up capital of a third party administrate or.
- Any transfer of shares exceeding five per cent of the paid up capital shall be intimated by the TPA to the Authority within 15 days of the transfer indicating the names and particulars of the transferor and transferee.

Every license granted by the Authority shall remain in force for three years. The Authority may revoke or cancel a license granted to a TPA for any of the following reasons:

- The TPA is functioning improperly and or against the interests of the policyholders or insurance company.

- The financial condition of the TPA has deteriorated and that the TPA cannot function effectively or that the TPA has breached any of the conditions of the TPA Regulation.
- The character and ownership of the TPA has changed significantly since the grant of license.
- The grant or renewal of license was on the basis of fraud or misrepresent action of facts and that there is a breach on the part of the TPA in following the procedure or acquiring the qualifications under the TPA Regulation.
- The TPA is subject to winding up proceedings under the Companies Act, 1956.
- There is a breach of code of conduct.
- There is violation of any direct ions issued by the Authority under the Insurance Act or the TPA Regulations.

Every insurer re-insures himself to protect against the risks to which it subjects himself in the conduct of insurance business. The general insurance company has been designated as the sole re-insurer in India. Every insurer is required to re-insure wit h an Indian re-insurer such percentage of the sum assured on each policy as specified by the Authority in this regard. The insurer is free to chose any re-insurer subject to the condition that such a re-insurer should enjoy a credit rating of a minimum of BBB of Standard and Poor or equivalent rating of any international rating agency. However, the placement of business by the insurer with any other re-insurer can be made only after obtaining the prior approval of the Authority. Every insurer is mandatorily required to retain the maximum premium earned in India commensurate with his financial strength and volume of business.

Every insurer should draw up a re-insurance programme in respect of all the lives covered by him. However, a programme of reinsurance on an original premium basis can be drawn only after obtaining the approval of the Authority. Further, a life insurer is not permitted to make any treaty arrangements with its promoter company or its associate or group company, except on terms, which are commercially competitive in the market and the prior approval of the Authority.

The profile of the programme, duly certified by the appointed actuary, should be filed with the Authority at least forty-five days before the commencement of each financial year. Additionally, the insurer should also submit the statistics relating to its reinsurance transact ions with the annual accounts to the Authority.

Every insurer who wants to write inward reinsurance business should adopt an underwriting policy for the purpose of underwriting inward reinsurance business. A note on the underwriting policy indicating the classes of business, geographical scope, underwriting limits and profit objective should be filed with the Authority.

Every insurer is required to maintain a retention, which is commensurate with its financial strength and volume of business. The Authority may require an insurer to justify its retention policy and may give directions to ensure that the Indian insurer is not merely fronting for a foreign insurer. Every insurer should cede such percentage of the sum assured on each policy for different classes of insurance written in India to the Indian re-insurer as may be specified by the Authority in accordance with the provisions the Insurance Act.

Every insurer is required to submit its reinsurance programme to the Authority for the forthcoming year within forth-five days before the commencement of the financial year. Additionally, the insurer should also file with the Authority a photocopy of every reinsurance treaty slip and excess of loss cover note in respect of that year together with a list of re-insurers and their shares in the reinsurance arrangement.

Insurers are permitted to place their reinsurance business outside India with only those re-insurers who have over a period of the past five years counting from the year preceding for which the business has to be placed, enjoyed a rating of at least BBB (with Standard and Poor) or equivalent rating of any other international rating agency. It is obligatory for all insurers to of fer an opportunity to other Indian insurers including the

Indian re-insurer to participate in its facultative and treaty surpluses before placement of such cessions outside India.

Any surplus over and above the domestic reinsurance arrangements class wise may be placed by the insurer independently with any of the re-insurers, subject to a limit of ten per cent of the total reinsurance premium ceded outside India being placed with any one re-insurer. In the even that the insurer would like to cede a share exceeding such limit to any particular re-insurer, in respect of specialized insurance, the insurer should seek the specific approval of the Authority in this regard.

Every insurer should also make an outstanding claims provision for every reinsurance arrangement accepted on the basis of loss information advices received from brokers/cedants and in cases where such advices are not received, on an actuarial estimation basis. In addition, every insurer should also make an appropriate provision for IBNR claims on its reinsurance accepted portfolio on actuarial estimation basis.

The Indian re-insurer is required to organize domestic pools for reinsurance surpluses in fire, marine hull and other classes in consultation with all insurers and should also assist in maintaining the retention of business within India. Such arrangements are required to be submitted to the Authority for approval. Further, the Indian re-insurer is required to retrocede at least fifty per cent of the obligatory cessions received by it to the ceding insurers after protecting the portfolio by suitable excess of loss covers. Every insurer wanting to write inward reinsurance business should have an underwriting policy for underwriting reinsurance business, which should be filed with the Authority stating the classes of business, geographical scope, underwriting limits and profit objective. Where there is a positive enactment of the Indian legislature, the language of the statute is applied to the facts of the case. However, the common law of England is often relied upon in consider action of justice, equity and good conscience.

A contract of insurance is a contract uberrimae fidei i.e. a contract of utmost good faith. This is a fundamental principle of insurance law. Both the parties to the contract are required to observe utmost good faith and should disclose every material fact known to them. There is no difference between a contract of insurance and any other contract except that in a contract of insurance there is a requirement of utmost good faith. The burden of proof to show non-disclosure or misrepresentation is on the insurance company and the onus is a heavy one. The duty of good faith is of a continuing nature in as much no material alteration can be made to the terms of the contract without the mutual consent of the parties. Just as the assured has a duty to disclose all the material facts, the insurer is also under an obligation to do the same. The insurer cannot subsequently demand additional premium nor can he escape liability by contending that the situation does not warrant the insurance cover.

The Insurance Act lays down that an insurance policy cannot be called in question two years after it has been in force for two years. This was done to obviate the hardships of the insured when the insurance company tried to avoid a policy, which has been in force for a long time, on the ground of misrepresentation. However, this provision is not applicable when the statement was made fraudulently. The Marine Insurance Act, 1963 ("Marine Insurance Act") lays down that the insured must disclose all the material facts before the contract is concluded.

The disclosures by the assured or by his agent should be true. The insured is deemed to know every circumstance, which in the ordinary course of business, ought to be known by him. The insurer may avoid the contract if the assured fails to make such disclosure or if the representation made is untrue. However, circumstances which diminish the risk, or which are presumed to be known by the insurer or information which is waived by the insurer or any circumstance which is superfluous to disclose by reason of any express or implied warranty need not be disclosed, in absence of any enquiry. In India the post contractual duty of good faith is very strict. The situation, though, has changed in England through a recent decision of the House of Lords. The decision in the Star Sea Case lays down that the duty of good faith in insurance contracts continues after the inception of the policy, but the duty is far less strict than it was prior to the commencement of the contract. This is because it would enable the insurers to avoid the whole policy ab initio for a post-contractual breach, which had no effect when the policy was drawn initially. However, this position has yet to be accepted by the Indian courts.

Representations are statements, made by one party to the other, either prior to or while entering into an insurance contract, of some matter or circumstances relating to it and which is not an integral part of the contract. These statements are said to have fulfilled their obligations when the final acceptance on the policy is conveyed.

A mere recital of represent actions made at the time of entering into the contact will not make then warranties. However, if representations are made an integral part of the contract they become warranties, and, in case of their being untrue, the policy can be avoided, even if the loss does not arise from the fact concealed or misrepresented. A policy of life insurance cannot be called in question on the ground of misrepresentation after a period of two years from the commencement of the policy.

In dealing with representations as circumstances invalidating a contract, consideration should be paid as to whether such represent actions are wilful or innocent and whether they are preliminary or for part of the contract.

The Insurance Act lays down three conditions to establish that the misrepresentation was wilful; (a) the statement must be on a material matter or must suppress facts which it was material to disclose; (b) the suppression must be fraudulently made by the policy holder; and (c) the policy-holder must have known at the time of making the statement that it was false or that it suppressed facts which it was material to disclose. The burden of proof of establishing that the insured had in fact suppressed material facts in obtaining insurance is on the insurer and all the aforesaid conditions are required to be proved cumulatively. In determining whether there has been suppression of a material fact it is necessary to examine whether the suppression relates to a fact which is in the exclusive knowledge of the person intending to take the policy and also that it could not be ascertained by reasonable enquiry by a prudent person.

A warranty may be distinguished from a representation in as much a representation may be equitably and substantially answered but a warranty must be strictly complied with. A breach of warranty will avoid the policy, although it may not relate to a matter material to the risk insured. Warranties may be express or implied, if it is condition implied by law. However, implied warranties are mostly confined to marine insurance. The Marine Insurance Act defines a warranty as a promise whereby the assured under takes that some particular thing shall or shall not be done, or that some condition shall be fulfilled, or affirms or negatives the existence of a particular state of facts.

The statements must be true in fact without any qualification of judgement, opinion or belief. The warranty should be in the policy or must be incorporated by reference. If any of the statements or representations made by the assured in the proposal have been made the "basis" of the contract and they are found to be untrue, the contract of insurance would be void and unenforceable in law, irrespective of the question whether the statement, concerned is of a material nature or not. However, non-compliance of a warranty is cxcused when, by reason of a change of circumstances, the warranty ceases to be applicable to the circumstances of the contract, or when compliance with the warranty is rendered unlawful by any subsequent law or when such a warranty has not been mentioned in the policy.

Conditions are terms which prescribe the limitations under which an insurance policy is granted and which specify the duties of the assured. They can be either conditions precedent or subsequent. Conditions precedent are those, which are essential for the creation of a valid contract, the non-satisfaction of which makes the contract void *ab initio*. Conditions subsequent relate to the continuance of a valid contract, the non-fulfilment of which leads to the avoidance of the contract from the date of the breach.

They can be further classified into express conditions and implied conditions. Implied conditions are those, which are implied by law to apply to every contract of insurance irrespective of any specific inclusion or reference to them such as insurable interest, good faith *etc.*

A condition, which seeks to reduce or curtail the period of limitation and prescribes a shorter period than that prescribed by law is void. However, the insured is absolved once it is shown that he has done everything in his power to keep, honour and fulfil the promise and he himself is not guilty of a deliberate breach.

An insurer cannot take recourse to a condition, which has not been mentioned in the policy to reduce his liability. However, an insurance policy may not curtail the right but may merely provide for forfeiture or waiver of any such right and such a right would be enforceable against either party.

Most kinds of insurance policies other than life and personal accident insurance are contracts of indemnity whereby the insurer undertakes to indemnify the insured for the actual loss suffered by him as a result of the occurring of the event insured against. Even within the maximum limit, the insured cannot recover more than whathe establishes to be his actual loss. A contract of marine insurance is an agreement whereby the insurer undertakes to indemnify the insured to the extent agreed upon.

Although the insured is to be placed in the same position as if the loss has not occurred, the amount of indemnity may be limited by certain conditions:

- Injury or loss sustained by the insured has to be proved.
- The indemnity is limited to the amount specified in the policy
- The insured is indemnified only for the proximate causes.
- The market value of the property determines the amount of indemnity.

Indemnity is a fundamental principle of insurance law, and the principle of Subrogation is a corollary of this principle in as much the insured is precluded from obtaining more than the loss he has sustained. The most common form of subrogation is when an insurance company pays a claim caused by the negligence of another. The doctrine of subrogation confers two specific rights on the insurer.

Firstly, the insurer is entitled to all the remedies which the insured has against the third party incidental to the subject matt er of the loss, such that the insurer can take advantage of any means available to extinguish or diminish, the loss for which the insurer has indemnified the insured. Secondly, the insurer is entitled to the benefits received by the assured from the third party with a view to compensate himself for the loss.

The fact that an insurer is subrogated to the rights and remedies of the insured does not *ipso jure* enable him to sue third parties in his own name.

It will only entitle the insurer to sue in the name of insured, it being an obligation of the insured to lend his name and assistance to such an action. An insurance policy may contain a special clause whereby the insured assigns all his rights, against third parties, in favour of the insurer. In case of subrogation, which vest by operation of law rather than as the product of express agreement, the insured would be entitled to only to the extent of his loss. The excess amount, if any, would be returned to the insured.

The doctrine of proximate cause is expressed in the maxim 'Causa Proxima non remota spectator', which means that the proximate and not the remote cause, shall be taken as the cause of loss. The insurer is thus has to make good the loss of the insured that clearly and proximately results, whether directly or indirectly, from the event insured against in the policy. The burden of proof that the loss occurred on account of the proximate cause, lies on the insured.

As per the Marine Insurance Act, unless the insurance policy states otherwise, the insurer is liable for any loss proximately caused by a peril insured against, but he is not liable for any loss which is not proximately caused by a peril insured against. An insurer would therefore be exempted from liability when the cause of loss falls within the except ions of the policy.

The Marine Insurance Act further states that the insurer is not liable for any wilful misconduct of the insured i.e. the assured cannot recover for a loss where his own deliberate act is the proximate cause of it. Further, in the event of loss caused by the delay of the ship, the insurer cannot be held liable, irrespective of the proximity of the cause.

The Consumer Protection Act, 1986 ("Consumer Protection Act") is one of the most important socio-economic legislation for the protect ion of consumers in India.

The provisions of this Act are compensatory in nature, unlike other laws, which are either punitive or preventive. Insurance services fall within the purview of the Consumer Protection Act, in as much, any deficiency in service of the insurance company would enable the aggrieved to make a complaint.

Disputes between policyholders and insurers generally pertain to repudiation of the insurance claim or the matters connected with admission of the claim or computation of the amount of claim. In the case of assignment of all rights by the insured to the insurer, the consumer forum and he courts generally refuse to accept the locus standi of the insured.

The courts have held that insurance companies do not fall under the definition of "consumer" under the Consumer Protection Act, as no service is rendered to them directly. Neither the subrogation nor the transfer of the right of action would confer the legal status of a 'consumer' on the insurer, nor can the insurer be regarded as any beneficiary of any service.

Therefore, the remedy available to the insurer is to file a suit in a civil court for recovery of the loss To constitute insurable interest, it must be an interest such that the risk would by its proximate effect cause damage to the assured, that is to say, cause him to lose a benefit or incur a liability. The validity of an insurance contract, in India, is dependent on the existence of an insurable interest in the subject matter.

The person seeking an insurance policy must establish some kind of interest in the life or property to be insured, in the absence of which, the insurance policy would amount to a wager and consequently void in nature. The test for determining if there is an insurable interest is whether the insured will in case of damage to the life or property being insured, suffer pecuniary loss. A person having a limited interest can also insure such interest.

Insurable interest varies depending on the nature of the insurance. The controversy as to the existence of an insurable interest between spouses was settled by the court, which held that such an interest could exist as neither was likely to indulge in any 'mischievous game'.

The same analogy may be extended to parents and children. Further, the courts have also held that such an insurable interest would exist for a creditor (in a debtor) and for an employee (in an employer) to the extent of the debt incurred and the remuneration due, respectively.

The existence of insurable interest at the time of happening of the event is another important consideration.

In case of life and personal accident insurance it is sufficient if the insurable interest is present at the time of taking the policy. However, in the case of fire and motor accident insurance the insurable interest has to be present both at the time of taking the policy and at the time of the accident. The case is completely different with marine insurance wherein there need not be any insurable interest at the time of taking the policy.

The general rule on the formation of a contract, as per the Indian Contract Act, is that the party to whom the offer has been made should accept it unconditionally and communicate his acceptance to the person making the offer. Whether the final acceptance is to be made by the insured or insurer really depends on the negotiations of the policy.

Acceptance should be signified by some act as agreed upon by the parties or from which the law raises a presumption of acceptance. The mere receipt or retention of premium until after the death of the applicant or the mere preparation of the policy document is not acceptance. Nonetheless, acceptance may be presumed upon the retention of the premium. However, mere delay in giving an answer cannot be construed as acceptance. Also, silence does not denote consent and no binding contract arises until the person to whom an offer is made says or does something to signify his acceptance.

When the policy is of a particular date, it would cover the liability of the insurer from the previous midnight preceding the same date. However, where there is a special contract to the contrary in the policy, the terms of the contract would prevail. Hence where the time of the issue of the insurance policy is mentioned, then the liability would be covered only from the time when it was issued.

8

INDIAN STATUS IN RISK INSURANCE

The insurance industry in India can be discussed in two ways – its historical background and its present state. Insurance in India is nothing new. It had its origins in the early 19th century with the arrival of British enterprise in India. Insurance, particularly non-life remained an urban oriented activity of the Insurance companies operating through their agencies.

Life Insurance Corporation of India

The insurance sector in India dates back to 1818 when first insurance company, The Oriental Life Insurance Company, was established, at Calcutta. Thereafter, Bombay Life Assurance Company in 1823 and Madras Equitable Life Assurance Society in 1829 were established. In 1912, the Indian Life Assurance Companies Act was enacted as the first statute to regulate the life insurance business. In 1928, the Indian Insurance Companies Act was enacted to enable the Government to collect statistical information about both life and non-life insurance businesses. The Insurance Act was subsequently reviewed and a comprehensive legislation was enacted called the Insurance Act, 1938. The nationalisation of life insurance business took place in 1956 when 245 Indian and foreign insurance and provident societies were first amalgamated and then nationalised.

The Life Insurance Corporation of India (LIC) came into existence by an Act of Parliament, viz. LIC act, 1956, with a capital contribution of Rs.5 Crores from the Government of India General Insurance Corporation Of India-The General insurance business in India started with the establishment of Triton Insurance Company Limited in 1850 at Calcutta. In 1907, the first company, The Mercantile Insurance Ltd. Was set up to transact all classes of general insurance business. General Insurance Council, a wing of the Insurance Association of India in 1957, framed a code of conduct for ensuring fair conduct and sound business practices.

In 1968 the Insurance Act was amended to regulate investments and to set minimum solvency margins. In the same year the Tariff Advisory Committee was also set up. In 1972, The General Insurance Business (Nationalisation) Act was passed to nationalise the general insurance business in India with effect from 1st January 1973. For these 107 insurers was amalgamated and grouped into four company's viz., the National Insurance Company Ltd., the New India Assurance Company Ltd., the Oriental Insurance Company Ltd. And the United India Insurance Company Ltd. General Insurance Corporation of India was incorporated as a company.

Current Scenario

In new economic policies formulated since 1991, globalisation, privatisation and liberalisation have become new buzzwords. Under new economic policies, many economic and financial reforms took place. Like liberalising licensing policy, attracting FDI, allowing foreign equity in public sector undertakings. The financial reforms restructured banking sector by allowing entry of new private and foreign banks. They also allowed private sector and commercial banks in mutual funds investment business, rationalising the EXIM policy and so on.

Insurance Sector Reforms

After the nationalisation of the life insurance industry in 1956 and the general insurance industry in 1972, the insurance industry confined only to the operations of LIC, GIC and its four subsidiaries viz. The National Insurance Company Limited, New India Assurance Company Limited, Oriental Fire and General Insurance Company Limited and United India Fire and General Insurance Company Limited. Over the years this state monopoly resulted in complacency, use of outdated technologies, inefficient and insufficient customer services and non-coverage of the potential market. Recognising this, the Government set-up a high-powered committee headed by Mr. R. N. Malhotra.

Malhotra Committee

Purpose

In 1993, Malhotra Committee, headed by former Finance Secretary and RBI Governor, was formed to evaluate the Indian Insurance Industry and recommend its future direction. The committee was set up with an objective of complementing the reforms in the Indian Financial sector.

The reforms were aimed at "creating a more efficient and competitive financial system suitable for the requirements of the economy keeping in mind the structural changes currently underway and recognising that insurance is an important part of the overall financial system where it was necessary to address the need for similar reforms."

Besides this, the Malhotra committee was asked to make recommendations for changing the structure of insurance industry, to make specific suggestions about how to improve the functioning of LIC and GIC and to recommend on regulation and supervision of the insurance sector in India. Besides this, the committee was asked to assess the strengths and weaknesses of the existing insurance industry and to make recommendations for changes in its functioning and the general policy framework keeping in mind the reforms under way in other parts of the financial sector.

Recommendations

In 1994, the committee submitted the report and gave the following recommendations:

Structure

- Government stake in the insurance companies to be brought down to 50%

- Government should take over the holdings of GIC and its subsidiaries so that these subsidiaries can act as independent corporations
- All the insurance companies should be given greater freedom to operate.

Competition

- Entry of private sector companies within well defined parameters of nature of business.
- Private Companies with a minimum paid up capital of Rs.1 billion should be allowed to enter the industry
- No Company should deal in both Life and General Insurance through a single entity
- Selective entry of foreign insurance companies preferably through joint ventures.
- Postal Life Insurance should be allowed to operate in the rural market
- Only one State Level Life Insurance Company should be allowed to operate in each state
- The insurance Act should be changed
- Controller of Insurance should be made independent
- Establishment of a strong and effective Insurance Regulatory Authority (IRA) as a statutory autonomous board.

Investments

- Mandatory Investments of LIC Life Fund in government securities to be reduced from 75% to 50%
- GIC and its subsidiaries are not to hold more than 5% in any company

Customer Service

- LIC should pay interest on delays in payments beyond 30 days
- Insurance companies must be encouraged to set up unit linked pension plans

- Computerisation of operations and updating of technology to be carried out in the insurance industry Overall, the committee strongly felt that in order to improve the customer services and increase the coverage of the insurance industry should be opened up to competition. But at the same time, the committee felt the need to exercise caution as any failure on the part of new players could ruin the public confidence in the industry. The recommendations of the committee were discussed at different forums. The recommendations to set up an autonomous IRA found wide support. Since enacting legislation for creating the statutory IRA was to take time, the then government constituted an interim IRA, pending the enactment of comprehensive legislation.

It was on the basis of this report that the then Finance Minister P. Chidambaram proposed the opening up of insurance to the private sector, including multinational companies.

IRDA Bill

The IRDA Bill was drafted keeping the Malhotra Committee recommendations in view and hence the government has ruled out privatisation of public sector insurance companies, LIC and GIC. The bill did not provide for any dilution of 100 percent government equity in the two premier companies.

The IRDA bill sought to give a statutory status to the interim Insurance Regulatory Authority and amend the 1938 Insurance Act, the 1956 Life Insurance Corporation Act and the 1972 General Insurance Business (Nationalisation) Act to open up the sector. It provides for a nine-member regulatory body with statutory powers. The bill also fixed minimum capital requirement for life and general insurance at Rs.100 Crores and for reinsurance firms at Rs.200 Crores.

The Malhotra Committee Report justified the entry of foreign insurance companies by arguing that if it is permitted, it should be done on selective basis preferably through joint venture with Indian partner. In 1999, the bill was finally passed and IRDA was formed to regulate and promote insurance business in India. The IRDA Act bestows the authority with powers to frame varies regulations, issue licenses, set capital requirements and solvency margins, prepare investment norms and inspect the books of private insurers independent of the government.

Liberalisation of Insurance Markets

Liberalisation of Insurance involves transformation of the industry from a Government monopoly to a competitive environment. Free markets allow for better resource allocation and creation of wealth and prosperity of people and the country. It enables development of health care, education and infrastructure of the country. In a liberalised insurance market, consumers are able to choose from different insurance providers having a wide range of products. A liberal insurance market is one in which the market determines who should be allowed to sell insurance, what, how and the prices at which these insurance products should be sold. The issues like market access and equality of competitive opportunity and national treatment will decide who will be allowed to sell insurance. Second and fourth items commonly deal with issues such as product, price and market conduct regulation. There are certain pre-conditions to make liberalisation of insurance effective:

- Sound competition law
- Efficient and reliable regulation
- Phased liberalisation
- Consistency and impartiality between competitors
- Optimum quantum of regulation
- Efficient disclose and dissemination of information to the society.

Insurance markets in India possess certain imperfections justifying the need for competition as well as regulation.

INSURANCE PLAYERS IN INDIA

Bajaj Allianz General Insurance Company Limited

It is a joint venture between Bajaj Auto Limited and Allianz AG of Germany. The company registered on May 2, 2001 to conduct General Insurance business (including Health Insurance business) in India. The company has an authorised and paid up capital of Rs.110 Crores and has a network of 31 offices across the country.

ICICI Lombard General Insurance Company Limited

It is a joint venture between ICICI Bank Limited India's second largest bank and Lombard Canada Limited, one of the oldest property and casualty insurance companies in Canada. ICICI Lombard offers a wide range of retail and corporate general insurance customised products. The company has over 100 branches across the country.

IFFCO-TOKIO General Insurance Company Limited

It is a joint venture between IFFCO and The Tokio Marine and Fire Insurance Company Limited, Japan Krishak Bharati Cooperative Limited (KRIBHCO), and Indian Potash contributing 49 percent, 26 percent and 5 percent respectively to its Rs.100 Crores capital. After getting the licence the company started operations and is a leading private General Insurance Company in India in launching innovative insurance cover for farmers called the "Sankat Haran Policy" It is operating from 20 cities in India.

National Insurance Company Limited

It was incorporated in 1906 to carry out general insurance business and nationalised in 1972.In the same year, 22 foreign and 11 Indian Insurance Companies were amalgamated with National Insurance Company Limited, as a subsidiary company of General Insurance Corporation of India. In 2002, with the passage of Insurance amendment Bill (2002), National Insurance Company has been delinked from GIC and has been functioning as an independent company. Apart from domestic insurance business the company also undertakes reinsurance and foreign operations.

New India Assurance Company Limited

The New India Assurance Company was incorporated on July 23, 1919 and commenced business from October 14, 1919. In 1972 the Government of India took over the management of the company along with all other non-life insurers in the country. New India Assurance was subsequently reconstituted taking over 23 companies. In 2002, with the passage of Insurance amendment Bill, New India Assurance Company Limited has been delinked from GIC and has been functioning as an independent company.

Oriental Insurance Company Limited

The Oriental Insurance Company Limited is a public sector company and is one of the four subsidiary companies of the General Insurance Corporation of India.

In 1956, Oriental became a subsidiary of the Life Insurance Corporation of India. On May 13, 1971 Government of India took over the management of all general insurance companies in India and nationalised the Oriental Fire and General Insurance Company under the General Insurance Corporation of India as one of the four subsidiaries. In 2002, with the passage of Insurance amendment Bill, the Oriental Insurance Company Limited has been delinked from GIC and has been functioning as an independent company.

United India Insurance Company Limited

United India Insurance is one of the four subsidiaries of the General Insurance Company carrying on general insurance business in India. In 2002, with the passage of Insurance amendment Bill (2002), United India Insurance has been delinked from GIC and has been functioning as an independent company.

Tata AIG General Insurance Company Limited

Tata AIG General Insurance Company Ltd. And Tata AIG Life Insurance Company Ltd. (collectively "Tata AIG") are joint venture companies between the Tata group and American International Group Inc. (AIG), the leading U.S. based international insurance and financial services organisation. It has a capital of Rs.125 Crores out of which 74 percent has been brought in by Tata Sons and the remaining 26 percent by American partner. Tata AIG General Insurance Company Limited claims to be the first Indian insurance company to offer a comprehensive policy to cover various risks in the IT sector.

Royal Sundaram General Insurance Company Limited

The joint venture between Royal and Sun Alliance Insurance and Sundaram Finance Limited started its operation from March 2001. Royal and Sun Alliance is one of the world's leading international insurance companies.

The Sun was established in 1710 and is the oldest insurance company in existence still trading under its original name. The Alliance was founded in 1824 and the Royal in 1845.

Cholamandalam General Insurance Company Limited

It is promoted by Chennai based Murugappa Group. The company is founded with Rs.105 Crores out of which 75 percent is being held by Tube Investment, a Murugappa group company. While Cholamandalam Investment and Finance Company Limited holds 15 percent stake and the rest is by other privately held Murugappa companies with 5 percent stake each.

Reliance General Insurance Company Limited

Reliance group has announced its plans to enter the Indian insurance sector – both in the life and general insurance businesses. Reliance Industries plans to bring in around Rs.300 Crores into its insurance venture through its financial arm Reliance Capital Limited.

The two companies will have an initial authorised capital of Rs.200 Crores each. This is the first Indian company without a foreign tie-up.

Export Credit Guarantee Corporation of India Limited

It was established in the year 1957 by the Government of India to strengthen the export promotion drive by covering the risk of exporting on credit. Being an export promotion organisation, it functions under the administrative control of the Ministry of Commerce, Government of India. It is the fifth largest credit insurer of the world in terms of coverage of national exports. The paid –up capital of the company is Rs.390 Crores.

HDFC Chubb General Insurance Limited

HDFC, India's premier financial services company and Chubb Corporation, leading global non-life insurer, entered into a joint venture agreement for non-life insurance in 2002. HDFC holds 74 percent and Chubb 26 percent in the joint venture company, HDFC Chubb General Insurance Limited with initial capital of Rs.100 Crores.

LIFE INSURERS

Alliance Bajaj Life Insurance Company Limited

Alliance Bajaj Life Insurance Company Limited is a joint venture between Alliance AG and Bajaj Auto Limited. The company was incorporated on March 12, 2001. The company received the IRDA certificate of registration on August 3, 2001 to conduct Life Insurance business in India.

Birla Sun Life Insurance Company Limited

It is a joint venture between Birla Group and Sun Life Corporation of U.S. The products of Birla Sun Life Insurance Company (BSLI) are distributed through a fully owned subsidiary– BSDL Insurance Advisory Services Limited (BSDL IAS) BSDL.

The company claims to have unique products, presenting a powerful combination of returns, liquidity, safety, tax benefits, transparency and convenience.

HDFC Standard Life Insurance Company Limited

HDFC and Standard Life was the first joint venture to enter the life insurance market, in January 1995. In October 1998, the joint venture agreement was renewed and Standard Life purchased 2 percent of Infrastructure Development Finance Company Limited (IDFC). The company as such, was incorporated on August 14, 2000 under the name of HDFC Standard Life Insurance Company Limited. HDFC are the main shareholders in HDFC Standard Life, with 81.4 percent, while Standard Life owns 18.6 percent. HDFC and Standard Life have a long and close relationship built upon shared values and trust.

ICICI Prudential Life Insurance Company Limited

The company was incorporated on July 20, 2000, with an authorised capital of Rs.230 Crores (paid up Rs.190 Crores). It is a joint venture of ICICI (74%) and Prudential plc U.K (26%). The company is on the top of the list of competitors to LIC. The company was granted certificate of incorporation on 26-11-2000 and it started its operations on 19-12-2000.

Life Insurance Corporation of India Limited

LIC was established in 1956 and is the dominant leader in life insurance in India. It has 7 zonal offices, over 100 divisional offices and 204 branches in India with over 6.50 lakhs agents.

Tata AIG Life Insurance Company Limited

It is capitalised at Rs.185 Crores of which 74 percent has been brought in by Tata Sons and the American partner brings in the remaining 26 percent. American Insurance Group (AIG) is the leading U.S. based international insurance and financial services organisation and the largest underwriter of commercial and industrial insurance in the United States.

AIG's global businesses also include financial services and asset management. Including aircraft leasing, financial products, trading and market making, consumer finance, institutional, retail and direct investment fund asset management etc.

SBI Life Insurance Company Limited

India's largest bank SBI and Cardiff S.A. a leading insurer in France have firmed SBI Life. It is a 74: 24 venture; with Cardiff the foreign partner contributing 24 percent paid capital of Rs.250 Crores. SBI plans to market the insurance products through select branches of SBI and its seven associate banks.

OM Kotak Mahindra Insurance Company Limited

The joint venture OM Kotak Mahindra Life Insurance started off with an initial net worth of Rs.150 Crores, with 74: 26 stake between KMFL and OM. Kotak Mahindra is one of India's premier financial services groups, with a range of over two dozen highly specialised products and services. Starting as a one-product company in the mid 80's, they have evolved into a full service financial conglomerate. Old Mutual pic. Is a leading financial services provider in the world, providing a broad range of financial services in the area of insurance, asset management and banking. It is a leading life insurer in South Africa, with more than 30 percent market share.

The partnership with Old Mutual plc. provides the Kotak Mahindra group with an international perspective and expertise in the life insurance business.

Max New York Life Insurance Company Limited

It is a partnership between Max India Limited, one of India's leading multi business corporations and New York Life, a Fortune 100 company. The paid up capital of the joint venture is Rs.250 Crores. Max India Ltd. is building businesses in the emerging knowledge based areas of Healthcare, Financial Services and Information Technology.

ING Vyasya Life Insurance Company Ltd.

It is a joint venture between ING, Vyasya Bank, one of India's leading private sector banks and GMR group. As per the joint venture agreement, Vyasya Bank holds 49 percent stake, ING 26 percent, and the GMR Group would hold 25 percent.

The paid up capital of the joint venture is Rs.110 Crores. Vyasya Bank has a very high degree of retail focus with good customer service. ING Group, with an asset base of over Rs.28, 42,000 Crores is a global financial institution of Dutch origin, which is active in the field of banking, insurance and asset management in more than 60 countries.

Aviva Life Insurance Company Ltd.

It is a joint venture between Dabur India and CGU, a wholly owned subsidiary of Aviva Pic, is capitalised at Rs.110 Crores. Aviva Pic is the largest life and general insurance group of UK and the world's largest insurer with worldwide premium income and retail investment sales of £28 billion. Aviva Life has tied up with ABN Amro, Canara Bank, Laxmi Vilas Bank and American Express for distribution of its products.

AMP Sanmar Assurance Company Ltd.

It is a joint venture between AMP having a stake of 26 percent and the Sanmar Group holding 74 percent. The Sanmar group is one of the largest industrial groups in South India. AMP Limited is one of the world's leading financial services businesses.

UNDERSTANDING ANNUAL REPORTS OF LIC AND GIC

The Annual Report of LIC

The contents of annual report of LIC are:

(1) Preamble Under Section 27 of the LIC Act 1956, LIC has to present its Annual report to the members. This also contains the names of the members of the Corporation and its various committees during the year.

(2) Scenario Economic In this, information is provided about GDP (Gross Domestic Product), GDS (Gross Domestic Saving), fiscal position, monetary conditions, inflation, equity market and external sector. What changes have taken place during the year in global life insurance business as well as domestic insurance market? After the opening up of the domestic insurance market in 1999 and with a level playing field provided by the new supervisory framework, what is the position of the state owned and private platers in the insurance business? How the changes in GDS, GDP and disposable income has affected the business performance of the insurance industry.

(3) Impact of Macro Economic Environment on Life Insurance Business Under this, the information is provided about impact of RBI policies and Government of India's Monetary and credit policies on insurance business. Like there is a RBI policy to reduce the exposure of Non-Banking Financial Institutions including LIC, in the call money market. As a result the Corporation has reduced its investment in call money market to meet RBI guidelines. Now, LIC has been

actively deploying its funds in other money market instruments like Repo and CBLO (Collateralized Borrowing and Lending Obligation). In addition, what is the impact of changes in the interest rate, inflation on life insurance business? Thus changes taking place on a global and national level affects the life insurance business.

(4) Working results the total working results of the Corporation are divided into two parts:

(1) New Business and

(2) Business in Force.

In new business the report discusses about the Number of Policies, Sum Assured, Annual Premium Receivable in Individual Assurance, General Annuity, Pensions Portfolio, Unit Linked business (Bema Plus and Future Plus) in India as well as out of India. It also gives information about Group insurance business including Social Security. In Social Security Schemes, the LIC provides insurance cover through Janashree Bima Yojana to 43 occupations like Beedi workers, Lady Tailors, Textile, Wood and Paper products, Printing, Physically Handicapped, Self-Employed persons.

The report also discusses about First Insurance, Rural Thrust, Alternate Distribution Channels, and Product Development. In First Insurance, in pursuance of the corporate objectives LIC provides insurance cover to more and more people who have no previous insurance on their lives. In Rural Thrust, LIC gives information about Life insurance cover provided to people of backward and remote areas. In Alternate Distribution Channels, the LIC provides information about how in competitive market environment LIC targets new market segments and high net worth individuals to increase its customer base. Banks have emerged as strong business partners amongst alternate channels in terms of first premium mobilisation. In order to meet the changing needs of customers, LIC offers a wide variety of products. Thus, in product development, the LIC gives information about new insurance products introduced and some existing withdrawn from the market after periodical review of its product portfolio.

In Business In Force in various segments, the LIC report says about Number of Policies, Sum Assured, and Annual Premium Receivable under Individual Assurance, General Annuity Pension Portfolio, Unit Linked (Bima Plus and Future Plus) in India as well as out of India. In Group Insurance Business the information is given about Number of Schemes, Number of Members, Sum Assured, Premium Income under Group Insurance including Social Security and Group Superannuation.

(5) Capital Redemption and Annuity Certain Business it provides information about Annuity Certain and Capital Redemption Policies in force.

(6) Statutory Statements regarding Policies Under this heading information in statements in the form "DD" prescribed under Insurance Act, 1938 is given about Number of Policies, Sum Insured and Annuities Per Annum, Single Premiums and Yearly Renewal Premium for Ordinary policies (Individual Assurance), Annuity Contracts, Unit Linked Plans (Bima Plus and Future Plus), Jeevan Suraksha, Group Insurance Policies and Group Annuity Contracts etc. in India and out of India in respect of premium paid during the tear for New Life Insurance business. Statutory Statements regarding Policies also provides information about Total Life Insurance business in force at the end of the year in the form of Number of Policies, Sum insured with Bonuses and Annuities per Annum, premium income for which credit has been taken in the Revenue Account in India and out of India.

(7) Life Fund, Surplus and Taxes Paid This provides information about life fund, valuation surplus, surplus retained, share of surplus and taxes paid to the Central Government for the last three years.

(8) Investments and Social Responsibilities This heading gives information about total investments of the Corporation in India and out of India. Besides investing in Stock Exchange Securities, Loans constitute one of the major avenues of investment for the Corporation's funds. Loans have been given to finance projects/ schemes for generation and transmission of electricity for agricultural and industrial use, housing schemes, development of road transport, piped water supply and sewerage projects in rural and urban areas and townships and industrial development.

LIC also fulfils its social responsibilities towards society at large.

To achieve this goal LIC provides security to as many people as possible. To meet this end, the Corporation has been promoting Social Welfare through socially oriented schemes. LIC invested and given loans to Central, State and other Government Guaranteed Marketable Securities and Infrastructure sector.

(9) Marketing Activities, Agents and Diversified Activities under marketing activities, LIC provides information about its operations in India and in Foreign countries. Also its operations through Foreign Subsidiaries/ Joint Venture Companies. In Agents heading, LIC gives information about total number of agents on roll, number of schemes launched by the Corporation to promote the cause of professionalising the agency force. In order to recognize agents who perform consistently year after year, clubs at five levels have been designated viz. Chairman, Zonal Manager, Divisional Manager, Branch Manager and Distinguished Agents by the Corporation. In order to motivate and recognize high performers a premium club called the "Corporate Club" has been formed. Besides providing insurance covers to lakhs of people, how LIC has diversified its activities through LIC Housing Finance Limited, LIC Mutual Fund Trustee Company Private Limited/ Jeevan Bima Sahayog Asset Management Company (JBS AMC) Limited.

(10) Policy Holders' servicing this heading provides information about how Corporation settles the claims of policyholders on maturity as well as on death. In case Claimants have any grievances, they can present their cases before Zonal/ Central Claims Review Committee. To impart transparency to the decision making process former High Court / District Court Judge is appointed as a sitting member of Review Committee. Also Corporation has Grievance Redressal Officers at Branch/ Divisional /Zonal / Central office to redress grievances of customers and for transparency.

(11) Public Relations and Corporate Communications Activities In order to improve public image and to boost the public confidence, Corporation has undergone a transformation, renaming its "PR and Publicity" department as "PR and CC" to revamp corporate image. AD campaigns through various media like Radio, TV, Internet, Press etc. were used to augment its sales and to enhance brand image. For this LIC has received many accolades from diverse entities.

(12) Personnel and Employee Relations In this information is provided about staff strength, new recruitments, relationship with employees and unions, ratio of women workers in the total strength of staff, reservation of SC,ST and OBC, Physically Handicapped and Ex – Servicemen Employees and Sports activities.

(13) HRD / OD initiatives / Training Statistics This heading provides information about training profiles of the Personnel of the Corporation. To sharpen the skills and capabilities of the personnel how training is imparted through in – house training centres, Management Development Centre, National Insurance Academy and Zonal and Divisional Training Centres. Besides this, to strengthen the entrepreneurial ability of the Managers to have better managerial perception and practices, Management Development Centre (MDC), the apex-training institute of LIC imparts training to Managers.

(14) Engineering Activities and Estates It gives information about new additions to the existing buildings and offices of the LIC. How Estate Portfolio of the Corporation progressed during the year, how much housing loans were given to employees for various staff housing schemes and agents housing schemes.

(15) Information Technology Initiatives This provides information about information technology initiatives undertaken by the Corporation to modernise their offices and to give better alternate options to the customers to do business with LIC like premium collection through ECS, E – Mail and Internet services, on line Data Store Project, a standardised package for Pension Policy Servicing etc.

(16) Internal Audit To help management to take corrective action and to ensure continuous improvement in the overall working of the offices of the Corporation, internal audit department is established by the Corporation. It periodically audits the workings of Branch, Divisional and Zonal offices and all offices of the Corporation.

(17) Inspection and Vigilance Inspection of all the branches, Divisional and Zonal offices in India are carried out by the Corporation. Besides this, Vigilance activities are also undertaken by the Corporation. Here the greater emphasis is on preventive vigilance through the dissemination of information on areas susceptible to vigilance besides expediting disposal of vigilance cases.

(18) Nominee Directors It provides information of directors nominated by the Corporation on the Boards of the Companies where it has substantial stake by way of Debt or Equity. Nominee directors are reviewed and guided by the Corporation from time to time. These Directors are Non – Executive Directors, not connected with day to day operational matters of the Company, who report on important matters discussed at the board meetings/other related committee meetings or any other issue which deserves attention of the Corporation.

(19) Corporate Governance The practice of good Corporate Governance enables the strengthening of the confidence of the stake holders, maintaining a healthy industrial climate within the organisation improving customer focus and withstanding the pressures of change in the external environment and in making LIC is great and dynamic organisation. This is achieved through various proactive measures, initiatives and guidance by the Government, namely, Board of Directors, Executive committee, Audit Committee, Investment Committee, Consumer Affairs Committee, Zonal Advisory Boards, Divisional level Policy holders Councils and LIC's employees and Agency force.

(20) Board Meetings and Central Management Committee As per regulations, Board meetings should be held at least once in a quarter. Board Meetings are generally held at corporate office of LIC to discuss policy matters to provide guidance and direction to management for Growth, Excellence and Corporate Governance. Board members have access to any information that they may like to have and the recommendations that may be prescribed or desired are implemented within the time frame. The Central Management Committee consists of all Executive Directors, Chief of Central Office and all the Zonal Managers. In the meetings Policy and Strategic issues are discussed and appropriate steps are taken to reformulate the strategies if thought necessary in view of the changes in the market environment.

(21) Zonal Advisory Board(ZAB) Zaps are constituted for each Zone, which are competent to discuss and review all matters and policy affecting the proper development of the LIC within due territorial limits of the Zone and make recommendations thereon.

(22) Policy Holder's Council Policyholder's councils are constituted in each division. Policyholder councils discuss all the matters, which relate to the servicing of the Policyholders. Items discussed are Service to the Policy

Holder, Outstanding claims, Progress of New Business in the Division, Publicity activities etc.

(23) Auditors Appointment of Statutory Auditors with the previous approval of the Central Government. In this the names and addresses of the firms are given.

(24) Plans In this, information about Annual Budget of New Business is given. This heading provides for what LIC wishes to do in the coming financial year under:

(1) Linked Business
   * Life Assurance
   * Pension Plan
   * Total linked Business

(2) Non-linked Business
   * Life Assurance
   * Pension plan
   * Total Linked Business

(3) Composite Business

(25) Acknowledgement In this LIC expresses its sincere thanks to the various Parliamentary Committees, the Union Finance Minister, and Union Minister of state for Finance, the Insurance division of the ministry of Finance and the IRDA for their active support, advice and cooperation on various committees and Board of Directors for their guidance and valuable suggestions.

BIBLIOGRAPHY

Arrow, Kenneth J.: *Social Choice and Individual Values,* New York, Wiley, 1951.

Campbell, J.Y., Lo, A.W.: *The Econometrics of Financial Markets,* Princeton University Press, 1996.

Chaudhuri, Pramit: *The Indian Economy: Poverty and Development,* New York, St. Martin's Press, 1979.

Dhingra, C.: *The Indian Economy: Resources, Planning, Development, and Problems,* Delhi, Sultan Chand, 1983.

Greer, Douglas F.: *Industrial Organization and Public Policy,* MacMillan Publishing Company, 1992.

Ishwar, C.: *The Indian Economy: Resources, Planning, Development, and Problems,* Delhi, Sultan Chand, 1983.

Little, I.M.D.: *India: Macroeconomics and Political Economy, 1964-1991,* Washington, World Bank, 1994.

Mongia, J.N.: *India's Economic Development Strategies, 1951-2000 A.D.*. New Delhi, Allied, 1986.

Pranab, K.: *The Political Economy of Development in India,* Delhi, Oxford University Press, 1984.

Sargent, Thomas J.: *Dynamic Macroeconomic Theory,* Harvard University Press, 1987.

Tirole, Jean: *The Theory of Industrial Organization,* MIT Press, 1988.

Williamson, Jeffrey G.: *American Inequality: A Macroeconomic History,* New York, Academic Press, 1980.

Xavier Sala-i-Martin: *Economic Growth.* McGraw-Hill, 1995.

INDEX

N

O

P

R

S

T

U

□□□